M000201025

# Rhetoric and Sexuality

# RHETORIC AND SEXUALITY

## THE POETRY OF HART CRANE, ELIZABETH BISHOP, AND JAMES MERRILL

*Peter Nickowitz*

RHETORIC AND SEXUALITY

First published in 2006 by
PALGRAVE MACMILLAN™
175 Fifth Avenue, New York, N.Y. 10010 and
Houndmills, Basingstoke, Hampshire, England RG21 6XS
Companies and representatives throughout the world.

PALGRAVE MACMILLAN is the global academic imprint of the Palgrave Macmillan division of St. Martin's Press, LLC and of Palgrave Macmillan Ltd. Macmillan® is a registered trademark in the United States, United Kingdom and other countries. Palgrave is a registered trademark in the European Union and other countries.

ISBN 978-1-4039-6849-4    ISBN 1-4039-6849-7

Library of Congress Cataloging-in-Publication Data is available from the Library of Congress.

A catalogue record for this book is available from the British Library.

Design by Newgen Imaging Systems (P) Ltd., Chennai, India.

First edition: February 2006

10 9 8 7 6 5 4 3 2 1

Printed in the United States of America.

Transferred to digital printing in 2008.

# CONTENTS

*Acknowledgments*                                                    vi

Introduction                                                          1
1  Chrysalis Unbound: Poems of Origin and Initiation               11
2  Anatomy of a Mother                                             53
   Coda: Literary Mothers                                          92
3  Burnt Matches, or the Art of Love                              101
Afterword                                                         145

*Notes*                                                           151
*Bibliography*                                                    169
*Index*                                                           175

# ACKNOWLEDGMENTS

I would like to record my gratitude to my colleagues and friends who helped me in manifold ways to complete this book: Tom Fink, Bill Handley, Carlos Hiraldo, Katie Hogan, Karlyn Koh, Isabel Garcia Lorca, Karen McKinnon, Bill Oliver, Ron Palmer, and Michael Silverman, and Farideh Koohi-Kamali, Lynn Vande Stouwe and Will Fain at Palgrave. I would also like to thank Professor Harold Bloom for his encouragement and support; Phillip Brian Harper and Carolyn Dever for their guidance and suggestions on the earliest drafts of this study. I thank Deborah Landau for her conversations on poetry and her unconditional friendship. Finally, I thank my parents, Arlen and Gail, and my sister, Allyson, for everything else.

I would also like to thank the publishers and editors of Hart Crane's, Elizabeth Bishop's, and James Merrill's work for their assistance. From *Complete Poems of Hart Crane* by Hart Crane, edited by Marc Simon. Copyright 1933, 1958, 1966 by Liveright Publishing Corporation. Copyright 1986 by Marc Simon. Used by permission of Liveright Publishing Corporation.

Reprinted by permission of Farrar, Straus, Giroux, LLC. Excerpts from *The Collected Prose* by Elizabeth Bishop. Copyright 1984 by Alice Helen Methfessel. Excerpts from *The Complete Poems 1927–1979* by Elizabeth Bishop. Copyright 1979, 1983 by Alice Helen Methfessel. Excerpts from *One Art: Letters* by Elizabeth Bishop, selected and edited by Robert Giroux. Copyright 1994 by Alice Methfessel. Introduction and compilation copyright 1994 by Robert Giroux.

From *Collected Poems* by James Merrill and J. D. McClatchy and Stephen Yenser, editors, copyright 2001 by the Literary Estate of James Merrill at Washington University. Used by permission of Alfred A. Knopf, a division of Random House, Inc. From *A Different Person* by James Merrill, copyright 1993 by James Merrill. Used by permission of Alfred A. Knopf, a division of Random House, Inc.

# INTRODUCTION

*The more I struggled to be plain, the more*
*Mannerism hobbled me.*

—James Merrill, *The Book of Ephraim*

Halfway through the twentieth century, Ralph Waldo Emerson's idea that the poet is a poem became gospel. Here is an example. In 1998, with flurry and fanfare, the English poet Ted Hughes published a collection of poems called *Birthday Letters*. These poems marked the first time that Hughes spoke publicly about his long-fabled and mythologized marriage to the American poet Sylvia Plath. Plath married Hughes in 1956, but, at the time of her suicide seven years later, the two poets had separated; Hughes was living with another woman. When Plath died, she became a feminist symbol, a figure of a woman driven to despair by an uncaring husband. Hughes's long silence on the subject of his life with Plath ended with the publication of *Birthday Letters* that was excitedly described as a response to, and literary dialogue with, Plath's *Ariel*. Indeed, many of Hughes's poems were written on the back of Plath's manuscripts, giving rise to charges that Hughes was erasing and rewriting Plath.

Seminars and lectures for both scholars and a public long transfixed by the Plath–Hughes saga marked the publication of Hughes's book, where its importance as poetry was debated, and where Hughes's contribution to the biography of Plath as a popular and literary figure was analyzed.[1] Yet, for poetry scholars and critics, the publication of *Birthday Letters* presented a new problem in the discourse of the criticism of poetry: how to talk about poems that clearly and reductively refer to very specific events in the poet's life. It seemed to be counterproductive to talk about "the speaker who says 'I' " in the Hughes poems and to insist upon the difference between the speaker who says "I" and the "I" spoken about or even the persona, the poet, behind the "I," because it was starkly apparent to readers that Hughes was the speaker in these poems. Similarly, it was futile to distance the "you" of the poems from Sylvia Plath; the speaker is speaking about her.

Certainly, for many people in the audiences of these discussions or for readers of the book, this critical collapse did not present a problem. As memoirs and autobiographies masquerading as novels become increasingly popular in American publishing, the lines between character and authorial voice are blurred, such that readers assume that the "I" in a poem *always* refers to the poet. This kind of reading where biography is crucial may be an unavoidable corollary to the confessional movement in poetry that is exemplified by Sylvia Plath's *Ariel* as well as Robert Lowell's poems beginning with *Life Studies* in 1959 and the poems of Anne Sexton.[2] M. L. Rosenthal defines a confessional poem as one in which "the private life of the poet himself, especially under stress of psychological crisis, becomes a major theme." The confessional poem is further characterized as one where the persona of the speaker is the naked ego, and where that ego is involved in a very personal world with particular, private experiences that are traditionally kept from public sight. Boris Tomashevsky writes that an autobiographical poem in contrast to a confessional poem is one that "mythologizes the poet's life in accordance with the conventions of his time. It portrays an idealized image of the poet, not what has occurred but what should have occurred."[3]

Within the connection between the "I" who speaks and the "I" spoken about, the poet must address his or her emotional responses to the world around him or her. For the poets writing in twentieth-century America, this is often accomplished by writing from personal experience. The danger in this is that poetry, or more specifically the criticism of poetry, approaches a solipsistic cast. In the chapters that follow, I consider the poems of Hart Crane, Elizabeth Bishop, and James Merrill. All three poets thematize aspects of, and/or events in, their lives. To varying degrees, however, these biographical themes are revised and masked primarily by rhetorical prowess. Crane is not a confessional poet. Bishop and Merill have some poems that are confessional, but they are not, generally speaking, confessional poets. Nonetheless, my readings of Crane, Bishop, and Merrill's poems are often with this mode in mind. Hart Crane and Elizabeth Bishop, for example, revise poems extensively to remove or to make ambiguous the biographical, whereas James Merrill's craft is often engaged in creating the illusion of direct self-representation, a "James Merrill," by describing a self that bears resemblance to, but is not necessarily the same as, the poet's self. The rhetorical language of Hart Crane, Elizabeth Bishop, and James Merrill renders ambiguously the biography and sexuality of each: the production of ambiguity serves to hide the self and hide sexual identity.

Biography figures prominently in my analysis because of the critical distinction already suggested between confessional and autobiographical poetry. Psychoanalytic theory provides the most coherent discourse available for interpreting biographical material. Theories of psychoanalysis by Sigmund Freud and of object relations by Melanie Klein require a discussion of the poets' lives because these theories are rooted in the idea that personal history informs adult experience. My intention is neither to psychoanalyze the poets, nor to provide insight into the development of homosexuality; rather I use the theories of psychoanalysis alongside the literary interpretation of the poetic texts I consider as a lens to consider questions about reading both kinds of texts. This recognizes the important distinction between Freud's and Klein's texts and those of the poets or of the other critics to whom I refer: Freud and Klein present a theory of human development, not one of literary critical analysis. I make this distinction clear in my discussions of Crane, Bishop, and Merrill and elucidate the salient features that such a difference engenders.

There are similarities in the biographies of these three poets, including wealthy parents, a love of travel bordering on restlessness, and homosexuality. Hart Crane was born Harold Hart Crane in July 1899 to Grace Hart and Clarence Arthur Crane, a successful Ohio businessman. The marriage, however, was fraught with problems; Clarence and Grace divorced when Hart was seventeen. Largely to avoid his divorced parents, who were often hostile and attempted to control the young poet, Crane left Ohio for New York City in 1916 and shuttled back and forth for a number of years as he worked on poems and searched for ways to earn a living. In New York, Hart Crane embraced the freedom the city offered to explore his homosexuality as well as the support of a network of artistic friends; this was the groundwork that allowed him to write, or, at least, to conceive of many of the poems that mark his considerable, although short, career. In 1926, he left New York to begin a period of extensive travel— Cuba, California, New York, Ohio, Europe, and Mexico—that culminated in his suicide by drowning off the coast of Havana in 1932. Throughout his life, Crane battled alcohol and a concomitant ambivalence toward his homosexuality. Fears that he would no longer be able to write poems also contributed to Crane's decline.

Merrill and Bishop only knew Crane through his poems; however, Merrill and Bishop met for the first time in the late 1940s at Bard College, where Merrill was teaching and Bishop was attending a poetry conference. Bishop and Merrill eventually became close friends in the late 1960s; Merrill even came to stay with Bishop at her house in Ouro Preto, Brazil. While certainly not as wealthy as Merrill, Elizabeth Bishop inherited money from her father's family, which afforded her a superior education and financial freedom for a number of years after she graduated from Vassar College in 1934. Bishop's father, William Thomas Bishop, died of Bright's disease when she was eight months old. Depressed and inconsolable, Bishop's mother, Gertrude Bulmer Bishop, was eventually committed to a mental institution when Bishop was five years old; she never saw her mother again. Bishop was raised by her elderly grandparents—one set in Great Village, Nova Scotia whom she loved and the other in Boston whom she found aristocratic, cold, and aloof.

Like Merrill and Crane, Bishop's adult life involved constant travel—Europe when she first graduated, New York, and Key West. In 1951, she met Lota de Macedo Soares while in Brazil and fell in love. Bishop lived in Brazil with Lota for sixteen years, until Lota's death in 1967. After Lota's death, Bishop returned to the United States but continued to travel living in Seattle, San Francisco, Ouro Preto, and Boston with a series of lovers. Her famous restlessness is often attributed to her search for an actual home from which she would not feel alienated. In addition, she often wanted to leave places in order to escape the consequences of embarrassing episodes caused by her alcoholic binges. If, as is commonly argued, her restlessness and alcoholism were attempts to reclaim a void left by the loss of her mother, then so were her lifelong friendships with a series of mothers and daughters, especially her mentor Marianne Moore and Moore's mother, both of whom Bishop visited frequently in New York.

James Merrill often joked that by the time he was five years old he was rich. As the son of Charles Merrill, a founder of the Merrill, Lynch & Company financial firm, and Charles's second wife, Hellen Ingram, Merrill was indeed rich and set up with a trust fund that ensured his financial freedom for the rest of his life. He grew up in New York City in an apartment on West 11th Street (mythologized in "18 West 11th Street" in *Braving the Elements*) and in a mansion in Southampton built by the architect Stanford White. Merrill studied at Lawrenceville, a private preparatory school, and at Amherst College. His father offered Merrill little choice but to attend Amherst, his alma mater, which is a sign of the pressure that Charles exerted over his son. Charles Merrill hoped that James would follow in his footsteps and work for the family firm; however, Charles soon realized that his son's interests and ambitions lay elsewhere. At Lawrenceville, Merrill began to write poems. His first collection, *Jim's Book*, was privately published by Charles (and later renounced as embarrassing juvenilia by the poet). His subsequent collection, *First Poems*, was published in 1951 when Merrill was twenty-five years old.

As an adult, Merrill's life was characterized by frequent travel. After spending several years traveling in Europe—about which he wrote in his memoir *A Different Person*—Merrill returned to the United States and moved to Stonington, Connecticut with his lover, David Jackson. They bought a house there, but soon collected others, spending parts of every year in Greece and, later, Key West, Florida.

As these brief sketches suggest, there are many points of similarities for these poets. I focus upon the poems of Crane, Bishop, and Merrill because of their collective importance to the tradition of American poetry, their creative output, their biographical similarities, their use of rhetoric, and their thematics. Hart Crane, Elizabeth Bishop, and James Merrill are each strong, individual and individualizing poets who share common genealogies of influence characterized by each poet's use of tropes of the closet, and of homosexual and maternal desire that are intertwined with images of ambivalence. The poems of Crane, Bishop, and Merrill, while also ambiguous regarding homo-sexuality, focus more centrally on the ambivalent figuration and repre-sentation of desire and loss, where rhetoric produces these ambivalent images in the service of confronting the poets' anxiety about homo-sexuality. In a letter to Robert Lowell that I discuss more fully in the second chapter, Bishop warns Lowell about the "infinite mischief" that comes from the mixture of fact and fiction. Bishop simultane-ously criticizes and enacts, does and undoes, this very "infinite mischief" when she, and Crane and Merrill, use rhetoric in this way.

The poems of Crane, Bishop, and Merrill are allusive, so it is espe-cially important to keep in mind the specter of poets such as Wallace Stevens, W. B. Yeats and T. S. Eliot, who were writing around the same time. The poetry of Hart Crane (1899–1932), Elizabeth Bishop (1911–1979), and James Merrill (1926–1995) extends across the twentieth century and, thus, perfectly illustrates the widely different styles of poetry that flood the American poetry scene. Crane's, Bishop's, and Merrill's poetry, while varied, derives from similar sources within the American canon of Walt Whitman, Emily Dickinson, Wallace Stevens, and William Carlos Williams. Despite the centrality of Crane, Bishop, and Merrill in American poetry, relatively little has been written about their work, and there is no previous study that discusses all three poets' works together.

When Hart Crane died in 1932 at the age of 32, he left behind two volumes of poetry, *White Buildings* and *The Bridge*. At the time of his death, he was working on a third collection, *Key West*, and also had manuscripts of uncollected poems—some of which had been published during his lifetime. Bishop's poetic oeuvre is similarly comprised of a relatively small number of poems. She published six collections, *North & South, Poems: North & South—A Cold Spring, Questions of Travel, The Complete Poems* (1969), *Geography III,* and *The Complete Poems: 1927–1979* as well as several short stories and translations, including *The Diary of Helena Morley* and an anthology of Brazilian poetry. James Merrill, on the other hand, was prolific; he published fifteen volumes of poetry, two novels, two plays, a collection of essays, and a memoir. The volume of Merrill's output creates a potential imbalance between him and Crane and Bishop, which I address through strategic selection of poems.

In each of the three chapters, I focus on specific themes in Crane's, Bishop's, and Merrill's poetry. My discussions of the individual poets are in a chronological order, Crane, then Bishop, and Merrill; I do not seek to prioritize any poet from this order but merely suggest the import of chronology on influence. I begin with a discussion of poems of initiation, especially Crane's "Repose of Rivers" and "The Broken Tower," Bishop's "In the Waiting Room" and "The End of March," and Merrill's "Scenes of Childhood" and "An Urban Convalescence." In the chapter, entitled "Chrysalis Unbound," I trace the dynamics of identification and repudiation as they are revealed through gendered images to create a drama of self-revelation. Poems of initiation describe a defining moment of a particular self-image and self-definition and are, therefore, especially useful in examining the ways poets construct themselves in relation to their art. I also examine the poets' use of architectural spaces, which figure in all six poems examined closely here, and which function as a defining locus of identity for Crane, Bishop, and Merrill. These poems are concerned with speakers who enact dramas of self-awareness within poetic narratives and who construct fantasies of enclosure within safe houses, towers, and rooms that remove the poet from the world. Once removed, the poet gives him- or her-self the space and the freedom to do the work of association and repudiation that is necessary for understanding one's identity.[4] While I do discuss the poets' relation to gendered images, a discussion of the differences that gender produces in poetry (i.e., between Bishop and Crane and Merrill) is beyond the scope of my examination.

The second chapter, "Anatomy of a Mother," focuses on a series of poems culled primarily from Crane's, Bishop's, and Merrill's first collections and from later collections that exemplify the poet's relation to, and representation of, the world outside of the speaker's self.

Because their imagery is rooted in psychological inquiry as much as it is in language itself, this examination looks at the poets' relationships to the figuration of the mother, and by extension, to a beloved. Crane's "Legend" serves as a guide into the hermeneutics of *White Buildings*, providing a key (a legend) into his poetic style, and it is a poem about the tensions between excitement for youthful love and the need for propriety and restraint in its expression. "Sunday Morning Apples" continues to guide the reader into Crane's language, here foregrounding the juxtaposition of concrete with abstract images. "Sunday Morning Apples" describes the origins of creative inspiration. From Bishop's work, I discuss "The Map," her two sestinas, "A Miracle for Breakfast" and "Sestina," as well as her poems of explicit loss, such as "At the Fishhouses," and "The Moose" from *Geography III*. Like Crane, Merrill often begins a book with a poem that provides an entrance into the prevailing theme of the collection; following Merrill's example, "The Country of a Thousand Years of Peace" introduces my discussion of *The Country of a Thousand Years of Peace* and the later poems, "The Broken Home," "Days of 1935," and "Days of 1971." Through close readings, I argue that the poets' rhetoric produces imagery that alternates between images of concreteness and abstraction.[5] In this way, their poetic language serves simultaneously to reveal and to conceal a dramatization of the poet's sexual, personal, and artistic identity. The figure of the mother is important to decode not only to reinforce her centrality in personal development but also to illustrate the degree to which associational meanings of poetic language are embedded in the poets' rhetoric.

In a coda to chapter two, I examine Crane's, Bishop's, and Merrill's literary precursors from whom they acquire their figurations of, and ideas for, the maternal. For example, I relate Walt Whitman's figure of the mother in his Sea Drift poems, "Out of the Cradle Endlessly Rocking" and "As I Ebb'd with the Ocean of Life," to Crane's figuration of the mother in his work. I then look at Marianne Moore's poem "Marriage" in order to position Moore as a figure on whom Bishop based her own representations of the mother. Merrill's figuration of the mother is based on Elizabeth Bishop, and for this discussion I look at his poem "The Victor Dog."

In the third chapter, "Burnt Matches," I consider love poetry. The poems of Crane, Bishop, and Merrill confound and resist attempts to define a group of poems called "love poems"; this is in part due to the poets' anxieties about the explicit revelation of homosexuality and homosexual desire. Indeed, the expression of love in Merrill's poems, for example, is complicated by his postmodern insistence on the artificiality of his work. For Merrill, as well as Crane and Bishop, there is always the reduction of theme to the prioritizing of language. In my analysis, this problem generates an exploration of the connection I see between rhetoric and thematic interpretations. I look at Crane's long sequence poems from *White Buildings*, "For the Marriage of Fautus and Helew," and "Voyages," and "The Tunnel" from *The Bridge* together with Bishop's "Love Lies Sleeping," "Insomnia," "It is Marvelous to Wake Up Together," "The Shampoo," "Crusoe in England," and "One Art" and Merrill's "Nightgown," "Between Us," "The Med Scene", "Days of 1964," and "Clearing the Title." I read these poems for instances in which the representation of love is figured in doublings of words or images. These moments recall psychoanalytic interpretations of love as rooted in narcissism and also the connection between love and psychic structures that produce a repetition compulsion. Through an analysis of poems of love in which the figure of the beloved is obscured to mask the homosexual content, I reflect upon the degree to which Crane's and Bishop's poetics of love cites as it blurs traditional love poems.

Homosexuality does not often figure explicitly in Crane's, Bishop's, or Merrill's work, which requires decoding to yield textual examples. Queer theorists have written extensively both about the ways to decode implicit instances of homosexual desire as well as about the figuration of the closet as a defining structure for homosexual invisibility.[6] In the poetry of Crane, Bishop, and Merrill, interior spaces are constructed as places in which to contain and to house the internalized homosexual anxiety that the poets exhibit. In addition, Freud, in *The Ego and the Id*, posits the importance of identification in the process of identity formation. While in *Love, Hate and Reparation*, Klein positions the mother as the child's first object of love and hate; the mother, therefore, remains a defining figure for every subsequent relationship the child has. Klein's constructs figure in Crane's, Bishop's, and Merrill's poetry of origin specifically as loss and ambivalence. When the tensions surrounding these identifications with and repudiations of gendered images, especially those involving the mother and the father, are decoded they produce insight into the construction of identity. Interestingly, maternal images are often combined with those of a beloved, creating complex structures of desire through a conflation of gendered imagery.

Through close readings of many of the central poems in Crane's, Bishop's, and Merrill's work, I elucidate the project of each individual poet and also draw some conclusions about American poetry during the course of the twentieth century. For example, I look at how identity becomes an increasingly central concern in American poetry at a time when the idea of the self was being challenged and redefined from all directions, from various sources, including the writings of Freud and of Michel Foucault as well as the world wars and post–World War II uncertainty.

I conclude in an afterword with a discussion of poetry that continues the traditions of, and follows the influence of, Crane, Bishop, and Merrill. As homosexual poets, Crane's, Bishop's, and Merrill's homosexuality can be read through a series of tropes and images within their poems, including the closet, the figure of the mother, and the lover. Yet, these tropes are constructed through language that reveals and conceals their import and makes their revelations ambiguous. I look at the work of Frank Bidart, Henri Cole, and Mark Doty. Through a discussion of their poems, I reveal a different treatment of homosexuality and homosexual themes. The densely allusive quality of many of Crane's and Merrill's poems, and of some of Bishop's, lends itself to a greater discussion of poetry in more generalized terms. The examination of Hart Crane, Elizabeth Bishop, and James Merrill extracts a precedent for these poets; I hope to lead readers to find analogous interpretations in the work of other poets.

# CHAPTER 1

# CHRYSALIS UNBOUND: POEMS OF ORIGIN AND INITIATION

*If you survive your childhood, you have enough material to write for the rest of your life.*

—Flannery O'Connor

Poems of initiation are windows into the imaginative life of the poet and reveal how art constructs the poet. As an example of a poem of initiation, picture the following scene. It is the New York coast, the early 1830s. A young, preternaturally mature boy looks out onto the rolling Atlantic Ocean. He is alone; as one of eight siblings he craves solitude. He is well-dressed in a shirt and short pants. It is summer and the sun unravels onto him. As if in a trance, he is listening to a bird singing, and, suddenly, the boy has a random epiphany. He declares: "Now in a moment I know what I am for, I awake." This line is Walt Whitman's from his poem "Out of the Cradle Endlessly Rocking." The speaker, as a young boy, fashions his initiation into poetry as an awakening—getting up from a slumber of being lost to a sudden acquaintance with his artistic vocation. The trope of Whitman's speaker's awakening is a rich one and, together with images throughout the poem such as that of the cradle, suggests a kind of rebirth or second birth out of the commonplaces, out of the world around him, and into a world of metaphoric substitutions, of artifice, and of heightened poetic language.

Poems of initiation thematize an entrance or an introduction into the poet's personal or artistic identity.[1] These poems often dramatize a specific revelatory scene, predominantly as a recollection of an event from early childhood. My concern in this discussion is with the figuration of *childhood* in poetic texts and not in the child. This distinction makes clear that I do not read the poems as biographical truths, but rather I discuss them as they represent tropologically the figuration of childhood. Poems of initiation describe a defining moment of a particular self-image and self-definition and are, therefore, especially useful material to examine the ways poets construct themselves in relation to their art. Sigmund Freud's psychoanalytic work on personal development in "Three Essays on the Theory of Sexuality" and "Female Sexuality" posits sexuality and the formation of one's consciousness as a series of competing associations and repudiations.[2] Freud, for example, theorizes that girls form an early attachment with the mother, whom they must later reject as a rival for the father's affections. Boys also form an attachment to the mother and feel aggression toward the father as a rival. This dynamic of associations and repudiations informs the drama of self-revelation and of poetic initiation in two poems by Hart Crane, "The Broken Tower" and "Repose of Rivers," two by Elizabeth Bishop, "In the Waiting Room" and "The End of March," and two by James Merrill, "Scenes of Childhood" and "An Urban Convalescence." These poems of poetic initiation invoke voices from each poet that are characterized by an early and, then, a mature speaker. In particular, they reveal the ways in which Crane, Bishop, and Merrill construct their origins with reference to an interior space. These spaces, here figured predominantly as houses, are rhetorically constructed at a point at which language fails to convey accurately the emotional intensity that the poet feels.[3] Crane, Bishop, and Merrill have written poems of initiation around dramatizations that require an identification and a repudiation in order to reify the poet's identity.[4]

Whereas I position identification as the opposite of repudiation, theorists such as Julia Kristeva use different structures. Kristeva, for example, places "denial" and "negation" in opposition to identification. In her model, the "denial of negation" of the melancholic subject, which she calls an improper mourning, is in effect a double negation that serves paradoxically to make the subject identify, as an introjection, with the lost object.[5] Thus, my conception of repudiation is closer to her idea of "denial" and/or "negation." Repudiation conveys the sense that these two dynamics work less to cancel each other out and more to produce ambivalence and thus parallels the relationship between the psychoanalytic and literature.[6]

In these poems Crane, Bishop, and Merrill attain artistic inspiration through a rethinking of the sexual in which they reinforce their respective voices by a repudiation of the gendered images that are in opposition to them. Because gender identification is problematic for these poets, however, each poet plays with his or her imagery in ways that appear rather to intermingle the seemingly distinct categories of gender identification. The theories of Freudian psychoanalysis are useful to this study because of Freud's focus on sexuality in childhood. My close readings of poems make clear, that sexuality in childhood is the key to a reading of these poets in order to understand their tropes of childhood as a liminal period when the self can be rewritten into a poetic self. Object relations theory, specifically the work of Melanie Klein, also addresses issues of childhood sexuality, especially on the role and figuration of the mother. Because I also discuss the differences surrounding gendered images, however, I foreground the work of Freud in this chapter because his work takes into consideration the gender difference of his subjects, whereas Klein's work generally disregards the gender of the subject, referring to a gender-neutral "infant" subject. Freud is a close reader of the body and of the conscious and unconscious mind (dreams). As a close reader, Freud provides an immediately recognizable link between my theoretical framework and the close readings of poetic texts.

Crane, Bishop, and Merrill were all predominantly homosexual in their choices of erotic objects. The troublesome emotions surrounding a homosexual awakening are precisely why Freud's focus on early sexuality is particularly relevant. Furthermore, the work of Melanie Klein offers insight into the adult experience through an examination of childhood, but she eroticizes the child differently. Freud's attention to early sexual drives lends support to the idea that sexuality is a salient aspect of identity from its beginnings and not simply from the onslaught of adolescence. Freud and Klein present theories of human development and not of literary critical analysis. This important distinction creates a gap: a theory of human development seeks to explain how the categories of men and women are formed, whereas a literary critical analysis based upon these theories seeks to explore the ways that such categories are constructed and represented in artistic texts. At the same time, this gap is often a problematic one, where the lines of the boundary are blurred. As Diana Fuss notes, "psychoanalysis . . . closely identifies with the literary insofar as it has already been anticipated by it, compromised from the start by the necessity of traveling through language and texts."[7] Because, as Fuss continues, "[it] erects itself, as a science, *against* the literary," psychoanalysis is fundamentally tied with it and, as I argue, at times the two appear to be conflated.

Indeed, Freudian interpretation is very often literary criticism. Poetry and psychoanalytic discourse are difficult; they require deciphering in order to decode their tropes and images into understandable forms. Both seem unknowable in their raw states; both require signposts, interpretation, and discussion. These shared qualities foreground the relationship between literature and psychoanalysis. What draws me to poetry, specifically here the poetry of Crane, Bishop, and Merrill, and what draws me to psychoanalysis, specifically the work of Sigmund Freud and Melanie Klein, is the parallel human dramas they present. Poems and psychoanalytic discourse present readers with fascinating parallel dramas—such a drama is clearly evident in case studies, though I hope my discussion of Freud's and Klein's work more generally reveals how readers can see their works as a whole as being dramatic. Indeed, my study not only helps us to read and to understand the language of Crane, Bishop, and Merrill but it also helps us to understand Freud and Klein in new ways because it reminds readers that Freud and Klein's work are literary. Though many literary critics have been reading Freud as a Modernist writer for years, this juxtaposition of poetry and psychoanalysis makes us see psychoanalytic discourse as a literary one.

The claim that Hart Crane, Elizabeth Bishop, and James Merrill were predominantly homosexual in their choice of a love object, carries with it the requirement of some evidence of their homosexuality. This requirement, however, is problematic since heterosexuality does not generally require proof by virtue of its normative status. Heterosexuality is standard and assumed, whereas homosexuality is often hidden behind and within structures, such as the trope of the closet.[8] Proof of homosexuality is often difficult especially when the subject has feelings of anxiety or ambivalence about his or her sexual identity. The closet is the defining structure for homosexual visibility and invisibility. The closet too, however, occupies an ambivalent position—it is both desired as a defining structure and hated because it reinforces homosexuality's second-class status to a normative heterosexuality. In this way, the figure of the closet functions rhetorically to reinforce, if not to reify, the notion that homosexuality needs to hide within it, as it simultaneously seeks to proclaim its presence. The closet is a trope that functions at a discursive level.[9] While closeting structures work to police and/or to control gestures and other extralinguistic forms of expression, the trope of the closet's discursive position is of particular interest here because of its connection to, and participation in, rhetoric. The proof of the homosexuality of Crane,

Bishop, and Merrill is in language—poems, letters, and biographical information. There is no "coming out" scene in which each can verbalize his or her status. The trope of the closet and rhetoric work together to solidify the proof over time, as a historical record in a way that gestures cannot.

What then constitutes textual evidence of each poet's homosexuality, and how much proof—textual or otherwise—is required? For example, do the names of each poet's lover and the poem in which the love is thematized provide sufficient evidence?[10] In the course of my discussions, I explore the relationships between Hart Crane and Emil Opffer, Elizabeth Bishop and Lota de Macedo Soares, and James Merrill and David Jackson as well as the specific poems in which these relationships are thematized. Explicit evidence of the homosexual status of Crane, Bishop, and Merril are shown through the discussions of poems of initiation that follow. This type of poem provides each not only with a space for a representation of origin but also with a connection to a poetic tradition because of the poem's genre. The paradigmatic poem of initiation in American poetry is Walt Whitman's "Out of the Cradle Endlessly Rocking." In "Out of the Cradle Endlessly Rocking" Whitman must repudiate the feminine and embrace a masculine identity before he can be celebrated as a poetic hero.

In her essay, "Rituals of Initiation in Whitman and Dickinson," Sandra Gilbert argues for a reading of "Out of the Cradle Endlessly Rocking," as an ode of poetic initiation in which the poet thematizes not only his self-definition but also the way in which he achieves such a self-image. Gilbert's work provides a model for my examination; however, my readings of Crane, Bishop, and Merrill depart from Gilbert's in that none repudiates and identifies with one gendered image over the other.[11] Rather, each poet conjoins the two and creates images that reveal an opposition and embrasure of both. Crane has to reify a masculine and feminine opposition in order to overcome a brokenness and gain access to the poetic. Gilbert writes:

> The famously incantory opening of "Out of the Cradle," . . . stresses not only the gift from, up, and out of the seashore that the poet remembers receiving, but also his own separation from the elements of nature, his emergence out, up, and from the mystically maternal forces emblematized by the endlessly rocking cradle of the deep.[12]

The poem celebrates the "multilingual" Whitman's accession to language; this is accomplished, however, through a consideration of gender identifications. "Out of the Cradle Endlessly Rocking" begins when the speaker in Whitman's poem strains to hear the song of the man-bird:

> Out of the cradle endlessly rocking,
> Out of the mocking-bird's throat, the musical shuttle,
> Out of the Ninth-month midnight,
> Over the sterile sands and the fields beyond,
>     where the child leaving his bed wander'd alone, bareheaded,
>     barefoot, . . .
> From the memories of the bird that chanted to me.[13]

The speaker is engaged in an effort to hear, and to make sense of, a song that is beyond the speaker's knowledge. The incantory opening lines of the poem set a scene in which the poet recalls a time in his youth when he was summoned to the shore "alone." The poet remembers that he came to the water's edge to observe, "Two feath-er'd guests from Alabama, two together," "the he-bird" and "the she-bird" (l. 26). The poet recounts that his job was to watch the birds and to listen to them and to make intelligible their songs: "And every day I, a curious boy, never too close, never disturbing them, / Cautiously peering, absorbing, translating" (ll. 30–31). The speaker remains here an observer. He is merely "translating" and repeating the bird's songs but not speaking his own words. In a movement that will prove to be unlike that of the poems under consideration by Crane, Bishop, and Merrill, the Whitmanian speaker begins his poem by leaving an enclosed space, the cradle, for the open expanse of the shore. The loss about which this poem speaks is constantly reflected in the loss of the safety of the cradle and the maternal comfort that the image implies. The speaker encounters the maternal, again, in the sea; however, here the maternal is not comforting as much as obliterating.

While the poet observes the birds, he notices a change take place: the she-bird is suddenly missing. The poet and the "he-bird" won-der what happened to her; is she dead, or did she simply leave? Rather than dwelling upon her fate, they choose simply to mourn her absence. The poet says: "I saw, I heard at intervals the remaining one, the he-bird, / The solitary guest from Alabama" (ll. 50–51). What the poet hears is the he-bird's poignant song of loss, an aria that lasts for fifty-eight lines of the ode.

The loss of the she-bird is an unreconciled and unreconcilable loss. She is gone; where she is no longer matters to the poet, because her loss enables a transcendence into the poetic aria. The aria changes the young poet enormously:

> The boy ecstatic, with his bare feet the waves, with his hair the
>     atmosphere dallying,
> The love in the heart long pent, now loose, now at last tumultuously
>     bursting,
> The aria's meaning, the ears, the soul, swiftly depositing,
> The strange tears down the cheeks coursing,
> The colloquy there, the trio, each uttering,
> The undertone, the savage old mother incessantly crying,
> To the boy's soul's questions sullenly timing, some drown'd secret
>     hissing,
> To the outsetting bard.   (ll. 136–143)

There is an erotic charge to the poet's connection to the he-bird that is reinforced through the poet's language. The anticipation of the verb reflects the ecstasy of the scene, "the boy ecstatic, with his bare feet the waves, with his hair the atmosphere dallying" (l. 136). The anticipation here is like that of erotic pleasure. The boy's "ecstasy," his "feet" that are "bare," and his "hair" flirting, "dallying," with the wind are images that foreground the sense of erotic play that the poet feels. Indeed, a brotherhood has been established between the two, a bond of understanding of loss and pain. The eroticism is based upon their brotherhood and emerges out of their shared understanding of anguish.

Before the poet can become too excited by his awakening knowledge of loss and its ensuing inspiration for poetic song, he must also learn of his own mortality. From the voice of the maternal sea, the source of life, comes the whispered knowledge of the inevitability of death: "the sea . . . Lisp'd to me the low and delicious word death, / And again death, death, death, death" (ll. 165, 168–169). Why does the speaker say that "death" is "delicious," a description that is reinforced through its repetition at the end of the poem: "That strong and delicious word [death]" (l. 182)? Indeed "death" is a democratizing aspect of existence. Everyone dies and, therefore, death erases all difference. The "delicious" quality of death seems to be analogous to the eroticism of loss: both death and loss are necessary to the poet to achieve poetic song: "My own songs awaked from that hour, / And with them the key, the word up from the waves, / The word of the sweetest song and all songs" (ll. 178–180). At the same time, "delicious" is an oral adjective, reinforcing its difference from loss and its potential status as rhetoric. The orality of "delicious" also highlights the degree to which "death" needs to be taken in, consumed, like food for the poet's creativity. Here, "death" is a requirement for the Whitmanian speaker to access poetic inspiration; death is a similar disruption that must occur for poetry to be created. The repetition of the word, "death" (ll. 169 and 173) serves to lessen the impact of the word; the reader no longer feels that "death" signifies a potentially sad and painful event, but rather, through its repetition, it comes to be a poetic device. At the same time, the repetition of "death" creates a linguistic space that mirrors the cradle itself, enclosing the ambivalent entrance into language that comes from significant loss.[14]

Whitman in "Out of the Cradle Endlessly Rocking" thematizes his poetic initiation through a separation from the maternal (the mother and thus, the feminine) as well as an ensuing knowledge of loss and death. The speaker's separation from, and understanding of, loss are forms of disruption that Crane foregrounds in many of his poems. Once the tensions between masculine and feminine imagery are pointed out, what do the tensions signify and what does one do with them? In "Group Psychology and the Analysis of the Ego," Freud offers further insight into the three ways that identification can function:

> First, identification is the original form of emotional tie with an object; secondly, in a regressive way it becomes a substitute for a libidinal object-tie, as it were by means of introjection of the object into the ego; and thirdly, it may arise with any new perception of a common quality shared with some other person who is not an object of the sexual instinct.[15]

The three forms of identification expand into a web for the ego in any number of recognitions. In the clinical scheme of psychoanalysis, a prolonged identification with the opposite sex brings about neurosis, or as Phillip Brian Harper points out in his discussion of this passage, it brings about male homosexuality.[16]

What, however, does identification signify in poetry? In Judith Butler's investigation of gender and gender identification, she writes:

> . . . identification is always an ambivalent process. Identifying with a gender under contemporary regimes of power involves identifying with a set of norms that are and are not realizable, and whose power and status precede the identifications by which they are insistently approximated.[17]

Butler, here, is discussing the implications of drag, but her ideas are relevant to this analysis of poems of initiation because she makes clear what is at stake in constructing oneself as a man or a woman. For Butler, gender identification is always an ambivalent process because there are always social and cultural costs involved. If a subject identifies as male, for instance, he is consciously and unconsciously the agent and the object of a series of culturally produced masculine stereotypes to which he is assumed to conform, and he would equally be presumed to stay away from those attributes that are traditionally female. For Crane, Bishop, and Merrill, this ambivalence is played out in the combination of gendered images within poems that dramatize selfhood. The ambivalence highlights their special position as marginalized homosexuals that posit them outside of the normative, heterosexual structure. Normative masculinity and femininity are for Crane heterosexual structures; Crane therefore reifies and repudiates both to illustrate his position outside of the heterosexual normativity they would otherwise signify. The reticent homosexuality of Crane and Bishop and of early Merrill foregrounds their ambivalence and functions as the force behind the problematic relationship between masculine and feminine imagery.[18] In this way, the masculine and feminine imagery serves as both an examination of the poets as well as of gender roles in general.

In some ways, Crane's final and masterful poem "The Broken Tower" can be seen as a reflection of a confused sexuality. The poem was written after Crane won a Guggenheim fellowship and decided to spend the term of its award living in Mexico. In the summer of 1931, Crane is called back to the United States, however, by the death of his father; when he returns to Mexico, he is reunited with Peggy Cowley, the soon-to-be ex-wife of Crane's friend Malcolm. Crane and Peggy Cowley had a brief affair: he in grief over his father and his lack of poetic output and she in grief over her divorce. Nonetheless the tense period in Mexico inspires Crane, who had not written a poem in two years, to write "The Broken Tower" in which he reflects upon his artistic career to date. The poem is composed of ten quatrains with a fixed rhyme scheme of a-b-a-b. Although he sent copies to several friends and to *Poetry* magazine, he did not hear any reaction to the poem and assumed readers did not like it. In fact, the copy Crane sent to *Poetry* was lost in the mail; the poem appeared in *The New Republic* a month after his suicide in May 1932. "The Broken Tower" is his final poem.[19] Like the auto-elegiac poems of Yeats, the first stanza begins with a tone of quiet composure:

> The bell-rope that gathers God at dawn
> Dispatches me as though I dropped down the knell

Of a spent day—to wander the cathedral lawn
From pit to crucifix, feet chill on steps from hell.[20]

These opening lines beautifully set the scene for the poem in which
the speaker is awakened by the cathedral bells that have rung at
"dawn." Despite the tranquillity of the scene, the words the speaker
chooses point toward a more serious tone; words like "knell," "pit to
crucifix," and "steps from hell" foreground the sense that the speaker
is not describing a tranquil morning walk, but rather one in which
intense emotions are brewing. A "knell" is not only the slow, ringing
sound of a funeral bell but also an omen of death or failure. The word
"knell" seems to invoke both meanings here; indeed, it is the ringing
of the bells that signals the poet's own potential failure as a poet.
Further evidence of foreboding can be seen in the description of the
poet who "wanders" the lawn, as if aimlessly and without any specific
destination. His wandering is not comfortable; he feels as if he has
"dropped down the knell." Also, he wanders with chilled "feet." He
is walking because he could not sleep or do anything else; there is a
poetic crisis at hand.

The poetic crisis appears through the first in a series of simultaneous
associations and repudiations in the poem.[21] The "bell-rope" calls to
"God"; the speaker aligns himself with religion and the protective edifice the cathedral appears to offer. Religion, like the closet, is an elastic
trope and foregrounds the poem's movement from one tropological
umbrella (religion) to another (the closet). Religion's only solace, however, is in the promise of the satisfaction of desire, wherein the anticipation of the communication with the divine is a continual process of
deferral. The speaker thus repudiates religion; his feet are "chilled." His
rejection is highlighted here by the sense that the cathedral offers no
solace to this poetic crisis. His walking around the grounds is an anxious
attempt to distance himself from the internal space of church.

The fearful assumptions suggested by the opening lines are proven
to be correct in the second stanza. The calm tone of the speaker is
broken by urgent questions:

Have you not heard, have you not seen that corps
Of shadows in the tower, whose shoulders sway
Antiphonal carillons launched before
The stars are caught and hived in the sun's ray?   (ll. 5–8)

This question, which addresses a "you," functions as a disruption in
the voice of the poem. The question makes the poem seem as if it were

an address to a specific person, as if the poem were a transcript of part of a conversation between two people. The representation of an urgent speaker questioning an addressee creates a fiction of presence, as if the dialogue were being said at the present time. The poet creates a fiction of representation that both disrupts the voice of the poem as well as causes the time in which the poem takes place to be called into question.

Disruption is also thematized through seemingly contradictory images. There is a "corps" "whose shoulders sway"; this is not a "corps" of people but of "shadows." Because the corps seem to sway, the poet gives life to them. But they are merely ghosts, spirits who have broken free from their bodies. Thomas Yingling hastily dismisses "The Broken Tower" as, "a poem that confesses the 'failure' of homosexual life and yearns for a return to origin, purity, and wholeness."[22] Yingling's reading oversimplifies the meaning of "The Broken Tower" by insisting upon its sexual meaning and ignoring its linguistic and representational import in Crane's poetic project. In fact, as my analysis suggests, the juxtaposition of gendered imagery makes ambiguous the poem's assertion of any sexual category. In the context of a poem of heterosexual aspirations, the shadow "corps" becomes a representation of disavowed objects of desire: men reduced to ghosts and therefore no longer desirable. Ghosts are not men; they are dead and not capable of being potential love objects. Yet, as a man, the poet could be one of these homoerotic "corps" of shadows that he repudiates. The corps move to the sound of the bells, the "carillons," which are "antiphonal" and produce an opposition of sounds. The omission of the preposition "to" between lines six and seven that connects the sway of the corps grammatically with the "antiphonal carillons," together with the sound of the bells as oppositional, are linguistic representations of ruptures. This rupture serves, at first, to destructure the poem and to reinforce the poet's crisis of a failed identity.

What is of such great interest to the poet, what makes him wander the cathedral lawn so early in the morning and what causes him to question the "you," the speaker says, are the bells. The poet writes:

> The bells, I say, the bells break down their tower;
> And swing I know not where. Their tongues engrave
> Membrane through marrow, my long-scattered score
> Of broken intervals . . . And I their sexton slave!
>
> Oval encyclicals in canyons heaping
> The impasse high with choir. Banked voices slain!
> Pagodas, campaniles with reveilles outleaping—
> O terraced echoes prostrate on the plain! . . .

> And so it was I entered the broken world
> To trace the visionary company of love, its voice
> An instant in the wind (I know not whither hurled)
> But not for long to hold each desperate choice.    (ll. 9–20)

The "bells" do more than simply "break down their tower," but they also "break down" the poetic line through their repetition, "The bells, I say, the bells." The break in the poetic line is a double one because of the insertion of, "I say." In her discussion of mourning, Julia Kristeva notes that "mourning conceals an aggressiveness towards the lost object." Her idea reinforces my reading of Crane's line of broken language as a decidedly masculine and aggressive act, revealing the poet's ambivalence toward the self and his language. A similar linguistic brokenness occurs in the Gerard de Nerval poem, "The Disenherited," that Kristeva analyses: "I am saturnine—bereft—disconsolate"; she, however, does not discuss the breaks as linguistic instances of aggression or ambivalence.[23] Crane's rhetorical phrase, "I say," reinforces the speaker's position within the confines of the bell's musical message. Similar to the bird's song in "Out of the Cradle," these "bells" are powerful signifiers of communication, so strong that the speaker compares their ability to communicate to that of people who can freely do so with "tongues." The tongues of the bells are violent and piercing; they cut through the skin and travel "membrane through marrow" right to the heart (Hart) of the listener. Indeed, the "bells" are such important communicators that the speaker declares himself to be their slave. These bells are feminine (because of their position in contrast to the masculine tower) as well as masculine ("bells/"balls) images. The speaker attempts to identify himself with the masculine and feminine "bells" and reject the fallible, masculine tower that, in the context of the poem, signifies homoerotic guilt and anxiety.

The "bells" have "tongues," but their language is "scattered" and "broken," so their communication is also unintelligible, proving the bells to be as inherently flawed as the tower. The crisis of the poem is one in which the poet feels that the bells are a signal of poetic inspiration or of the poetic gift in Crane himself; unfortunately, the bells' speech is unknowable, and so the poet cannot gain access to their inspiring communication. It is the desperate state of having missed the vital communication of the bells that compels the poet to enter what he calls "the broken world." This world is a fantasy that the poet creates. It is both an ideal and idealized place that he desires as well as one that he rejects, because it is flawed and "broken."

The brokenness of the world is reflected in the dismembered, decentered body that is here described as, "Membrane through marrow, my long-scattered score / Of broken intervals," and is recalled in Crane's earlier poem "At Melville's Tomb." "The Broken Tower" serves as a reworking of several shared themes within these two poems. In "At Melville's Tomb" the speaker is watching the sea from a ledge because the "dice of drowned men's bones" rests on the sea floor.[24] The numbers on the dice "beat on the dusty shore and were obscured" (l. 4). Like the "long-scattered score / Of broken intervals" in "The Broken Tower," the bones constitute a "scattered chapter"; the sailor's bones represent the men's inability to communicate their stories (l. 7). The "scattered chapter" is an incomplete message, dissipating and retaining its secret message. Images such as the "scattered chapter" of "At Melville's Tomb" and the "long-scattered score" of "The Broken Tower" are characteristic of Crane.[25] These images reify the poem as taking place within a disseminated narrative that requires rupture for poetic progression. This rupture stems from the theme of identification and repudiation, because the "scattered score" invokes the rhythm of the speaker's poetic line. That is to say, the disseminated narrative reflects the tension between his identifications and repudiations. The poet wants and desires the "score," which is his poetic gift; yet, it is troublesome and flawed. The brokenness of the "intervals" forces the desire for its rejection.

The idea of "brokenness" is not only an image within these particular poems but also is a description of Crane's poetic practice in general.[26] Crane's sexual and creative identities and the ambivalence in which they figure result from the same source of anxiety. This interconnectedness of sexual and artistic identities derives from Freud's drives theory, Eros/love and Thanatos/death.[27] Sexual identity is primarily involved in the Eros drive. Artistic identity can be seen as an instinct of destruction because the creative act is one of aggression, whereby the artist seeks to re-create and re-write the world out of a dissatisfaction with it. The struggle between these two drives for life and for destruction is represented by the poets as ambivalent, interconnected identities. Why exactly does Crane's poetry require thematic ruptures, and what does it mean to require them? The ruptures certainly reflect a self in turmoil, specifically over Crane's ambivalent attitude toward his sexuality. Crane wrote "The Broken Tower" while he was living in Mexico City and having his first and only known heterosexual affair with Peggy Cowley. In Cowley's memoir of her time with Crane, she writes that they were "home" to each other. Yet, the affair produced a bad bout of drinking and doubt in Crane's remaining weeks before his suicide.[28] Crane's images and instances of poetic ruptures reflect a ruptured speaker. To the degree that Crane's entrance into poetic discourse requires a destructuring of his language, it is no doubt that his poetic gift would prove burdensome. For this reason, Crane's depiction of poetry in the fourth and fifth stanzas of "The Broken Tower" is precarious. It seems to signal the death of his poetry, when he writes: "Oval encyclicals in canyons heaping / The impasse high with choir. Banked voices slain! / Pagodas, campaniles with reveilles outleaping—" (ll. 13–15). The "voice" of poetry is, here, "slain," and in the following stanza, the voice is said to register only, "An instant in the wind" (ll. 14, 19). To fragment this image of the voice on the wind, the poet adds that the voice is directionless, as if he does not even know whose voice it is: "(I know not whither hurled)" (l. 19). The query into the sufficiency of language and its temporary inability to represent identity is also seen in Bishop and Merrill.

Crane's images are not only representative of ruptures, of tensions between associations and repudiations, but also of language itself. Words themselves are broken by a series of dashes throughout the poem. Crane uses compound words such as, "bell-rope" and "long-scattered," in which he foregrounds rupture by writing them with a dash in between the two words. He also uses a series of dashes (in lines 3, 15, 24, 27, 28, 34, and 35) and ellipses (in lines 12, 16, 32, and 38) throughout the poem to represent a lapse from discourse. Dashes and ellipses appear when the poet fails to find the right words to express his feelings; these punctuation marks signify the inexpressibility of certain strong emotions.[29] The use of dashes and ellipses to separate phrases and sentences fractures language itself, inserting a break or gap within the otherwise grammatically whole line of poetry.

Crane reflects upon his earlier self, who, he feels, has failed, and he represents this self poetically as a loss. The knowledge of the necessity of loss and death in order to access the creative imagination for poetry is problematic in "The Broken Tower"; this is in part because of the connection to sexuality: "The steep encroachments of my blood left me / No answer (could blood hold such a lofty tower / As flings the question true?)" (ll. 25–27). Crane conceives of loss and death in combination with sexuality, all of which are represented as "brokenness." He believes that access to poetic writing requires brokenness; however, he is unwilling to reconfigure it flippantly as a poetic image. He seems to be searching for the most appropriate form of "brokenness," but is uncertain how best to represent it. The poet is overburdened here by his own poetic gift.

Once the poet elucidates a series of ruptures in the first six stanzas of his ten-stanza poem, he is free to end with images of construction. The opposition of the female presence, "or is it she / Whose sweet mortality stirs latent power(,)" (ll. 27–28) to the earlier shadows of masculine presence offers a final disruption that allows for the reconciliation of the many poetic fractures that come in the final lines of the poem. The female presence is a nurturing one that heals his fractured language and broken images:

> And through whose pulse I hear, counting the strokes
> My veins recall and add, revived and sure
> The angelus of wars my chest evokes:
> What I hold healed, original now, and pure . . .  (ll. 29–32)

The former fractures are now "healed," and the poet has a renewed sense of himself, "revived and sure." At the same time, the female presence complicates the sexual matrix of the poem, because traditionally the male poet should position the feminine as the erotic object. The poet does not posit the "she" as an object of desire; rather he aligns himself with her nurturing ability. Then, the speaker repudiates her for his lack of sexual interest, noting that the powers she arouses are "latent," not manifest. Also, her presence is comprised of questions; there is nothing sure or specific about her.

The female presence allows the poem to end with a tone of equanimity and with a construction that takes place *within* the poet, who "builds, within, a tower." The speaker concludes the poem, as he says:

> And builds, within, a tower that is not stone
> (Not stone can jacket heaven)—but slip
> Of pebbles,—visible wings of silence sown
> In azure circles, widening as they dip
> The matrix of the heart, lift down the eye
> That shrines the quiet lake and swells a tower . . .
> The commodious, tall decorum of that sky
> Unseals her earth, and lifts love in its shower.  (ll. 33–40)

This "tower" is first defined by negation. It is *not* like the broken tower of the cathedral, because that tower is made of stone and has shown itself to be fallible. Such a tower gave rise to his crisis. Rather, this tower that exists within the speaker is a "visionary" one, of contradictory and religious beauty. It is made of "slip / Of pebbles,—visible wings of silence."[30] Crane aligns himself with the feminine and earthly, the "slip / Of pebbles," and repudiates the violent ruptures of the masculine.

Crane's final construction is built within "the matrix of the heart." A matrix is a place from which something originates and takes its form. This new tower will take its form not only from the poet's "heart" but also certainly from "Hart" himself. The repetition of the word "lift" in lines thirty-seven and forty raises the question of who is lifting and what exactly is being lifted. One kind of "lift" is contradictory, "lift down," while the second is through the image of the "unseal(ed) earth," "lift love." The image of lifting, together with those of the "matrix," "shrines," and "love in its shower," suggest a religious and erotic tone. This tone is different from the religion of the "cathedral" at the beginning of the poem and is more like a spiritual or visionary one.[31] It is with the assistance and beauty of God that the poet is finally able to overcome the crisis of rupture that called him so early in the morning to the cathedral lawn and to construct a poetry from within himself. While the poet constructs a combination of gendered images here, it is important to note that the poet nonetheless figures each image in normative ways. For example, the words "tall" and "sky" are masculine; the masculine "sky" is inverted, however, as an open, invaginated and thus, "commodious," space. Its "shower" is paradoxically lifted from where the "earth" "unseals." In the closing of the poem, the speaker has entered into poetic discourse and seeks to mend the ruptures of the previous lines by the intermingling of the formerly opposing masculine and feminine imagery. Therefore, the poet reifies both feminine and masculine images. The final "shower" is a baptism that marks an approval of the coupling of the masculine and the feminine imagery and confirms the religiosity of the poem's conclusion.[32] The movement from one interior space, the broken tower, to another, the tower within, carries the reader progressively further into the consciousness of the poet to a linguistic space that allows for the poem's conclusion.

If "The Broken Tower" characterizes Crane's late poems of initiation, "Repose of Rivers" is an early example of Crane's poetry that thematizes initiation through a brokenness. While "Repose of Rivers" does not make use of an explicit architectural structure, as is the case with the other poems under consideration here, there is an attempt to define a space that contains the strong voice that recounts and asserts his problematic sexual initiation.[33] This is not to suggest that all spaces within Crane's poetry are figurations of the womb; however, through the space's association with words and phrases, the womb becomes one of several important significations. Crane's poems often end with a unionization of masculine and feminine images, highlighting the womb's position as constituting one of several significations.

Like "The Broken Tower," "Repose of Rivers" is composed of a tension between the speaker's competing identifications and repudiations. Unlike "The Broken Tower," "Repose of Rivers" was published in the poet's lifetime; it appears in his first collection, *White Buildings*. This auto-elegiac lyric is composed of twenty-three lines and has no fixed rhyme scheme; even the line lengths vary. The coupling or the juxtaposition of the words in the poem's title, the stasis of "repose" and the motion of "rivers," foregrounds the central linguistic break of the poem.[34] In each of the previously discussed poems, "The Broken Tower" and "Out of the Cradle Endlessly Rocking," there is a lesson for the poet to learn from an outside source in order to gain access to poetry. In "Repose of Rivers," nature holds a secret from which the poet must learn. The natural world, specifically the wind, attempts to communicate to the poet. Crane's discussion of the wind appears like a quotation of nature, where the wind is nature's language:

> The willows carried a slow sound,
> A sarabande the wind mowed on the mead.
> I could never remember
> That seething, steady leveling of the marshes
> Till age had brought me to the sea.    (ll. 1–5)

The sound or voice of the "wind" is compared to a "sarabande," which is a movement of music in triple time and a stylized, Spanish dance. The voice of the "wind" is musical and graceful with its "slow sound" (l. 1) and, at the end of the poem, "steady sound" (l. 23). Yet, there is something sinister and violent about the wind, which is capable of a "seething, steady leveling," as if the wind were a bulldozer "leveling" the marshes for some construction. Why does the poet write that he can never "remember" the wind's "leveling of the marshes"? The wind seems to represent more to the poet than merely pleasant sounds of rustlings through leaves. This idea is conveyed through the passive way in which the speaker describes his being "brought" to the sea; the "leveling" and "age" conspire to bring him. The speaker's lack of agency in this action conveys the sense that this was against his will. It appears that the poet cannot "remember" the wind because he prefers to forget its violence while he is young.

The sounds of the wind as well as the image of the "pond" into which the poet enters and hurriedly leaves are inspirational, although their memories are sources of melancholy (l. 15):

> Flags, weeds. And remembrance of steep alcoves
> Where cypresses shared the noon's

> Tyranny; they drew me into hades almost.
> And mammoth turtles climbing sulphur dreams
> Yielded, while sun-silt rippled them
> Asunder . . .
>
> How much I would have bartered! the black gorge
> And all the singular nestings in the hills
> Where beavers learn stitch and tooth.
> The pond I entered once and quickly fled—
> I remember now its singing willow rim.   (ll. 6–16)

The images of wind and the pond appear to communicate secrets to the poet. Nature, like the poet, does not openly declare itself; rather its secrets are hidden or encoded within the natural.

"Repose of Rivers" seeks to transcend the intangible mysteries of the natural world into physical things. The poet constantly represents the wind not simply as an unseen, barely heard entity but as something concrete. He speaks of the wind as a "sarabande"; he also refers to the wind as "flaking sapphire," such that the reader pictures not only a deep "sapphire" blue but also sees and feels the weight of the stone that is a "sapphire." The image of the wind as flakes of a stone conveys a sense of the materiality of the wind and of its considerable force; it is "flaking," losing pieces of itself. Thus, he describes the wind as a force that both requires shelter from it and provides a shelter by its physicality. Similarly, dreams are burdened with the weight of "sulphur," and the sun is loaded in the sky heavy with rays of light, "sun-silt." Crane's project to transform the natural world into something that can be handled or touched reflects nature's role in his poetry as the concealer and revealer of secrets. The poet's desire to imbue nature with physical attributes, he hopes, will allow nature to hand him its information. Having transformed these ethereal, natural images into concrete ones, Crane can hold these natural containers of information in his metonymically significant hands.

"Repose of Rivers" is an auto-elegiac poem in which the poet recalls his early childhood as well as his introduction to his imaginative life. While the poem is concerned with a recollection of a creative life, it also is a consideration of the poet's sexuality, a homosexuality that the poet desires but has never completely realized. This is a reading shared by several critics, such as Harold Bloom, Robert Martin, and Thomas Yingling, who all read the poem as dealing with a homosexual self-acceptance or an authorization of identity.[35] This reading of the poem as one that represents the construction of the poet's identity is surprising when its twenty-three lines are closely examined. Crane's language is surprisingly opaque and distancing for a poem that chronicles the self: the reader must question the level of self-knowledge set forth in such non-revealing terms. The introduction of the subject self, the "I," is through suppression: "I could never remember" (l. 3). This line functions as a central clue to the puzzle of the poem. What is it about the natural world that is so troubling he cannot remember it?

"Repose of Rivers" manifests the speaker's coming to terms with his homosexual identity through a series of poetic images, such as the "pond." The speaker describes his desire for the realization of a homosexual union in terms of entering a pond: "The pond I entered once and quickly fled— / I remember now its singing willow rim" (ll. 15–16). These lines suggest a discussion of creative opportunity, where the "pond" is a symbol for poetry itself. These lines, however, also have a sexual import, describing a life of homosexuality indulged in but, then, "quickly fled." The sexual overtones of this image are reinforced by the image of the "Flags, weeds" (l. 6), images that recall Whitman's eroticization of the flags and sprigs in "When Lilacs Last in the Dooryard Bloom'd." The "Flags" and "weeds" are phallic symbols; however, the threat of castration of these phallic symbols is hinted at only through the destructive power, the "monsoon," of the wind. The "flags," signifying a claim of territory or of sovereignty, are also symbols of communication, signs to render a piece of information intelligible through extralinguistic means. In this way, the "flags" serve a similar function to the "bells" of "The Broken Tower" to transfer information.

In "The Broken Tower," Crane thematizes a brokenness that is necessary for him to achieve poetic inspiration; in "Repose of Rivers," Crane contextualizes a similar brokenness. Here, breaks in the poetic lines interrupt the flow of brokenness. The speaker foregrounds his feeling of brokenness most centrally in the image of the forbidden waters of the pond: "The pond I entered once and quickly fled." The images of rupture are continued in "The monsoon" that "cuts across the delta," making the geography reflect the poet's own sense of rupture. Also, "the wind flaking sapphire" is an image in which the concrete, "sapphire," is fragmented into flakes. Equally, the description of the oppressive weather in the poet's memory of the Caribbean constitutes a representation of a rupture. The poet says: "And remembrances of steep alcoves / Where cypresses shared the noon's / Tyranny; they drew me into hades almost" (ll. 6–8). What the poet seems to be remembering of this island is the labor that was required to move under the "noon's( ) tyranny," the oppressive heat of the sun. He compares the heat of the island to "hades." Interestingly, Crane chooses not to capitalize the name of the mythological city of the underworld, "hades"; this decision, simultaneously allowing and denying, suggests that the poet wants more to invoke a condition of deathly, weighty heat and less to bring to mind the Greek mythological place. Indeed, the many images of ruptures undo any attempt to ground the poem in a specific or stable place.

The poem continues with images of fragmentation: "And mammoth turtles climbing sulphur dreams / Yielded, while sun-silt rippled them / Asunder . . ." (ll. 9–11). The light of the sun's rays are broken by the tangible "silt" of the hot, heavy air. This second stanza ends with the word, "Asunder," in a prestigious position on a line shared only with an ellipsis. Asunder means to separate in direction or position, foregrounding again a movement toward rupture within the poem. The ellipsis after "Asunder," however, points toward the unknown direction of the separation. Does "Asunder" point toward the sexual options of homo- or heterosexuality that will be addressed in the third stanza? Regardless of its contextual import, the ellipsis signifies a break from language; it represents through punctuation the poet's temporary lapse from the ability to express himself with words and highlights the connection between language (poetry) and sexuality.

As Crane contrasted his images of homosexual desire with remembrances of heterosexual love in "The Broken Tower," he again opposes masculine images with feminine ones. If the many references to trees, "cypresses" (l. 7) and "willow(s)" (ll. 16, 23), together with the "weeds" and "flag" are phallic symbols, they are contrasted with the remote, interior spaces: the bower, "alcove," that remains "steep" for example. The association of these interior spaces along with other words around them make these places appear unpleasant: words like "hades," "alcove," "gorge," and "gulf gates" are associated and qualified by negative words like, the heat's "tyranny," smells of "sulphur," and darkness. These interiors recall a feminine space, which is foreign and uncanny. At the same time, these interior spaces provide a freedom from the ambivalence of the phallic symbols. The phallic images serve to reinforce the speaker's acceptance of a homosexual identity— an acceptance that does not come without the labor and the pain of a series of ruptures.[36]

"The Broken Tower" and "Repose of Rivers" are concerned with poetic initiation and self-definition and, therefore, discuss how Crane's masculine voice is developed. Whereas traditionally masculine voices are established through a repression of the feminine and an identification with the masculine, Crane uses the opposition between the masculine and the feminine as one of many images of fragmentation in his poetry. Ruptures and breaks in images and language are required for Crane to gain access to poetic language. In this way, an entrance into Crane's poetry is a rupture as the poetry itself is comprised of ruptures. The achievement of poetic initiation and self-definition derives from a breaking down of their worlds, destructuring images in order to restructure them through poetic language.

There is a similar tension between identification and repudiation in the poems of Elizabeth Bishop; however, with Bishop this tension reflects a complicated sexual matrix. Rather than destructuring the world, Elizabeth Bishop's speaker uses the outside world for support in the construction of her identity. In Bishop's "In the Waiting Room," the logic moves from matter-of-fact observation at the beginning of the poem to a poetic language at the end that is characterized by rhetorical elevation of diction, such as in the lines, "Outside, / in Worcester, Massachusetts, / were night and slush and cold" (ll. 95–97). The poem starts with a description of the poem's setting:

> In Worcester, Massachusetts,
> I went with Aunt Consuelo
> to keep her dentist's appointment
> and sat and waited for her
> in the dentist's waiting room.
> It was winter. It got dark
> early.[37]

In these opening sentences, the speaker sets the scene for the poem. It is a crepuscular moment, when it is in the process of becoming "dark," a time of impending change. The speaker is in both a literal and a figurative space, a "waiting room" that functions as a kind of chrysalis out of which she will emerge with a new sense of self.

The waiting room becomes a space within the poem in which the speaker both identifies with, and becomes anxious over, the inevitability of sexual maturation:

> My aunt was inside
> what seemed like a long time
> and while I waited I read
> the *National Geographic*
> (I could read) and carefully
> studied the photographs:
> the inside of a volcano,
> black, and full of ashes;

then it was spilling over
in rivulets of fire.
Osa and Martin Johnson
dressed in riding breeches,
laced boots, and pith helmets.
A dead man slung on a pole
—"Long Pig," the caption said.
Babies with pointed heads
wound round and round with string;
black, naked women with necks
wound round and round with wire
like the necks of light bulbs.
Their breasts were horrifying.
I read it right straight through.
I was too shy to stop.   (ll. 11–33)

The speaker is a young girl who excitedly proclaims her ability to read. Like Whitman's speaker in "Out of the Cradle," Bishop constructs her subject self as a young child and plays with the notion of a young speaker constructed by a poet who is writing from the vantage point of a much older age. The speaker sits with a magazine, "*National Geographic*," and grows horrified at the images before her: "black, naked women with necks / wound round and round with wire / like the necks of light bulbs" (ll. 28–30). The combination of the images of the "babies" and the "women" seems overpowering because the poet gets the sense that the "babies" begin with "string" around their necks and progress to "wire"; there is no sense of freedom from the two forms of constriction—"string" or "wire." Both convey the possibility of asphyxiation.[38] The sense of being closed in is heightened by the repetitions of sounds and words within those three lines that betray the speaker's complicated relationship to the sexual import of the images before her, especially in the repetition of the phrase "wound round and round." These images are both playful and commonplace, like "light bulbs," but also threatening through a fear of the electricity that makes the bulbs work. She is specific about the magazine she reads, "*National Geographic*," which is both comforting because of its familiarity as a popular magazine as well as frightening in the "otherness" of the exotic images inside. Her fear and identification become explicit in the next line: "Their breasts were horrifying" (l. 31), but still she keeps reading: "I read it right straight through." The speaker's focus on the female breasts also points to an erotic interest that further frustrates her, conveyed when she says that she is "too shy" to put down the magazine. She is simultaneously drawn to as well as afraid of the breasts. The tension between these two views of the breast, the nurturing breast of the mother/aunt and the rejecting breast, produces an ambivalence.[39] In this way, the waiting room is a figurative place in which the poet waits for the signs of sexual maturation, the "breasts" of the native women and the babies they hold, to show their mark on her. She waits for sexuality and for sex, as a wish and a fear at once excited and anxious.

The African women and babies are "black" and "naked"; through their nakedness they are images of an explicit erotic potency. The eroticism is reinforced by the speaker's attention to the "inside of a volcano" that suggests a vaginal space. Yet, the blackness of the women and the destructive, obliterating potential of the "volcano" undercut the erotic allure here with a threat of danger. This threat of danger is continued in the setting of the poem outside of the dentist's office that produces the speaker's aunt's cry of pain (l. 37). The "otherness" of the native women is contrasted with the images of the husband and wife, white, English explorers, "Osa and Martin Johnson," who are dressed "in riding breeches, / laced boots, and pith helmets" (ll. 21–22). Their description complicates the sexual matrix of the poem, because they are described without sexual differentiation. The husband and wife are de-eroticized; any visual signifiers of gender difference that can traditionally be read through clothing are erased. The erotic potential of Osa and Martin Johnson is channeled into a socially acceptable form and, therefore, masked behind the institution of marriage. Their identical outfits form a visual signifier of their status as married. They are a stiff, matching pair.

In the middle of the poem, the identifications of the speaker become even more explicit.[40] The first is an identification with her aunt as a maternal figure. The speaker hears her aunt's cry of pain from inside the dentist's office and conflates the sound with her own anguish over her sexual initiation: "Without thinking at all / I was my foolish aunt, / I—we—were falling, falling" (ll. 48–50). The explicitness of the association, "I—we," serves both to reinforce the association as well as to introduce a resistance to it. She tries to say simply "I" but cannot help but conflate herself with her aunt. Why is the child with her aunt and not her mother, and why are there no references to the child's mother at all? There is only a surrogate mother, her aunt. While it seems clear from her published comments on the poem's "truthfulness" that Bishop was trying to follow the facts of her life, she could have engaged in some imaginative invention, as she did with the issue of the magazine and her aunt's name.[41] The absence of a literal mother figure drives the speaker to impose a heightened maternal import upon the aunt and the images of native women. With only these "virtual mothers," the speaker must simultaneously form an attachment to and repudiate the mother figure.

The second explicit identification is between the speaker and her self, where the speaker asserts herself as an individual through the performative statement:

> But I felt: you are an I,
> you are an *Elizabeth*,
> you are one of *them*.
> *Why* should you be one, too?
> I scarcely dared to look
> to see what it was I was.

Why does she "scarcely dare" to "see what it was [she] was"? What is she afraid of here? Perhaps it is the uncanny, "unlikely," nature of self-hood. The poet does not sound convinced that she will definitely become "one of them" because she asks herself, "why should you be one, too(.)" She is uncertain that she will be like the "black, naked women" or like her "foolish, timid" aunt and this makes her afraid. She wants to be like them. These lines serve as a fulcrum, balancing the poem and the poet. They are reminiscent of Stephen Dedalus's prayer-like mantra in James Joyce's *Portrait of the Artist as a Young Man*, where Stephen utters his name and his geographical position to ground himself:

> Stephen Dedalus
> Class of Elements
> Clongowes Wood College
> Sallins
> County Kildare
> Ireland
> Europe
> The World
> The Universe.[42]

These are verbal attempts to battle a feeling of being overwhelmed by the outside world and confused by one's place in it. Bishop's speaker tries to situate herself in time, in "Worcester, Massachusetts" and in "February 1918." David Kalstone has written that Bishop's writing must document the literal truth, because the " 'literal' representation kept almost inconceivable pain within bounds."[43] The literal weight of the "truthfulness" of the date, the place, and the issue of the magazine functions as an anchor for the poet, grounding her to concrete facts as an antidote to the instability of the self. As her sense of individual identity is forming, she immediately attempts to connect it with a whole. This struggle to connect is threatened by the dizzying sensation of the "round, turning world" which, together with the waiting room, feels like "a big black wave," without features or differentiation.

Bishop's drama of initiation into selfhood is a strategic fiction. Bishop engages her ingenious style, her reticent manner characterized by unpretentious language, and her very controlled assertion of perspective to create the illusion of a naive (in the sense of being uninitiated), six-year-old speaker, who boasts, albeit parenthetically, that she "can read" and who feels slightly uneasy in the world of "grown ups." However, this six-year-old girl is a fictional character, created late in the poet's life, appearing in Bishop's last volume of poetry, *Geography III*.[44] Childhood is recalled to invoke an illusion of innocence. Rather than creating a poem that reflects upon a past state of affairs within the presence of the poem, as in "Crusoe in England," Bishop invents a fiction that recreates the past within the poem's presence, although the speaker is confronting issues of identity that characterize a more typically adult crisis.

The recreation of this fictive scene in which a child is confronted with her own self in the form of her name, "you are an I, / you are an *Elizabeth*," presents a moment of a realization of identity as described by Jacques Lacan in "The Mirror Stage" in which the self is constituted through an act of vision.[45] For Bishop, the vision is not the image of the self in a mirror but the image of the self's name. As she writes the poet sees her own words: "You are an *Elizabeth*," and thereby assumes her image. Her name, "Elizabeth," is therefore significant because it announces her gender in a way that a reflection of herself—at the time of the poem she is almost seven years old—is too young to reinforce her gender identity. The poet reconstructs an image of herself through a recognition of her linguistic act. In this light, the feeling of being engulfed "beneath a big black wave" and feeling "unlikely" represents the poet's resistant reaction to her realization of herself as an individual "I" and her feeling of the instability of that selfhood. The role of the speaker's gaze, her act of vision that brings about identity, is a problem for her not only because the gaze is a masculine gesture but also because she does not know where to look. After her declaration of selfhood, her eyes wander: "I gave a sidelong glance / -I couldn't look any higher- / at shadowy grey knees" (ll. 66–68). Her eyes travel from her self-declaration back to the site of biological sex; she cannot look "any higher" than the crotches of the other people in the waiting room, reinforcing the immediacy of the facts of life. She is drawn to the factic proof of her inevitable maturation.

The degree to which the speaker's recognition is through language reinforces her statement, "you are an I, / you are an *Elizabeth*," as a performative speech act. This declaration enacts its own selfhood in the way that it is a citation or repetition of the paradigmatic performative speech act, "it's a girl." When the doctor announces the gender of the infant at the moment of its birth, the doctor's statement works to codify the gender identification of the baby.[46] From then on, the infant enacts her girlness. Similarly, the speaker recognizes and conforms with the image of herself as represented by her name and, thus, asserts her individual identity. "In the Waiting Room" does not simply reflect a Freudian case study but creates a scene representative of the case study that reinforces the linguistic role in the recognition of identity. At the same time, the speaker does not just say you are an I and you are a girl, but "you are an *Elizabeth*." She needs to enact her Elizabeth-ness whatever that may mean. This mystery of selfhood is scary.

As in the drama of the Mirror Stage, "In the Waiting Room" focuses on a child's point of view. By contrast, in "The End of March," Bishop treats the subject of identity from the perspective of a mature speaker. "The End of March" is a shore ode, a traditional American form practiced by poets such as Walt Whitman, Hart Crane, and Wallace Stevens. The poem is auto-elegiac in tone, reinforcing the sense of maturity in the speaker's voice. The speaker walks on the beach with other people; it is cold, and she describes the day as an unlikely one for their walk:

> It was cold and windy, scarcely the day
> to take a walk on that long beach.
> Everything was withdrawn as far as possible,
> indrawn: the tide far out, the ocean shrunken,
> seabirds in ones or twos.
> The rackety, icy, offshore wind
> numbed our faces on one side;
> disrupted the formation
> of a lone flight of Canada geese;
> and blew back the low, inaudible rollers
> in upright, steely mist.   (ll. 1–11)

As the poem opens, we do not yet know its crisis. Something is forbidding, making the speaker feel "numb." Perhaps the "Canada geese" makes her think of her childhood in Nova Scotia. The world in this first verse stanza seems uninviting: "Everything was withdrawn as far as possible, / indrawn: the tide far out" (ll. 3–4). Like the ocean, the speaker herself is "withdrawn"; she is introspective. This interior space of consciousness prefigures the images of the poet's dream houses later in the poem.

In the second verse paragraph, the natural world around the speaker is described in foreboding images that continue those in the poem's opening:

> The sky was darker than the water
> —*it* was the color of mutton-fat jade.
> Along the wet sand, in rubber boots, we followed
> a track of big dog-prints (so big
> they were more like lion-prints.) Then we came on
> lengths and lengths, endless, of wet white string,
> looping up to the tide-line, down to the water,
> over and over. Finally, they did end:
> a thick white snarl, man-size, awash,
> rising on every wave, a sodden ghost,
> falling back, sodden, giving up the ghost. . . .
> A kite string?—But no kite.    (ll. 12–23)

There are a series of disturbingly odd images in this second stanza, beginning with the "water," which is described as "the color of mutton fat jade," a sickening color and one that looks forward to Bishop's description of the water in "At the Fishhouses," which is discussed in the following chapter. The next, almost surreal image is that of the "lengths and lengths" of "endless," "wet, white string." Like the "dog-prints" where there is no sign of a dog, the kite string is a trace but there, too, is "no kite." The stanza ends with the most disturbing of the images—a drowned person. The "ghost" is "man-size" and "awash." James Merrill writes that the parenthetical sentence, "Many things about this place are dubious," alerts the reader to a "double meaning."[47] In this way, the "sodden ghost" is an image of a drowned woman, her hair floats in the "tide-line" like "wet white string." The lines describing the string are broken by a parenthetical interruption and by commas, characteristic of the language of loss. The image of the drowned person, an erotic object and a maternal figure, like the dream house of the next stanza, functions as an image of unattainable desire, a figure of a woman to whom the speaker is erotically attracted but is unable to reach.

The image of the "sodden ghost" disrupts the speaker. She breaks into a new stanza and describes a fantasy of removal from the world.

The poet contemplates her "crypto-dream-house," her "proto-dream-house," her fantasy of a solitary life of reading and drinking:

> I wanted to get as far as my proto-dream-house,
> my crypto-dream-house, that crooked box
> set up on pilings, shingled green,
> a sort of artichoke of a house, but greener
> (boiled with bicarbonate of soda?),
> protected from spring tides by a palisade
> of—are they railroad ties?
> (Many things about this place are dubious.)    (ll. 24–31)

Like the deception of the string as a drowned woman, the "railroad ties" are dubious: the poet reflects on her "ties" to the outside world. The dream house is boarded up; her fantasy is an impossibility both on the level of the writtenness of the poem as well as the improbability of achieving such a dream. The paradoxical image of the house, the ideal place, which is boarded up reflects the tension produced in the image of the breasts that are both nurturing and rejecting. Presumably one would want access to the ideal place as one would want the nurturing breast of the mother; why, then, does the speaker prevent herself these satisfactions? Melanie Klein argues for the presence of a "good breast" and a "bad breast" based upon the breast that is nurturing (good) and the one that is frustrating and depriving (bad). Klein writes:

> I recognized also that the oral-sadistic relation to the mother and the internalization of a devoured, and therefore devouring, breast create the prototype of all internal persecutors; and furthermore that the internalization of an injured and therefore dreaded breast on the one hand, and of a satisfying and helpful breast on the other, is at the core of the super-ego.[48]

Klein continues in this essay to explain that the ego must work to "synthesize" the good/loved with the bad/hated—for Klein, this is an effort for the infant to come to terms with the fact that the mother is more than the good breast or the bad breast and that she is more than a synthesized breast. While Klein offers a useful model for the way that individuals can reconcile a seemingly disturbing state of ambivalence, she does not specify between male and female infants. Therefore, it is unclear if Bishop's reaction to the ambivalence of the breast might be different from that of Crane or Merrill because of her gender. The image of the boarded up house and the nurturing and rejecting breast must bring up sad memories of loss for the poet. Also, the "kite" and reference to "Canada" are associated with images of childhood and maternal comfort. These images undoubtedly serve to reinforce the elegiac tone of the poem. The description of the dream house begins with its distance; it is not easy to reach it. If it were not for this third stanza, "The End of March" would resemble a poem like "At the Fishhouses"; both poems are concerned with description of the cold, dark water that is here the color of "mutton-fat jade." The third stanza is a departure from her descriptive style, because it indulges in a fantasy that betrays a sadness and a feeling of isolation, which she also appears to desire. What do these houses signify? She writes:

> I'd like to retire there and do *nothing*,
> or nothing much, forever, in two bare rooms:
> look through binoculars, read boring books,
> old, long, long, books, and write down useless notes,
> talk to myself, and, foggy days,
> watch the droplets slipping, heavy with light.    (ll. 32–37).

The repetition of words, "nothing" and "long," creates a linguistic space that mirrors that of the dream-house itself. It is a liminal space that is a fantasy of completeness and isolation. Yet, the isolation is tempered by the reference to "binoculars," which serves both to connect the poet to the outside world and to keep the outside world at a distance, allowing for uninterrupted peace and solitude. Her nights would be filled with warm drinks, "*grog à l'américaine*"; she writes: "I'd blaze it with a kitchen match / and lovely diaphanous blue flame / would waver, doubled in the window" (ll. 39–41). Like the "fluttering stranger," the piece of ash on the grate in Coleridge's "Frost at Midnight," the wavering flame atop the drink is a comforting source of relief to the solitude of the introspective inquiry of the poem.[49]

Nevertheless, the poet reinforces the simultaneous desire for, and impossibility of, her dream. She describes the inside of the house:

> There must be a stove; there is a chimney.
> . . .
> A light to read by—perfect! But—impossible.
> And that day the wind was much too cold
> even to get that far,
> and of course the house was boarded up.    (ll. 42, 48–51)

The limits that the poet imposes upon her own dream, "the house was boarded up," reinforces the tone of loss and absence within the poem.

This loss is also highlighted by the poet's construction of a dream that is of an isolated, but nonetheless domestic scene. The theme of domesticity is underscored by the speaker's language, such as "mutton-fat," "artichoke," "bicarbonate of soda," "kitchen match" and the warm hearth of the "stove" and "chimney." These are all items from the domestic world that create a sense of home, place, and permanence.

The dream of a home foregrounds the movement of the poem from the outside to the inside; indeed the crisis of "The End of March" takes place inside the poet's consciousness, in her introspective reveries. This is in contrast to "In the Waiting Room," where the crisis is directed outward to the room and the external realization of her individual identity through the vision and utterance of her name. In both instances, it is through a simultaneous need for association and rejection of associations to the world that the self is constituted. The poem ends with a return to the outside as well as a return to gendered images; this time the images are conveyed through the poet's literary allusions:

> On the way back our faces froze on the other side.
> The sun came out for just a minute.
> For just a minute, set in their bezels of sand,
> the drab, damp, scattered stones
> were multicolored,
> and all those high enough threw out long shadows,
> individual shadows, then pulled them in again.
> They could have been teasing the lion sun,
> except that now he was behind them
> —a sun who'd walked the beach the last low tide,
> making those big, majestic paw-prints,
> who perhaps had batted a kite out of the sky to play with.     (ll. 52–63)

The "damp" stones recall the image of the "sodden ghost" and reinforce a connection between her image and the images of this final stanza, where the speaker comes to terms with these gendered images and uses them toward the completion of her poem.

Whereas in "In the Waiting Room" the speaker gains a knowledge of her individual self through an identification with, and repudiation of, the mother figures around her, in "The End of March" Bishop grounds herself not only through the mother and erotic object of the drowned woman but also through a connection to her literary past. Her use of the traditional form of the shore ode connects her with that literary tradition. Also, she includes references to Emily

Dickinson, who is invoked through the image of the "long shadows."
Wallace Stevens is alluded to through the image of the "lion sun":
compare, for example, Bishop's "The End of March" with the title
and images of the "sun" and the "lion" in Wallace Steven's "The Sun
This March." Here, Stevens's speaker says: "The exceeding brightness
of this early sun/ Makes me conceive how dark I have become," (ll.
1–2); Bishop's speaker, however, is not concerned with how "dark"
but with how "withdrawn" she has or could become.[50] Nevertheless,
Bishop changes the tone of these appropriated images by rendering
them playful ones; indeed the speaker's tone through most of the
poem is jocular, especially in her parenthetical comments. For example, the poet wonders at the end of the poem if it was the formidable,
Stevensian lion sun who "batted a kite out of the sky" with his paw.
Also, the Dickinsonian "long shadows" that had symbolized mortality, here, are innocently cast from stones in the sand. If Bishop
acquires her title from a reworking of Stevens's, what does her revision signify? Bishop may have been playing with the children's rhyme
in which March is said to come in like a lion but go out like a lamb
when she revised the image of the lion to reflect such a change. The
end of March is also the beginning of spring, and this conveys the
sense that with the renewal of the season the poet might lessen her
"withdrawn" thoughts.

The "dubious(ness)" of "The End of March" allows for an interpretation of the poem as one that concerns the poet's craft. Bishop's
speaker both aligns herself with, and distances herself from, the series
of gendered images. The drowned woman and the allusions to poetic
forbearers functions as desired objects as well as ones about which she
is wary. In this way, a central difference among Crane's and Merrill's
and Bishop's poetry becomes clear. For Crane and Merrill, the figure
of the mother is connected with the homoerotic, but not directly
because of the mother's female status. The femininity of the mother is
in opposition to the masculinity of their erotic objects. For Bishop,
the mother and the homoerotic are directly conflated; both are
eroticized as female objects of desire.

As is the case in Bishop's poems, the image of the real world that exists
at a distance is also invoked by James Merrill in "Scenes of Childhood."
In this poem, there is a clear succession of images in which the poet
develops an understanding of his own self-disclosures, reminiscent of
"In the Waiting Room." "Scenes of Childhood" is comprised of fifteen
stanzas of eight lines each and is in two parts. In the first part, mother
and son are together watching displaced representations, home

movies, of themselves as they were thirty years ago. In the second part, the poet is alone and reflecting on the heated encounter in his past and the confrontation with his mother. Merrill describes the film with Oedipal overtones, as an erotic triangle of mother–father–son. The poem is included in the 1962 collection *Water Street* that is named after the street on which Merrill and his lover, David Jackson, shared a house in Stonington, Connecticut. The poem's return to the scene of childhood is ironically positioned against the significations of the book's title and conveys the sense that the speaker is able to return to his "scenes of childhood" because he is far removed from them in his own secured home on "Water Street." There is also in the title the irony of a street made of water. The poem opens as the speaker's mother turns out the lights and he runs the film of "a real noon's field's / Crickets and gnats" (ll. 7–8). Sexuality exists beneath the well-manicured surface of Merrill's lines:

> Under the risen flood
> Of thirty years ago—
> A tree, a house
>
> We had then, a late sun,
> A door from which the primal
> Figures jerky and blurred
> As lightning bugs
> From lanterns issue, next
> To be taken for stars,
> For fates. With knowing smiles
> And beaded shrugs
>
> My mother and two aunts
> Loom on the screen. Their plucked
> Brows pucker, their arms encircle
> One another.
> Their ashen lips move.
> From the love seat's gloom
> A quiet chuckle escapes
> My white-haired mother
>
> To see in that final light
> A man's shadow mount
> Her dress.   (ll. 22–43)

The speaker both presents and plays with a Freudian drama of sexual maturation; he, for example, calls his family the "primal / Figures," suggesting that they are both prime characters as well as characters creating a sort of primal scene. The poet's language, "love seat" and "mount(s) her dress," foregrounds the eroticism of the scene. At the same time, the father is merely a "shadow." He is not real; therefore the impression of a fantasy being created is heightened. The fantasy here is reinforced by the speaker's language that is meant to suggest the distance of time between the speaker as he is now and the speaker as he was when the home-movie was filmed. Phrases like "a house // We had then" and words like "jerky," "taken for stars," and "ashen lips" foreground the sense in which the poet and his family exist in two worlds here: the world as they are, watching the movie, and the world of artifice in which they are like actors in a fiction, black and white, ash-looking film.

As the poet continues his description of the film, the film changes from a displaced version of the speaker's self to one in which he is confronted with violence:

> . . . And now she [the mother] is
> advancing, sister—
> less, but followed by
> A fair child, or fury—
> Myself at four, in tears.
> I raise my fist,
>
> Strike, she kneels down. The man's
> Shadow afflicts us both.
> Her voice behind me says
> It might go slower.
> I work the dials, the film jams.
> Our headstrong old projector
> Glares at the scene which promptly
> Catches fire.   (l. 43–56)

The speaker denies, at first, that it is he who "follows" his mother like a "fury."[51] Merrill generates an ambiguity in these lines as to whether the child raises his fist and strikes the mother, which would mean that she kneels down from the child's blow, or whether the child strikes the father, and the mother kneels down to help the fallen man. In either interpretation, it is the father who inspires the child's rage. It is his "shadow," described in alienating terms as "the man's" instead of as "my father's," that "afflicts" the speaker. Like the father who is merely a "shadow," the child is also a fantasy. He is both "fair" and a "fury," composed of opposites. The description draws the reader into the narrative by raising questions; why is the child "fair," a "fury," and "in tears?" The violence and potential violence of the scene causes the

speaker to establish a distance between himself and his cinematic figure in the poem; indeed the poet is uncomfortable with the violence.

   The violence and aggression of the child running with his "fist"
raised surprises the poet and engenders a break in the poem's narrative: the mother insists on adjusting the projector, and the film jams
and catches fire. The image of the burned film reinforces the guilt and
aggression with which the poet views his past. With the night's enter-
tainment cut short, the poet remains alone with his thoughts, running
toward a similar moment of self-realization to that which occurs in
Bishop's "In the Waiting Room." The poet, however, does not simply
present a violent encounter with his father in order to recreate a scene
of Oedipal rage; rather, once he is alone with his thoughts, he returns
to contemplate his father:

> Father already fading—
> Who focused your life long
> Through little frames,
> Whose microscope, now deep
> In purple velvet, first
> Showed me the skulls of flies,
> The fur, the flames
>
> Etching the jaws—father:
> Shrunken to our true size.

The image of the father is comforting; he is the sole masculine figure
beside the speaker in the film that is otherwise populated with women,
his "mother and two aunts." Words like "fading" and "focused" reinforce the dynamics in which Merrill revises his scene; "fading" conveys
the sense of the poet's aggression toward his father. The word registers
his anger in a passive manner. Conversely, "focused" provides the other
part of the poet's conflicting relationship with his father; "focused"
highlights the speaker's embrasure of the father. In the second part of
the poem, the poet provides an interesting revision of the Oedipal
drama. He has fought with the father; however, in the end, it is the
mother who has been repudiated and sent away, while the father
remains in the form of embracing thoughts. It is this simultaneous
aggression and affection for the father that permits the examination of
him—not under a "microscope" that reveals his ugly flaws but
"shrunken to [their] true size." This is to say, the poet addresses the
figure of the father in realistic and mortal terms. The figure of
the father functions as a father and an erotic object, as the
mother/drowned woman did for Bishop's speaker.

As the poem moves toward its conclusion, the speaker's ruminations on his father become a source for qualified identification with
him and lead to further memories from childhood. Because the
speaker considers the father in his "true size," aware of his faults and
virtues—the word "fall" invokes the image of Adam and of masculinity in a general conceit (l. 92)—he reflects on his relationship with his
father and its connection to his own identity:

> A minute galaxy
> About my head will easily
> Needle me back. The day's
> Inaugural *Damn*
> Spoken, I start to run,
> Inane, like them, but breathing
> In and out the sun
> And air I am.
> The son and heir!   (ll. 97–105)

The spoken invective "*Damn*" releases a literal "dam," a floodgate,
which sets the poet on the path toward the poet's realization of, and
coming to terms with, his familiar origins. These lines represent a
quintessential moment in Merrill, who was a fan of puns, in which the
reader can feel the poet's delight in being able to make such a glori-
ous pun (sun/son and air/heir). Merrill's readers are meant to get all
of his self-conscious jokes, allusions, and puns and thereby share in a
strong sense of the interaction with the literary tradition to which the
poet feels an attachment. At the same time, the declaration of himself
as a "son and heir" is a moment of connection and realization of his
own identity. The lines work toward the kind of self-awareness of
Bishop's "you are an I, / you are an *Elizabeth*"; however Merrill's
speaker no longer identifies with his familiar origins:

> . . . In the dark
> It makes me catch my breath
> And hear, from upstairs, hers—
> That faintest hiss
> And slither, as of life
> Escaping into space,
> Having led its characters
> To the abyss
> Of night. Immensely still
> The heavens glisten. One broad
> Path of vague stars is floating

Off, a shed skin
Of all whose fine cold eyes
First told us, locked in ours
You are the heroes without name
Or origin.   (ll. 105–120)

Unlike Bishop's seven-year-old girl who identifies with her aunt as a surrogate mother, Merrill's speaker acknowledges his mother's utterance ("hiss") as separate from his own ("breath"). The mother, too, is allowed to return, so that the speaker allows for the maintenance of conflicting desires between him and the figures of the mother and father. The mother's utterance is not a signifier of life, but is described as being "as of life," not life completely. The mother's breath that is like "life / Escaping" provides the speaker with a Whitmanian knowledge of the import of life and death and allows for the poem's ending.

It is this simultaneous repudiation and identification of his mother and father that leads "Scenes of Childhood" in a dramatically different direction from that of "In the Waiting Room," where the parental figures are substitute ones. "Scenes of Childhood" ends with two lines that sound self-consciously like a moral or a summation of a point of crisis: "You are the heroes without name / Or origin." "The heroes" are either the speaker, because he has confronted and survived his family and his artistic past, or the parents themselves, because the word is plural. The violence of the confrontation is reinforced through the burning film and the threat of displacement from the pastoral world of the fields and fireflies that characterize the summer days of his youth. Merrill does not simply bring up the images of his past to house them in poetry but invokes them in order to repudiate them. The poet's revision of the drama of maturation involving the figurations of the mother and father reveal his simultaneous identification and repudiation of them; this combination of responses permits the poet to move beyond the drama they engender and reinvent himself in the poem's motivating close: "without name / Or origin" other than that of the poet. This ending is curiously reminiscent of many poems of initiation where the poet seeks to illustrate his or her selfhood by repudiating the past and fashioning a poetic self that derives only from a poetic "origin."

The theme of the combination of repudiation and identification continues in "An Urban Convalescence," where the object of the speaker's concern is not his family but his former literary style. "An Urban Convalescence" also appears in *Water Street*; it is the opening poem for the collection. The first half of the poem is composed of a series of stanzas of different lengths; the second half is a series of seven quatrains

that represents the speaker's shift from free verse and malady to structure, rhyme, and composure. The title implies an illness from which the
speaker is recovering, but it is more a metaphoric illness than a real one.
The speaker goes for a walk and encounters the rubble of a demolished
building; his illness is likened to the "shabby stone(s)" that are now a
pile. His observations bring on memories and internal questions:

> Out for a walk, after a week in bed,
> I find them tearing up part of my block
> And, chilled through, dazed and lonely, join the dozen
> In meek attitudes, watching a huge crane
> Fumble luxuriously in the filth of years.
> Her jaws dribble rubble. An old man
> Laughs and curses in her brain,
> Bring to mind the close of *The White Goddess*.    (ll. 1–8)

The language of the poem's opening is combined with humor at the
folly of the scene observed by the speaker: "As usual in New York,
everything is torn down/ Before you have had time to care for it"
(ll. 9–10). The theme of the building that is being torn down before
its prime is presented, at first, as a reflection of a postmodern, depth-
less view of the city and, by extension, of art.[52] There is also a play
with gendered images, most notably the "crane" that the poet surprisingly figures as feminine, "Her jaws." The "crane's" femininity
subverts our expectations of traditional gender images because the
reader expects the aggressive and destructive machine to be masculine. The "crane" is a playful moment in the poem especially as it
refers to the poet's literary predecessor "in the filth of years," Hart
Crane. The grammar of lines six and seven foreground the importance
of gender in the poem: "An old man / Laughs and curses in her
brain." The syntax confuses here; is it the "old man" who laughs in
"her" brain? The reader is also surprised by the man's age; why is he
"old"? The "old man" is the "crane's" operator; he sits in her "brain."
The poet's use of confusing grammar highlights the import of gender.
    The poem is filled with various confusions. The speaker is confused,
and the poet is as well, represented through internal contradictions and
questions. The speaker begins by trying to remember the building that
was demolished: "Was there a building at all?" then two lines later,

> Wait. Yes. Vaguely a presence rises
> Some five floors high, of shabby stone
> —Or am I confusing it with another one
> in another part of town, or of the world?—    (ll. 12 and 14–17)

These internal questions reflect the speaker's unsure sense of self, a self that is in the process of thinking. The questions and contradictions also reinforce the malady of the poet.

Indeed as the speaker continues, it becomes clear that the external scene reflects an internal state of affairs. While the speaker tries to recall the building that was torn down, he closes his eyes and imagines he sees a "lintel," the building's frame with a "garland" in the edifice. He says: "When did the garland become part of me" (l. 23), suggesting that the building is, or reflects, an internal state of affairs. This question leads to the first of several frissons that the poet describes, "Then shiver once from head to toe" (l. 25). The speaker enters farther into his consciousness and into memory as he tries to recall a woman, "the small, red-nailed hand," whom he can picture but not recall. She is invoked by negation that not only reinforces the speaker's uncertain consciousness but also disrupts the line of poetry:

> Also, to clasp them, the small, red-nailed hand
> Of no one I can place. Wait. No. Her name, her features
> Lie toppled underneath that year's fashions.
> The words she must have spoken, setting her face
> To flutter like a veil, I cannot hear her now,
> Let alone understand.    (ll. 32–37)

The woman's presence, invoked through her detailed absence, functions in opposition to the masculinity of the building that is "still erect." The difference between the "still erect" building and the speaker's interior building is that the speaker's has been emasculated, torn down. This memory produces a second frisson in the speaker, as represented through phrases like the "structure shudders" and "soundlessly collapses" and words such as "fluttering" and "quiver" (ll. 40, 41, 36, and 47). The speaker's "shudder" comes in part because the speaker compares his internal, demolished building with the masculine one still standing. He also compares himself with the figure of the woman and feels a sense of lack. The speaker does connect the woman and the building through language: "her features / Lie toppled." At the same time, the poet is at his apartment in New York; this is presumably 18 West 11th Street, his family's townhouse in the city, which Merrill inherits.[53] In this way, the figure of the woman also is an image of the poet's mother. Her "red nails" convey the sense of her glamour and undercut her maternal import. Toward the later part of the poem the speaker reinforces the import of place, during the poem's "scene":

> Indoors at last, the pages of *Time* are apt
> To open, and the illustrated mayor of New York,
> Given a glimpse of how and where I work,
> To note yet one more house that can be scrapped.
>
> Unwillingly I picture
> My walls weathering in the general view.
> It is not even as though the new
> Buildings did very much for architecture. (ll. 60–67)

The speaker's apartment, which is "where [he] work(s)," becomes a part of the poem; yet, the speaker's thoughts about its fate are ambivalent in nature and reflect his ambivalence toward the masculinity and femininity associated with the external and internal buildings of the poem's beginning.

Indeed, the connection between confusion and ambivalence brings about the climax of the poem, a break in the line that reduces the otherwise long stanzas to one that is only two lines (ll. 58–59). The speaker continues to represent his consciousness as confused through contradictory images, such as "motes of stone," and further examples of internal questions:

> Upon that book I swear
> To abide by what it teaches:
> Gospels of ugliness and waste,
> Of towering voids, of soiled gusts,
> Of a shrieking to be faced
> full into, eyes astream with cold—
>
> With cold?
> All right then. With self-knowledge. (ll. 52–59)

As was the case with Bishop's "The End of March," things here are "dubious" as well, specifically the admission that he is concerned with "self-knowledge." The contingency of time, where even stone buildings of the mind can decay in forgetfulness, and where the identifications with images of masculinity and femininity become ambivalent ones proves to be the disturbing "self-knowledge" the speaker is reluctant to accept. After the word, "self-knowledge," the tone of the poem changes to one of uncertainty. The remainder of the poem is a series of seven quatrains with a fixed rhyme scheme (a-b-b-a). The speaker moves inside where the structure permits a fixed rhyme

scheme that serves to help cure the poetic malady. The poet moves
from what J. D. McClatchy describes as "exposure to enclosure and
doubt, from what life teaches to what art questions."[54] Why the need
for enclosure, and what is the connection between enclosure and the
meditation on the poet's art?

The movement from the street to "indoors" represents a movement into the poet's consciousness to emotions that are beyond language, where a facile phrase merely "enhances then debases" what the
poet feels (l. 76). That is to say, language cancels itself out and leads
nowhere in a way that is similar to the gendered images and contradictions; however, in those instances, the conflicting images were per-
mitted to coexist rather than cancel each other out. This loss of
language echoes the crisis of Bishop's speaker in "In the Waiting
Room" who fumbles for words to describe her fate of growing old,
symbolized by the image of sagging breasts: "How—I didn't know
any / word for it—how 'unlikely' . . ." (ll. 84–85). Intense emotion
and instability rupture the poets' abilities in both cases to find suitable
language for description. The ending of Merrill's poem provides an
antidote to this linguistic malaise: "the dull need to make some kind
of house / Out of the life lived, out of the love spent" (ll. 86–87).
Also, within this house, the figures of masculinity and femininity exist
conjoined, signified as "her hand in his" (l. 85), and this union of gendered images produces a state of affairs that seems to be useful to the
poet. The need to go inside, "indoors," into the desired "house," if it
were already to exist, is because that is where "life" and "love" exist,
and to be in such a house would mean self-knowledge. Similarly, the
"home movies" in "Scenes of Childhood" allude to a house that
is concerned with self-knowledge; however, the confrontation with
self-awareness in the home movie forms the crisis, rather than resolves
it. By understanding his identity as a poet, the speaker can take
possession of his elusive house.

Indeed architectural spaces, figured in these six poems as houses,
function as a defining locus of identity for Crane, Bishop, and Merrill.
"The Broken Tower," "Repose of Rivers," "In the Waiting Room,"
"The End of March," "Scenes of Childhood," and "An Urban
Convalescence" are concerned with speakers who enact dramas of
self-awareness within the poetic narratives and who construct fantasies
of enclosure within safe houses, towers, and waiting rooms that
remove the poet from the world. Once removed, the poet gives him
or herself the space and the freedom to do the work of repudiation
and identification that is necessary for understanding one's identity. In
presenting these six poems as dramatizations of the recognition of

identity, Crane, Bishop, and Merrill are not repeating structures that construct selfhood but are creating dramas about them and participating in the evolution of categories of identity. In so doing they represent the confluence of forces that comprise such identities, such as through the tensions in gender representations and sexuality. While this discussion gestures toward a potential theory of poetic difference based upon gender difference—other than the one generated by the eroticization of the mother—Crane, Bishop, and Merrill resist such attempts through their recognition of both the masculine and feminine imagery they employ.

# CHAPTER 2

# ANATOMY OF A MOTHER

Readers of Hart Crane's poetry sympathize with Harriet Monroe. The founder and editor of *Poetry* magazine from 1912–1936 was confused by unclear imagery when Crane submitted to her "At Melville's Tomb," an admittedly difficult poem but one that is representative of the poet's style. Not averse to the idiosyncrasies that characterize the tenets of modern poetry, Monroe championed many of the emerging poets of her day: Wallace Stevens, T. S. Eliot, Marianne Moore, as well as Hart Crane. But she did initially wonder about the successfulness of Crane's verse, and, from the poet's response in a letter written in 1926 that is held up in Crane's oeuvre to be central to the understanding of his poems, she accuses him of being, among other things, "elliptical" and "obscure."[1] Readers of Crane can understand Monroe's reservations in publishing his work, because Crane often requires explanation. In fact, many of his letters contain glossaries for his images. Similarly, James Merrill's poetry is often described as politely ambiguous with a drawing-room tone that many readers find idiosyncratic, at best, or distancing, at worst. Readers of Elizabeth Bishop, however, are almost never dumbfounded by her style; rather they remark on her lucid descriptions and detailed observations. Randell Jarrell, reviewing Bishop's first book *North & South*, postulates that beneath her poems there is written "*I have seen it.*"[2] In different ways Harriet Monroe and Randell Jarrell help to delineate these poets' style and, in so doing, point out that Crane, Bishop, and Merrill use language in ways that suggest narratives beyond the existing written words of poems.

   The poetic language that characterizes the poems of Hart Crane, Elizabeth Bishop, and James Merrill involves a movement between concrete and abstract imagery that at once expresses and conceals what can be said to be the autobiographical impulse of the poet. The autobiographical impulse provides a way to discuss biography and how it is used to create an individual's identity as it is figured in poems. This impulse can be as explicit as describing a personal experience or it can be a desire to express a sensation, arising out of a factual experience but that does not include a representation of the experience itself. The connection between sexual and creative identities in these poets' work that I illustrated in chapter 1 adds a further nuance to this impulse. In order to analyze the poetic projects and language of these idiosyncratic poets, I begin my discussion looking at their early collections and, then, at later poems.

Crane's first volume, *White Buildings*, provides an introduction to his impacted style that exhibits these shifts between concrete and abstract images. This shift is also apparent in Bishop's first book, *North & South*, where one of the central characteristics of her idiosyncratic rhetoric—the assertion of, and play with, perspective—is established. Merrill's second book, *The Country of a Thousand Years of Peace*, illustrates similar shifts in the images I describe. In these volumes, the movement between the concrete and the abstract functions simultaneously to express and to conceal various factual details about the poets' lives, in particular complicated modes of desire for same sex lovers and for the figuration of the Mother.[3]

The connection between homoerotic and mother-erotic desire reveals the degree to which ambivalence plays a crucial role in both of these structures of desire in the poetry of Crane, Bishop, and Merrill. Specifically, desire for the mother functions as a basis for homoerotic desire. The juxtaposition of these desires also serves to reinforce their connection with, and frequent representation as, loss. Indeed, the combination of mother-erotic and homoerotic desires clarifies the generalized interrelatedness of desire and loss. Psychoanalytic discourse also reinscribes this combination, when it asserts that love is always countered with opposing impulses of ambivalence, hatred, and destructiveness. Drawing a parallel between images of the Mother and those of homosexual desire serves to illustrate the way the ambivalent reaction to one is extended to the other, creating a violent, or disseminative, gap as well as a distant tone in the speakers of the poems.[4]

In the previous chapter, I focus my attention on a series of poems of initiation, or of poems that dramatize the recognition of the poet's identity, and discuss the expression of identity as the result of a movement between identification and repudiation on the part of the speakers. Freud is especially useful in this discussion because he theorizes that identification is at the heart of the formation of identity. In *The*

*Ego and the Id*, Freud posits the importance of identification, writing that the identification with the father is "an individual's first and most important identification, his identification with the father in his own personal prehistory."[5] Using Freud's theory of the importance of identification, the examination of poems in the first chapter decodes the representation of the poets' selves in their work, specifically in terms of the formation of an artistic and sexual figuration of the self. Building on these ideas in this chapter, I explore the poet's relation to and representation of the outside world. Because I see their imagery as based in psychological inquiry, this examination looks closely at the poets' relationships to the figure of the mother and by extension to other people in the social, natural, and political spheres. To this end, the work of the British psychoanalyst, Melanie Klein, is especially useful.

According to Melanie Klein, ambivalence toward the Mother is an inherent aspect of developmental growth. In her essay "Love, Guilt and Reparation," she writes:

> The baby's first object of love and hate—his mother—is both desired and hated with all the intensity and strength that is characteristic of early urges of the baby. . . . Because our mother first satisfied all our self-preservative needs and sensual desires and gave us security, the part she plays in our minds is a lasting one.[6]

The relationship with the Mother is a primeval one from which all other relationships are based. An infant learns how to interact with other people in part from experiences it has with the mother. For example, the infant begins to shape its own sense of self in response to the way the mother relates to the child. Klein's theories concern the pre-Oedipal infant—the infant who remains non-gender specific throughout her discussions of development. I relate Klein's idea about the primacy of the mother to the poems in order to see various figurations in them as recreations of her.

In opposition to Klein, Freud places gender identification at the heart of the formation of identity. Klein speaks of a non-gendered "infant"; Freud makes it necessary in his theories to distinguish between "boy child" and "girl child."[7] For Freud the neonate comes into the world with mechanisms for the ego, the id, and the superego. The capacity for these three modes to develop stems from the Oedipal stage, in which gendered identifications and repudiations are key: boys identify with their father, eventually coming to see him as a rival for the mother's affections, whereas girls, at first, identify with the mother but then at some point switch to see her as a rival for the affections of her father whom she loves. The gender of the child and of the parent is crucial in Freud's structure of development, whereas Klein's view of development concentrates on contrasting impulses: love and hate. These capacities are brought about through their connection with love and death drives and through alternations between satisfaction and frustration with respect to the mother and the breast. Indeed the child is unable to recognize the mother in this pre-Oedipal stage as encompassing anything more than her breast; she is not even all breast but merely a part. The mother and father are necessary but not for gender-based identification as was the important case with Freud's model for hoe gender identity becomes reified.

The mother is also at the root of the creative impulse: "The desire to re-discover the mother of the early days, whom one has lost actually or in one's feelings, is also of the greatest importance in creative art."[8] Following this logic, the desire to create a poem is an unconscious re-creation of the first loved person. Once the child grows and becomes less dependent solely upon the mother for the gratification of primary needs, he or she takes notice of objects around him or her. These objects are sometimes given special significance because of the similarity to the mother that the child imposes on the object. This process in which the child says that two seemingly unrelated things are similar, in which an object (a blanket or a ball) is like the mother because the object provides the child with sentiments like those the mother produces (comfort, pleasure), introduces metaphor into the child's world. This first experience with metaphor can be the basis for the desire to create in later life, whereby the connections introduced by the metaphor produce surprise and pleasure. Klein links this desire to create with the desire to explore new, geographic territories and the desire for scientific exploration; all are attempts to rediscover the lost mother. Klein's theories about the fundamental psychic position of the Mother and her preexisting presence as an introjected spirit that one wants to re-create or reexamine are enlightening in conjunction with Crane, Bishop, and Merrill given their problematic relationships with their mothers. In each of their poetries, Crane's, Bishop's, and Merrill's Mothers are represented through a defining loss. Indeed, in each of their poetries, the representation of Crane's, Bishop's, and Merrill's mothers are attempts to create a distinctive poetic language, which I discuss as their rhetoric, to reexamine and replace the Mother as a defining loss.

Because Klein and Freud present a theory of human development and not of literary critical analysis, their work produces its own limitations when applied to literary texts. Complicating this theoretical gap,

Freud's project to render the body and dreams readable and knowable in works such as his *On Dreams* often is the antithesis of the modernist poetic project as exemplified by Crane (as well as other poets such as W. B. Yeats and Rainer Maria Rilke). While Freud and psychoanalytic discourse secularizes terms like dreams, the modernist poet provides images to make them unknowable. In this way, scientific knowledge seems to work against poetic knowledge, as it is represented through Crane's dream-like verse. This limitation requires the assertion of a gap between an actual, biographical mother and a figurative Mother, where "Mother" signifies both the biographical and the metaphoric position. The fact that Klein does not present a gendered theory of subjectivity presents a further limitation; thus, the differences between Crane's, Bishop's, and Merrill's poems that stem from gender cannot easily be detected with help from her work. There are moments of theoretical collapse in both Freud and Klein, where their theories fail to answer important questions of development and motivation.[9] Freud and Klein, for example, cannot produce satisfying answers to questions about the nature of gender difference or same sex desire.

Crane, Bishop, and Merrill are not self-consciously engaged in the representation of gender. In the early decades of the twentieth century when Hart Crane was writing the poems that became his first volume, he, like other poets of his generation, specifically T. S. Eliot, was concerned with the role of science and technology in daily life; such institutions were increasingly changing the way individuals lived their lives and conceived of themselves. For Hart Crane, poetry is not bound by historical place, or by the things or events in it; rather, these things make their way into poetry only in the way they impress themselves upon the mind of the poet. Crane's poetic views here can be seen as a challenge to Eliot's. In his letters, Crane writes that a primary objective in writing his long poem *The Bridge* is to oppose the realism of Eliot's *The Waste Land*. This idea is summarized by the editors of Crane's letters: "Eliot also meant 'negation' to Crane, a denial of the life-affirming potential in modern culture that was already Crane's theme."[10] In Crane's essay "Modern Poetry" he writes: "the function of poetry in a Machine Age is identical to its function in any other age." That is to say, poetry presents "the most complete synthesis of human values remain[ing] essentially immune from any of the so-called inroads of science."[11] The mind of the poet then is primary. Everything else is merely useful only to the extent to which it impacts the poet's imagination.

Science, as an institution, requires absorption, and, in order to achieve that, the poet must surrender to the sensations of the world around him.[12] Through this process, the poet is able to subsume the world around him into material for poetry. In Crane's view, "some of the most intense and eloquent current verse derives sheerly from acute psychological analysis, quite independent of any dramatic motivation."[13] The "psychological analysis" foregrounds the crucial role the Mother assumes because of her central position in psychic thought and development. The lack of "dramatic motivation" that the poet notes is meant to bolster his argument for the use of "abstract statement and metaphysical representation," for words to be used in seemingly illogical and, therefore, new ways. This seems to be in keeping with the poetic philosophy that Crane writes in a letter to Harriet Monroe in which he attempts to explain his poem "At Melville's Tomb":

> I may very possibly be more interested in the so-called illogical impingements of the connotations of words on the consciousness (and their combinations and interplay in metaphor on this basis) than I am interested in the preservation of their logically rigid significations at the cost of limiting my subject matter and perceptions involved in the poem.[14]

Nonetheless Crane's focus on an interior source—that may be the result of psychological analysis and discovery or that may be the result of unintelligible sensations—posits the poet's experience as central to the creative project. Crane's penchant for abstract statement and metaphysical representation reflects a psychological tension, whereby he applies rhetorical devices in order to render linguistically the ambivalence he feels toward his demanding mother.

The loss of the Mother is complicated and commingled with the existence of the closet, the structure that encapsulates Crane's complicated homosexuality. Crane, Bishop, and Merrill were predominantly homosexual in their choice of love object, a fact that complicates their sexualities because of their conflicted views of homosexuality. Even James Merrill, who came into his sexual identity later in the century, favors discreet references to his sexuality—at least until his later work in which he speaks openly about his lover, David Jackson.[15] Both personal as well as societal constraints forced Crane to embrace the closet in both his life and his art, as a central, if unconscious, metaphor.[16] As I discussed previously (chapter 1), the closet is a defining structure, which, although necessary, maintains an ambivalent position. The closet requires a "proof" of homosexuality, if only to stabilize an identity from which one is alienated; this foregrounds the special circumstances of a homosexual identity, which differs from its heterosexual counterpart, because heterosexuality generally requires no evidence of its existence. Rather, evidence of heterosexuality is masked beneath commonplace, social institutions such as marriage and inheritance.[17] Yet, the closet itself figures rhetorically here not only as an elastic term that can include one or many persons but also as a defining structure for otherwise undefinably varied individuals.[18] In this way, the closet can be seen as a highly effective metaphor for the poets because of its secured status as rhetoric.

Because of his complex relationship with his Mother and with his homosexuality, Crane's poetry requires an analysis that unpacks the tensions within his rhetoric in order to produce textual instances of their impact upon the poet's consciousness. *White Buildings* provides several examples of this dynamic, particularly with the opening poem, "Legend." As with "To Brooklyn Bridge," the proem to his second collection, *The Bridge*, "Legend" serves as an introduction that informs the reader how to make sense of the poems that follow. Like a legend on a map, "Legend" is a brief description of, or a key to, the poetic language that composes Crane's work. In this sense, "Legend" also refers to the type of story—a legend or myth—that is handed down from generation to generation among a particular people. This type of story historically serves to explain or interpret experiences that are seen as collective.

The beginning of the poem disorients the reader, because the speaker does not situate himself in an immediately recognizable place:

> As silent as a mirror is believed
> Realities plunge in silence by . . .
>
> I am not ready for repentance;
> Nor to match regrets. For the moth
> Bends no more than the still
> Imploring flame. And tremorous
> In the white falling flakes
> Kisses are,—
> The only worth all granting.
>
> It is to be learned—
> This cleaving and this burning,
> But only by the one who
> Spends out himself again.   (ll. 1–13)

The opening lines of this poem shift between a concrete assertion or image, "As silent as a mirror is believed," and an abstract image,

"Realities plunge in silence by." A rhetorical trickery characterizes these lines. The poet writes, "As silent as a mirror is *believed*" (italics mine), which is to say that someone might think a mirror is silent, but, to the speaker, it is not. Indeed, a mirror does have extralinguistic powers of communication. Jacques Lacan, for example, in his theory of the Mirror Stage posits the mirror as the vehicle for the production of agency through which the self comes to see its identity through nonverbal means.[19] The communication of the mirror in these lines is a "reality" that is undisclosed, because it is concealed in the silences of the reflection. Here, the mirror is a kind of initial closeting structure that functions to contain these silences.

The second closeting structure containing the revelation of desire is established through a repetition of words. In lines one and two, "silent" and "silence" is joined by "twice" repeated in line fourteen, "again" in lines thirteen and sixteen, and "drop" in line twenty. The "mirror" of the first line appears again in line eighteen and is also alluded to in "eidolon," a word, which given its unusualness, "bleed-ing eidolon," exists self-consciously within the poem. There is also a repetition of sounds; "falling flakes" in line seven, and the gerunds "cleaving" and "burning" in line eleven. These repetitions of words and sounds create a liminal space in the poem, encapsulating the undisclosed object of the "regrets," the "kisses." The image of the "moth," which is perhaps a linguistically condensed "moth(er)," that bends toward a flame, alludes to passion in the same way that the lover contains the Mother. A reference to "kisses," which is highlighted by its position at the beginning of its line, and "smoking" make clear that the poet is talking about sexual desire. Indeed, sexual desire is the import of "only by the one who / Spends out himself" (ll. 12–13). Who "spends (himself) out," but a person who has been spent out by sexual gratification?

"Legend" is a poem about the tension between excitement for youthful love and the need for propriety and restraint in its expression. The poet sees the need for restraint because love "is to be learned." Crane's poem and its poetic language adopt the restraint necessary to discuss the problematic desire of the poem; indeed, the speaker goes so far as to thematize this in lines such as "Unwhispering as a mirror" (l. 18). Is an "unwhispering" a shout or a veiled whisper? Here the negation of language, in the hushed tones of a whisper, reinforces the speaker's position in relation to his desire, signaling its inexpressibility. Ann Douglass postulates that "the literal text of much of Crane's finest short poetry is an undisguised if enjambed account of gay love-making"[20] While I think the opacity of the poet's imagery makes a reading of these poems as being definitively about "gay lovemaking" difficult to illustrate, I would argue that these poems are about homoerotic desire and would extend this idea to include all of his poetry: Crane's poems are always either explicitly or implicitly involved in the thematization of homosexual desire. At the same time, because Crane resists grounding "Legend" in concrete images, specifically the lack of an expressed object of desire, the poem embraces a metaphysical and avoidant representation of love. The language of the concluding stanza of the poem makes this abstraction clear:

> Then, drop by caustic drop, a perfect cry
> Shall string some constant harmony,-
> Relentless caper for all those who step
> The legend of their youth into the noon.   (ll. 20–23)

This final stanza illustrates that as the poem progresses, the speaker moves away from shifts between concrete and abstract images that characterize the beginning of the poem and relies solely upon abstract ones. This practice allows for Crane's associational meanings that he describes in his explanation to Harriet Monroe in which he explains his "logic of metaphor." In this way, one could certainly read this poem as being about the inexplicable love for the poet's Mother, which, like homosexual desire, is considered a socially inexpressible form of love, and one that requires concealment. Following this logic, the "mirror" and the "constant harmony" reflect the poet's face in the Mother's image.

"Legend" is a guide to the hermeneutics of *White Buildings* because it introduces the reader to the interminglings of concrete and abstract imagery that Crane uses and teaches his readers what needs to be done in order to unpack them. Many of the poems that make up this collection are not principally concerned with the expression of love for another person. "Sunday Morning Apples" for example is a poem written for Crane's friend, the painter William Sommer. The poem is initially about the apples that grow at Sommer's country house and appear in a still life that Sommer is painting. These two different apples—those in nature and those in art—allow for the speaker to juxtapose imagery of the physical (nature) and nonphysical (art). Unlike in "Legends," the juxtaposition in "Sunday Morning Apples" appears on the same line of poetry. The first line of the poem reads, "The leaves will fall again sometime and fill(.)" The line begins with a concrete image of autumn, the season when leaves fall from trees and apples ripen. This opening line also has a metaphoric import, in which the poem enters the rhetorical language of poetry through the reference to the recurrence of time, "will fall again." Recurrent time refers to the time that is representative of the artistic space—of the poem and of the painting that the speaker describes—where the reader, or viewer, enters into the cyclical presence of the poem regardless of the number of encounters with it.

The end of "Sunday Morning Apples" associates the theme of nature, the apples, and creative inspiration with a sexual import:

> I have seen the apples there that toss you secrets-
> Beloved apples of seasonable madness
> That feed your inquiries with aerial wine.
> Put them again beside a pitcher with a knife,
> And poise them full and ready for explosion-
> The apples, Bill, the apples!    (ll. 15–20)

These lines continue the narrative of the apples as a metonym for nature that have "secrets" to be revealed because of their magical ability to produce creative inspiration. Yet, concurrent with a description of a still life, "a pitcher with a knife," is a scene of sexual excitement, where the "knife" is a phallic symbol that is "poise[d] . . . full and ready for [sexual] explosion." Words like "madness" and "aerial wine" create a Bacchic scene. That the poem concern's the poet's friend, Bill, creates a homosocial feel at best. The sexuality of this description, however, does not have the same homosexual content that is present in more overt poems in *White Buildings*, such as "Black Tambourine," "Repose of Rivers" or "Recitative." The overwhelming presence of the apples that frames this final stanza foregrounds a different reading for this poem, one that invokes the figuration of the poet's Mother. The apples represent the breast and by extension the Mother. As the editors of Crane's letters make clear, Crane's relationship with William Sommer extended beyond that of friendship in that the poet viewed Sommer as a parental figure. Sommer was an older man; he was a teacher and a mentor for the young poet.[21] It does not require too much displacement and condensation for the poet to conflate the paternal Sommers with his Mother, if only as a wish-fulfillment fantasy in which the poet imagines what it would be like to have a supportive parental figure without the constant manipulations for affection and devotion that characterize his actual relationship with his parents.

Melanie Klein explains the way a person can easily forge unconscious connections between objects and the figure of the Mother:

> The process by which we displace love from the first people we cherish
> to other people is extended from earliest childhood onward to things.

In this way we develop interests and activities into which we put some of the love that originally belonged to people. In the baby's mind, one part of the body can stand for another part, and an object for parts of the body or for people. In this symbolical way, any round object may, in the child's unconscious mind, come to stand for his mother's breast. By a gradual process, anything that is felt to give out pleasure and satisfaction, in the physical or in the wider sense, can in the unconscious mind take the place of this ever-bountiful breast, and of the whole mother.[22]

In a passage that underscores the inherent differences between a theory of human development by contrast to one of literary critical analysis, Klein describes a "process" of displacement akin to metaphor, except that for her it is an unconscious reaction whereas for the poet it is conscious. Crane intends for such interplays of meaning. In light of Klein's theory, Crane's apples, the "round object," which as a poetic image already refers to the mother's breast, here takes on the ambivalent status that the breast occupies in Klein's model. The ambivalent breast/"apples" resonates, then, with Crane's similar attitude toward the Mother and sexuality. Their secrets, their apparent unintelligibility, stem from the fact that the safety of the Mother is lost, and this loss produces an anxiety in the speaker. The apples are thus a paradoxical image that themselves are "straddling / Spontaneities" (ll. 10–11). The apples are a site of a simultaneously concrete (physical) and abstract (nonphysical) image.

Despite a great deal of critical praise when *White Buildings* was first published in 1927, Crane himself was uncertain about the collection. He wrote to his friend, Yvor Winters, who reviewed the book for *Poetry*, "My *White Bldgs* [*sic*], now out, shocks me in some ways. I think I have grown more objective since writing some of those poems. . . ."[23] Part of the poet's shock, which he admits in another letter, comes from his inclusion of several poems in the collection in order to fill out the book. Crane is also responding to what he might have seen as his youthful poems as he was twenty-eight when the book came out. His assertion that he has "grown more objective" in his writing illustrates his anxiety about the highly subjective and revelatory status of *White Buildings* and predicts the overarching path of *The Bridge* toward the mystical span that he envisions. One major accomplishment of this first collection is to provide a lesson over the course of its twenty-three poems in how to read and to interpret Crane's difficult style, which was frequently criticized when individual poems began to appear in magazines.

The letters of Hart Crane illustrate his complex family life and begin the process of a literary representation of Crane and of his mother. Throughout the letters, the poet's relationship with his mother figures centrally, often as a motivation behind much of his geographical restlessness. As soon as he could, Crane moved to New York City from Columbus, Ohio, in part to get away from the volatile struggles between his mother and father that ended in their divorce the following year. The move occurred in December of 1916, when he was seventeen years old and also about to matriculate to Columbia College. Crane quickly sided with his mother after his parents' separation, but their relationship deteriorated into one of manipulation and struggles to prove their mutual love. Ann Douglass characterizes Crane's relationship with his parents: "behind the skirmish with the father lay the battle with the mother; Father was shadowboxing, but Mother was the real match."[24] The lengthy, regular correspondence between mother and son read like love letters. Breaks in correspondence, especially periods of silence from Grace Hart Crane, were used to punish the poet. Crane used his given name, Harold Hart Crane, until in March of 1917 when Grace wrote to her son to congratulate him on the publication of his poem "The Hive." She writes:

> In signing your name to your contributions & later to your books [Harold Crane], do you intend to ignore your mother's side of the house entirely? That was the only thing I criticized about it. It seems to me that Hart or at least H. should come in some where- . . . How would 'Hart Crane' be? You see I am already jealous, which is a sure sign I believe in your success.[25]

Couching her advice in the language of a congratulatory and supportive letter, Grace Hart Crane's assurance that she "believes in [Crane's] success" is nonetheless tempered by her suggestion that he change his name. Her suggestion, however, does clarify the kind of relationship that the two have.[26] After the separation from her husband that pushed Grace to attempt suicide, Crane officially signs his allegiances with his mother, when he changes his name to "Hart Crane." Much has been written about the potential for puns with this change: the name, "Hart," signifies that his "heart" lies with his mother. The irony is not lost on mother and son who occasionally joke about their names, "Grace/grace" and "Hart/heart." Indeed, Hart was not the only one to change his name. Grace suggested that her son write to her as "Grace," instead of mother. Paul Bowles writes in the introduction to Crane's selected letters *O My Land, My Friends*: "Beginning in January 1917, she [Grace Hart Crane] signed her letters to him with her first name, 'Your dearest Grace.' The new signature, replacing 'Mother,' was an invitation to her son to replace her former husband (his father) in her affections" (p. xvi). While these biographical anecdotes reveal an unusually close and troubling mother–son dynamic, they illustrate the way in which the poet, with the help of his mother, transforms himself. His change in name signals his entrance into and his figuration in his highly complex rhetorical structure, a structure that Crane does not limit to his poetry but extends to him. His change from "Harold" to "Hart" illustrates his transformation to rhetorical status. And interestingly the change is to a less explicitly gendered name: "Hart"—like Hilda Doolittle's new modern identity as H. D.—is not a name that is immediately recognizable as male or female.

Whereas in Crane's speakers the figure of the Mother serves to complicate the expression of erotic desire, the Mother in Elizabeth Bishop's poetry figures centrally as loss. Klein's writing helps clarify that the Mother is represented in Bishop's poetry through objects designed to replace the Mother. In my discussion of Bishop's rhetoric, I focus on her observation of details on a map, and of objects around the speaker in the domestic and natural worlds, applying to this Klein's notion that scientific discovery, or exploration, is connected with the desire to replace the loss of the Mother. The speaker's exploration of objects works as a desire to recreate the Mother.[27] In this way, the feelings of sadness and loss that are present in the poems are clarified by locating instances of the Mother's implicit, textual presence/absence. Just as the specter of the mother exists behind every relationship, the Mother is also present in the language of Bishop's poems. In addition Klein's rejection of Freudian theories of regression, and her assertion of an absence of history and historical time, serves to shed light on the ways that Bishop manipulates perspective and shifts between images of expression and concealment. Bishop creates speakers who occupy Klein's "total situations" and explicitly embrace the tensions they produce.

In her infamous letter to Robert Lowell in response to his book, *The Dolphin*, Elizabeth Bishop, quoting from Thomas Hardy, argues passionately against what she feels is the "infinite mischief" that comes from a "mixture of fact & fiction," when Lowell quotes from personal letters to compose his poems: "What should certainly be protested against . . . is the mixing of fact and fiction in unknown proportions. Infinite mischief would lie in that. If any statements in the dress of fiction are covertly hinted to be fact, all must be fact, for obvious reasons."[28] Bishop was responding to Lowell's use of private letters from his wife in his poems without her permission. The mixture of fact and fiction is mischievous to Bishop, whose writing raison d'etre ascribes to the literal truth. For her, the facts of a poem are central to its creation. Nonetheless, Bishop makes use of this mischievous mixture at the same time as she disavows it. The manipulation of facts for Bishop—to present them as if there were no alterations—is a point of departure from Crane who changes the facts in his poems to create images that distort the impropriety of their revelations.

Critics and biographers of Bishop have written about her adherence to the truthfulness of her experience within her poetry.[29] Bishop strives in her poetry to remain accurate and responsible to the "truthful" representation of an experience or scene about which she writes. The nature of Bishop's "truthful" rhetoric figures most notably in the observation of details and is written in the language of everyday speech. Nonetheless, I propose that this stance is a rhetorical one, and therefore a strategic fiction. Bishop's reliance on "truthfulness" functions as one way that the poet asserts a perspective. As the perspective of her speakers constantly shifts, however, this truthfulness paradoxically highlights its own figurative status as rhetoric.

Bishop's reliance upon truth is further complicated when it is held up alongside her relationship to confessional poetry. Bishop describes her feelings about the confessional mode in a letter to Lowell:

> In general, I deplore the "confessional"—however, when you wrote *Life Studies* perhaps it was a necessary movement, and it helped make poetry more real, fresh and immediate. But now—ye gods—anything goes, and I am so sick of poems about my students' mothers & fathers and sex lives and so on. . . . one surely should have a feeling that one can trust the writer—not to distort, tell lies, etc.[30]

It is clear from comments such as this that Bishop distrusted the confessional movement; however, her relationship to Lowell, one of the movement's central practitioners, betrays a certain tolerance for it. Bishop's last volume of poetry, *Geography III*, published in 1976, does more than that; it is her most decidedly confessional work. Bishop's reliance on the documentation of the literal truth functions awkwardly within the confines of explicitly confessional, or apparently autobiographical, poetry, producing a rhetoric that approaches the "infinite mischief" about which she warned Lowell in her 1972 letter. Yet, Bishop's explicit intolerance for confessional poetry highlights her general aversion to revealing aspects of her personal life; she nonetheless does this, albeit through veiled expressions. The label "confessional poetry" brings to mind the work of Michel Foucault who explores the confessional as a major technique for producing truths and, thus, lies at the heart of individuation.[31] Bishop would certainly have been horrified by Foucault's thesis that sexuality, although commonly assumed to be a private and an intimate matter, is in fact culturally constructed according to the political aims of the society's dominant class. Sexuality is not only a secular concern but also a concern of the state. Bishop's desire for "closets, closets, and more closets"[32] runs counter to unraveling the paradoxes of sexuality that Foucault's project makes clear in which legal, scientific, and religious authorities simultaneously repress as they produce sexual behaviors. While Bishop appears to enact, albeit parodically, a Foucaultian response, Barbara Johnson notes a gender difference inherent in this question of the confessional: "When men employ the rhetoric of self-torture, it is read as rhetoric. When women employ it, it is confession. Men are read rhetorically; women literally."[33] While it seems true that many critics are reluctant to speak of her language as rhetoric, Bishop's own focus on the literal creates an interesting juxtaposition to Johnson's argument and the poet's continued refusal to be a part of collections of women poets' anthologies interestingly complicates this question further.

Bishop's poetry is not as straightforward as it seems; the poems must have some other function than merely to document and tell the story of her life. Victoria Harrison argues, "[Bishop's] writing is nonetheless a record of how the world impinged daily on her life: war, issues of class and race, feminism, and lesbianism enter her writing not as confessional and not within larger political frames, but as everyday relationships among ordinary subjects."[34] Harrison focuses attention on Bishop's life in order to examine the way that Bishop encodes and reveals it in her poetry. Bishop was not entirely averse to straightforward revelations of her private self and did write several prose memoirs of which "In the Village" is the most notable example. It is also possible to look at the rhetoric of the poems and find encoded within them aspects of the "truth" from Bishop's life. The poems of *North & South* are hard to classify, because Bishop writes them in a variety of styles and forms—a sestina, her version of a series of blues lyrics, and a double sonnet. Anne Colwell describes the collection as being concerned with perception and "the body as mediator of reality."[35] In "Love, Guilt and Reparation," Melanie Klein offers a possible explanation for why Bishop is so concerned with place, with homes and homelessness, and with a geographical restlessness that is foregrounded in this first collection by its title, *North & South*: "In the explorer's unconscious mind, a new territory stands for a new mother, one that will replace the loss of the real mother."[36] Geographical exploration is a central theme in all of Bishop's work and is often represented in terms of her homelessness and love of travel. Klein's work is useful to the extent that she reinforces the centrality of the Mother's position in psychic thought and development; however, Bishop's poetry illustrates the limitations of Klein's model.[37] "The Map," for example, figures the combination of homoeroticism with mother-eroticism to illustrate the ambivalence inherent in both.

"The Map," which opens the collection of *North & South*, is the first example of Bishop's rhetorical practice of revelation and concealment through the assertion of a particular perspective. The poem is the first in a series of poems that confronts the reader with a reevaluation of a familiar object—here a map. The first stanza establishes this play in perspective that the narrator generates:

> Land lies in water; it is shadowed green.
> Shadows, or are they shallows, at its edges
> showing the line of long sea-weeded ledges
> where weeds hang to the simple blue from green.
> Or does the land lean down to lift the sea from under,
> drawing it unperturbed around itself?
> Along the fine tan sandy shelf
> is the land tugging at the sea from under?    (ll. 1–8)

Bishop's speaker begins the poem with an assertion of a way of seeing the map before her.[38] The "[l]and lies in water"; rather than the land occupying a primary position, it is the water that is the prime body. This destabilizing gesture—the reader does not seem to be settled on *terra firma*—is negated by the repetition of words from one line to the next: "shadowed," "shadows," "weeded," "weeds." The repetition of words resettles the reader. The speaker further destabilizes the reader from his/her expectations by including a fixed end rhyme scheme only in the first and third stanzas (abbacddc). Even that rhyme scheme is not accurate because the a and c rhymes are repetitions, "green" (ll. 1 and 4) and "under" (ll. 5 and 8).

At the same time, the internal question in the second line, "or are they shallows," serves to draw the reader into the language of the poem and contrasts the disquieting nature of shifting perspectives. Unlike the questions that comprise the last four lines of this first stanza, this internal one lacks a question mark. It is the first sign that the poet is trying to represent a mind at work, not a mind composing in tranquillity as was the mode of many poets, most notably Wordsworth.[39]

The second stanza shifts perspective to one in which the speaker closely examines the map in front of her:

> The shadow of Newfoundland lies flat and still.
> Labrador's yellow, where the moony Eskimo
> has oiled it. We can stroke these lovely bays,
> under a glass as if they were expected to blossom,
> or as if to provide a clean cage for invisible fish.
> The names of seashore towns run out to sea,
> the names of cities cross the neighboring mountains
> -the printer here experiencing the same excitement
> as when emotion too far exceeds its cause.
> These peninsulas take the water between thumb and finger
> like women feeling for the smoothness of yard-goods. (ll. 9–19)

Here the perspective is one of close observation. "Newfoundland" seems to be but a "shadow"; or is this the same shadow of the edges in the first stanza? The speaker notices how the names of towns and cities extend beyond the scale allotment of space, like "when emotion too far exceeds its cause." Under what circumstances does "emotion too far exceed() its cause"? This odd simile, which comes in the middle portion of this twenty-seven-line poem, points toward an alternative reading of this poem as one of subsumed desire. For Bishop passionate emotion of any kind, whether it is erotic desire or desire for the Mother, occupies an ambivalent status because it is both wanted and not wanted. In her reading of the poem, Victoria Harrison writes, "Whether 'The Map' suggests desired or actual love can only be conjectured, but in either case the sea lifting the land 'unperturbed around itself' and the bays that we may stroke are sensual, even sexual."[40] The speaker's language of intimacy, the land that cuddles with water, attains its peak when she again makes a comparison in the middle stanza: "These peninsulas take the water between thumb and finger / like women feeling for the smoothness of yard-goods" (ll. 18–19). A legend to Bishop's metaphoric representation, the land is precisely like "women" because the poem thematizes intimacy between women. Thus, the "mapped waters" are "more quiet than the land is" (l. 20) because the land is not quiet; it proclaims itself symbolic of female intimacy.

Bishop's speakers appear to prefer quiet and solitude, despite the fact that these states of affairs are associated with desire. The juxtaposition of desire with an image of silence and/or solitude functions to undercut the desire and sets up roadblocks for its textual satisfaction. In "The Map," the "mapped waters are more quiet than the land is" (l. 20), is a state reminiscent of the representation of Paris in the series of poems in the middle of *North & South* that take place there: "Paris, 7 A.M.," "Quai d'Orléans," "Sleeping on the Ceiling," "Sleeping Standing Up," and "Cirque d'Hiver." One might not think of a city often associated with vivaciousness in connection with quietness; however, the Paris in these five poems is one reflected upon in the poet's consciousness—an interior, rather than an exterior description of the city.[41] In "Sleeping on the Ceiling" the speaker boldly declares: "It is so peaceful on the ceiling!" To sleep on a ceiling, as opposed to a bed, is easier for the speaker because it is a desexualized place. It is also upside down and so produces an impossible situation. The solitude and silence of the ceiling are in opposition to the erotic potential of the bed. Triggered by her skewed perspective, the speaker's fertile imagination transforms the ceiling into a park and the chandelier into a fountain; the speaker is content because she is alone, "not a soul in the park." The speaker, however, is not entirely alone, for in the final stanza she uses a "we": "But oh, that we could sleep up there" (l. 15). This "we" is a fantasy, a spectral figure of a lover, with whom the speaker can sleep, but it is also a dream of the speaker's Mother, a nurturing figure who will rescue the speaker from the encroachments of the insects that "tunnel" and "go under" the wallpaper.[42]

"Sleeping on the Ceiling," however, is an unusually explicit example of the language of intimacy from this first volume. More representative is "A Miracle for Breakfast," which continues Bishop's project in *North & South* of shifts in perspective and of close examination of objects, both techniques that highlight the poet's ambivalence toward desire. In this poem, written in a classical form called a sestina that creates a weaving of repeated words, the reexamination of objects takes place in a domestic setting and provides an opportunity for the poet to reflect upon her childhood. The sestina comes out of an experience that the poet records in her notebook in January 1935:

> This morning I discovered I had forgotten to get any bread and I had only one dry crust for breakfast. I was resigning myself to orange juice and coffee and no more when the door-bell rang. I pushed the button, and up the stairs trailed a weary-looking woman, shouting ahead of herself: "I don't want to sell you anything—I want to give you something!" I welcomed her at that, and was presented with a small box containing three slices of "Wonder Bread," all fresh, a rye, a white, and whole-wheat. Also a miniature loaf of bread besides—The only thing I disliked about the gift was that the woman opened the box, held it under my nose, and said "Smell how sweet!" But I breakfasted on manna-[43]

In "A Miracle for Breakfast" the temporary problem of hunger and deprivation motivates the speaker's imaginative mind to expand upon this chance happening, no doubt fed by the frequent sight of Depression-era bread lines around New York City. Lines, words, and phrases double back on themselves. The first four stanzas of the poem read:

At six o'clock we were waiting for coffee,
waiting for coffee and the charitable crumb
that was going to be served from a certain balcony,
-like kings of old, or like a miracle.
It was still dark. One foot of the sun
steadied itself on a long ripple in the river.

The first ferry of the day had just crossed the river.
It was so cold we hoped that the coffee
would be very hot, seeing that the sun
was not going to warm us; and that the crumb
would be a loaf each, buttered, by a miracle.
At seven a man stepped out of the balcony.

He stood for a minute alone on the balcony
looking over our heads toward the river.
A servant handed him the makings of a miracle,
Consisting of one lone cup of coffee
And one roll, which he proceeded to crumb,
His head, so to speak, in the clouds—along with the sun.

Was the man crazy? What under the sun
was he trying to do, up there on his balcony?
Each man received one rather hard crumb,
which some flicked scornfully into the river,
and, in a cup, one drop of the coffee.
Some of us stood around, waiting for the miracle. (ll. 1–24)

Opening with a scene that invokes the lines of soup kitchens of the Depression era, the speaker is reduced to a cultural "we" that is "waiting for coffee and the charitable crumb" (l. 2). Within the confines of the strict and repetitive rhyme scheme—"coffee," "crumb," "balcony," "miracle," "sun," and "river"—the poem shifts from a concentration on physical things to one in which the physical is made to perform the tasks of the spiritual.[44] In this sense, the word "miracle," foregrounded within the title, performs as a fulcrum for the poem, balancing the tension between the two realms—the physical and the spiritual—that the poet depicts. At the beginning of the poem, the "miracle" is a reference to the miracles of God in *The Bible*. Similarly the second "miracle" describes the speaker's hope that she will receive not just a piece of bread but a whole, buttered loaf and alludes to the biblical story of Jesus feeding the multitudes. In the third stanza, however, "miracle" becomes a kind of communion. The transformation in the ways that the speaker sees the "miracle," or the different kinds of miracles that she describes, serves as a central shift in the poem's perspective. As the poem subtly moves from a realistic observation to a spiritual rumination, Bishop points toward the mind's ability to alter reality through the imagination.

If "The Map" is concerned with a projection of desire revealed through its language, "A Miracle for Breakfast" provides a more complex model of desire. "A Miracle for Breakfast" is a modern, metaphysical contemplation on the transformation of everyday objects into objects with a spiritual purpose. The air of unintelligibility of these foods, the "crumb" and the "coffee," that are domestic items foregrounds a more general sense of the unintelligible nature of the home (and for the Mother that the home represents) for Bishop's speaker.[45] Yet the poem is also about the desire for sustenance, "coffee." The "crumbs" can also refer to the Eucharistic bread of religious ceremonies. In that the crumb and the coffee are so necessary for survival that their acquisition is a miracle, these things invoke the sustenance of the mother's breast.[46] To read the "crumb" and "coffee" as pleasure-giving objects that are reminiscent of the maternal breast aligns them with ambivalence and the destructive impulses that accompany the love for the mother. This would reconcile the discrepancy between the reportage tone of the speaker, "I can tell you what I saw" (l. 25), and the spiritual revelation, the "miracle," that moves the poem along through the otherwise static nature of the sestina's formal structure.

The shift in perspective from realistic scene to spiritual contemplation is characteristic of Bishop and illustrates the ways the poet draws her readers into her subjective view of the world around her. Bishop undoubtedly learned this art of transformation from realistic scene to one of spiritual contemplation in her poems from English Renaissance poetry, which she loved to read, especially the poems of George Herbert. In his poem "The Collar" Herbert begins with a speaker who is fed up with himself, strikes the table before him and launches into a description of his rage; this realistic scene, however, moves into a religious confrontation by the end of the poem.[47] David Bromwich has observed, in an essay that questions the concealments in Bishop's poems, that her work "compels our attention without giving the reasons why."[48] Her work commands the reader's attention at the site of her simultaneous expressions and concealments. Such a site is one in which perspective becomes self-conscious, or where the reader can be especially conscious of her change in perspective.

To understand the genealogy of these perspectival shifts, it is useful to return to the work of Melanie Klein to explore her idea that the past and the present are one. Klein reconceives traditional psychoanalytic notions of personal history and time. There is not so much a regression to a phase as Freud theorizes in structures such as the Oedipal phase, but the readoption of a position: "what she is observing, describing and theorizing is the very absence of history and of historical time"[49] Juliet Mitchell explains: "Where in Freud repression is a defense that creates a past and a symptom is a return of that past, Klein is appropriately more interested in the defenses which have no such dimension of time past and with atemporal inhibitions of the ego, not with symptoms."[50] Mitchell further explains that Klein differs from nineteenth-century thinkers such as Freud, who explain the present through the past. In this way, Klein focuses on a *defense* that takes place in the present, not a repression of a memory. The shifts that character-ize Bishop's poetry do not represent temporal or spatial movements; rather, these occur within the presence of the poem. Bishop's speakers seem to exist on a lateral plane with the images they invoke.

Whereas "A Miracle for Breakfast" contemplates the transformation of everyday objects into objects for a spiritual purpose, "Sestina," Bishop's second triumph over the form, is concerned with memory. Bishop wrote "Sestina" when she had the distance of time and of geog-raphy from which to look back on her orphaned life in Nova Scotia from the distance of her life in Brazil. According to Bishop's biogra-pher, " 'Sestina,' originally titled 'Early Sorrow,' works directly with the terms of 'In the Village' [Bishop's prose memoir] and Elizabeth's childhood . . . and also of her recent reading and thinking about child psychology, in Benjamin Spock, Melanie Klein, Arnold Gesell, and others."[51] "Sestina" makes for interesting comparisons to her earlier sestina "A Miracle for Breakfast." Again she chooses commonplace words to carry her through the traditional form: "house," "grand-mother," "child," "stove," "almanac," and "tears." The first stanza sets the scene of the poem in the grandmother's kitchen:

> September rain falls on the house.
> In the failing light, the old grandmother

sits in the kitchen with the child
beside the Little Marvel Stove,
reading the jokes from the almanac,
laughing and talking to hide her tears.

She thinks that her equinoctial tears
and the rain that beats on the roof of the house
were both foretold by the almanac,
but only known to a grandmother.
The iron kettle sings on the stove.
She cuts some bread and says to the child,

*It's time for tea now;*   (ll. 1–13)

The poem opens with the appearance of a common scene of a grandmother and child in a kitchen while an autumnal rain falls outside.
However the speaker's language quickly conveys the scene's strangeness,
for example, the status of the "tears" and of the time that is represented in the poem through the almanac. The reader does not know
the gender of the child, which does allow for some ambiguity as to
whose "tears" they are. The grammar of the stanza suggests that the
tears belong to the grandmother, but the series of displacements that
the tears go through in the subsequent stanzas make that uncertain.
Also, the reader wonders why the grandmother "hide[s] her tears."
With each repetition of "tears" the speaker enacts a different displacement. In the first stanza, the tears are the grandmother's but they are
a source of embarrassment. The grandmother tries to hide them from
the child. In the second stanza, the tears are still attributed to the
grandmother, "her . . . tears," but they are qualified as "equinoctial."
Here "equinoctial," because of its context in connection with the
"rain" and the "almanac," means a storm occurring at the time of the
equinox. The poem is set in September, so this must be a storm during
the autumnal equinox. Thus, although the tears are still the grandmother's, they are compared to the driving rain that "beats on the roof
of the house." In the remaining stanzas, the "tears" are anything but
real tears attributable to any particular person; the speaker has displaced
them from the grandmother to metaphor. For example in the third
stanza "tears" describes the droplets of water on the teakettle.

The transformation in the image of tears is one of a series of changes
in perspective that occurs through this poem. The speaker's perspective
moves from a position in which she is aligned with the child and
knows that the tears are being hidden to one in which she is aligned
with the grandmother and hides, through the series of displacements,
the tears herself.

The "almanac" also figures in the poet's manipulation of perspective in the poem. The "almanac" represents time. Time, and the passage of time, is a recurrent theme in Bishop's poetry and one that always involves anxiety.[52] In the image of the "almanac," Bishop contains time in a manageable form; this rhetorical containment allows her to overcome the anxieties of time. In this way, Bishop continues her theme of the contemplation of, and potential for, changing reality. Many of the poems of *North & South* are concerned with changing the speaker's perception of reality, especially "A Miracle for Breakfast," "The Man-Moth," "Paris, 7 A.M." and the two sleeping poems, "Sleeping on the Ceiling" and "Sleeping Standing Up." In "Sestina," the almanac that in the first three stanzas appears oppressive in its prophecies and cleverness is transformed into a playful fantasy. It becomes "birdlike" (l. 19), as it "hovers" still with a potential for threat. The speaker renders the almanac a more playful figure by changing her perspective of it—both in terms of the language in which it is characterized and physically in terms of where the almanac is placed within the poem's scene.

The speaker's perspective changes again when she foregrounds the connection between the grandmother and the child. In the fifth stanza the speaker says: "With crayons the child draws a rigid house / and a winding pathway. Then the child / puts in a man with buttons like tears" (ll. 27–29). This drawing of a "man with buttons like tears" is again a simple displacement. The child, having learned through observation of her grandmother's unease with overt expressions of emotion, projects her own tears onto her drawing. The grandmother and the child are connected through their sadness; the source of their sadness is the absent mother, who, like the almanac, seems to "hover" as a textual presence.

The poem ends with a description of the child's second drawing, "another inscrutable house," which is equally an act of projection as the first drawing. When the speaker says "*another* inscrutable house" (emphasis added), she highlights her view that this present house in which the scene takes place is also "inscrutable." Its unintelligibility comes from the fact that there is a lack of normalcy due to the mother's unexplained absence. The grandmother and the child are both crying but are uncomfortable with their emotions and seek to displace them. The two acts of projection by the child when she draws her pictures are complicated when the figure of the child is viewed as a projection herself. This central shift in the poem's perspective derives from the speaker who projects and distances her memory into a scene in which she is the child.

When "Sestina" is read with the specter of the absent Mother as the implicit source of the collective grief of grandmother, child, and speaker, the objects of the poem—the stove, almanac, and house—take on added significances. As Melanie Klein would argue, the speaker focuses her attention on these objects because they are replacements for the Mother. The transformation of the almanac also can be a fantasy to recreate the Mother as well as act out the speaker's anger toward the Mother for her absence.

When Bishop's first collection *North & South* was going to be published in the summer of 1946, the poet planned to be out of the way of potential critics by returning to Great Village, Nova Scotia for the first time since her mother's death in 1934. Although Bishop was able to visit with her beloved Aunt Grace, according to her biographer she was miserable, clearly troubled by painful memories of her mother. It was at this time that she began to take notes for the poem that was to become "At the Fishhouses." The poem first appeared in *The New Yorker* the following year and was collected in her second book, *Poems: North & South—A Cold Spring.* Many of Bishop's contemporaries—as well as her readers over the years—consider "At the Fishhouses" to be one of her most remarkable poems. The poem is concerned with reflections about her mother, the loss of her beloved life in Key West, and her relationships there with Marjorie Stevens and Pauline Hemingway; yet, the most notable aspect of the poem is its complete lack of affect in the face of the *froideur* she quietly describes.

The central feature of Bishop's rhetoric in the poem is its function to create a liminality. The poem begins in a crepuscular moment, "in the gloaming," where the light is on the edge of darkness. This twilight is continued in the series of images that are of an "apparent translucence"—"the silver of the benches"; "beautiful herring scales"; "creamy iridescent coats of mail, / with small iridescent flies crawling on them" (ll. 18, 15, 22, and 24–25). These words create the effect of "translucence," of a shimmering, where the light twinkles in a sort of continuing motion that is reflective of the speaker's liminal position.

The speaker talks to an "old man," a fisherman who was a friend of her grandfather's; however her interests are not in the people so much as in the landscape that surrounds her, especially the water. She turns her attentions to the water and enters into a meditation:

> Cold dark deep and absolutely clear,
> element bearable to no mortal,
> to fish and to seals . . . One seal particularly

I have seen here evening after evening.
He was curious about me. He was interested in music;
like me a believer in total immersion,
so I used to sing him Baptist hymns.
I also sang "A Mighty Fortress Is Our God."    (ll. 47–54)

The "total immersion" jocularly seems to say that the speaker believes in an "immersion" of faith;[53] however, the speaker is more a believer in the "total immersion" of homosexual love or of the affect that is created through its absence. There is an absence here of love, reinforcing her sense of loss. Such images of love and loss are complicated by the poem's final images of "the cold hard mouth" and "the rocky breasts" (ll. 80–81). These two images not only combine masculine and feminine imagery in surprising ways but also function to invoke the Mother, whose ambivalent status is reflected in the harshness of the adjectives. If the sea, here, is representative of the speaker's consciousness, its forbidding nature, "Cold dark deep and absolutely clear," is attributable to her refusal to give her overriding emotions a place within the poem. The coldness of the water, her consciousness, denies any human company and any immediate sense of affect. When the description is repeated, "Cold dark deep and absolutely clear," the speaker changes the subsequent line instead of continuing the repetition: "the clear gray icy water . . . Back, behind us, / the dignified tall firs begin" (ll. 60–62). The "gray icy water" characterizes excessiveness, whereas it is the "tall firs" that provide the contrast to the water and are "dignified."

The sense of coldness and loss that makes the water uninhabitable and that permeates the *froideur* of the Nova Scotia landscape affects the speaker's judgment of the world and extends to her sense of "freedom" and "knowledge." The poet describes her idea of freedom through the water:

> . . . The water seems suspended
> above the rounded gray and blue-gray stones.
> I have seen it over and over, the same sea, the same,
> slightly, indifferently swinging above the stones,
> icily free above the stones,
> above the stones and then the world.    (ll. 65–70)

The indeterminacy of the color "gray" (neither black nor white) reinforces the liminality of the translucent images. The water is "free" above the "stones" but "icily free"; the element that makes it "bearable to no mortal" remains with it and negatively colors the sense of freedom. At the same time, the speaker considers communing with

the water: "If you should dip your hand in," and "If you tasted it"
(ll. 71 and 76). Having already established the water's unbearable
coldness, such suggestions seem ridiculous, but reinforce the continuation of the role of ambivalence. If the water represents the poet's
Mother, then she would want to taste and to touch her, to take her in,
in an effort toward companionability and in an erotic gesture.

In the final lines of the poem the speaker disavows the eroticism of
the feminine images by juxtaposing them with masculine and aggressive
adjectives:

> It is like what we imagine knowledge to be:
> dark, salt, clear, moving, utterly free,
> drawn from the cold hard mouth
> of the world, derived from the rocky breasts
> forever, flowing and drawn, and since
> our knowledge is historical, flowing and flown.   (ll. 78–83)

This description is not the way most people would "imagine knowledge to be." The poet's "we" is actually an attempt to distance herself
from the "I" to remove from the poem any further potential for affect.

The feelings of loss that "At the Fishhouses" evoke are present in
one of Bishop's poems, "The Moose," from her final collection
*Geography III*. The speaker in "The Moose" rides, "From narrow
provinces / of fish and bread and tea," in "a bus" that "journeys
west" (ll. 1–2 and 26). This is the same Nova Scotia landscape of
"At the Fishhouses." "The Moose" is a long poem, twenty-eight stanzas
of six lines each; the lines are short and characteristically lacking in
affect. Through much of the poem the speaker entertains reveries
about her childhood and her grandparents, until she is pulled out of
her thoughts by a moose:

> A moose has come out of
> the impenetrable wood
> and stands there, looms, rather,
> in the middle of the road.
> It approaches; it sniffs at
> the bus's hot hood.
>
> Towering, antlerless,
> high as a church,
> homely as a house
> (or, safe as houses).
> A man's voice assures us
> "Perfectly harmless. . . ."

Some of the passengers
exclaim in whispers,
childishly, softly,
"Sure are big creatures."
"It's awful plain."
"Look! It's a she!"

Taking her time,
she looks the bus over,
grand, otherworldly.
Why, why do we feel
(we all feel) this sweet
sensation of joy?    (ll. 133–156)

The gendered depiction of the moose as a "she" is highlighted by repetition, "antlerless." The moose's femininity, like the "rocky breasts"
and "cold hard mouth," subverts expectations of gender representation and at the same time illustrates the moose's representation as a
Mother figure. Also in similar terms to "At the Fishhouses" the figuration of the mother is surrounded by contrasting imagery that recalls
her ambivalent status; here, she is "big," "high as a church,"
"homely," "plain," "harmless," "grand," and "otherworldly." The
moose emerges from woods that are "impenetrable"; this seems to
add to her otherworldliness. Why does the speaker feel "joy," and is it
a joy at the moose's otherworldliness? The "joy" comes from the
moose's largesse. It seems that it is her otherworldliness, her uncanny
nature that the poet finds endearing and reminiscent of the figuration
of the mother. The poem's final images are smells, "there's a dim /
smell of moose, an acrid / smell of gasoline," that themselves recall
the idea of memory through its ephemeral qualities. Rather than combine or juxtapose the moose's femininity with masculine imagery, the
poet erases the moose's trace with the sent of "gasoline." This poetic
gesture nonetheless counters the femininity of the moose with the
masculine aggression of the "gasoline."

Bishop composed the majority of her poems that reflect upon her childhood experiences when she had the perspective of a comfortable home
in Brazil from which to contemplate the machinations of time. This position of objectivity established by a geographical remove is reminiscent of
the one that Crane required to complete his long poem, *The Bridge*,
which also deals in part with the poet's musings on time. Crane first conceived of *The Bridge* in 1923, believing he could write the six-part poem
in a year. Crane suffered from a malaise of creative inactivity and could

not write successful parts of the poem until he spent time in Isle of Pines, Cuba. *The Bridge* took seven years to complete and was expanded in its scope from the original six parts. Crane's letters illustrate his thoughts on time in connection with his poem: "The form of my poem rises out of a past that so overwhelms the present with its worth and vision that I'm at a loss to explain my delusion that there exist any real links between that past and a future worthy of it."[54] Crane is in part expressing a concern that "a future" will not provide an audience of readers who are "worthy" of his poem. But he is also commenting on the number of specters, of figures from a past state of affairs, which are subsumed within the poem. One example of a past figure that informs the sequence of the poem is that of Walt Whitman. Whitman is invoked in many places, most notably in the fourth section, "Cape Hatteras":

> yes, Walt,
> Afoot again, and onward without halt,-
> Not soon, nor suddenly, -no, never let go
>      My hand
>          in yours,
>              Walt Whitman-
>                  so-   (ll. 229–235)

While some of Crane's contemporaries such as Allen Tate dismissed this conclusion for its sentimentality, these lines foreground the poet's intention to be included within an American tradition of poetry, as they also reinforce Crane's continued attempts to re-create a familiar figure. Here the figure is a masculine one, but its expression of emotional companionability connects it with earlier images of the Mother in *White Buildings*.

The poet uses other kinds of figures to invoke a specter of the past in "To Brooklyn Bridge." Images of the world of business, of the technology of the modern city (the "subway"), of the bridge itself, and of the erotic figures of the "bedlamite" and of the "shadow" in the cruising arena "by the piers," are invoked at the beginning of the "Proem" in order to provide material for a transfiguration through the prayer-like, final stanza and a half of the poem:

> *The City's fiery parcels all undone,*
> *Already snow submerges an iron year . . .*
>
> *O sleepless as the river under thee,*
> *Vaulting the sea, the prairies' dreaming sod,*
> *Unto us lowliest sometime sweep, descend*
> *And of the curveship lend a myth to God.*   (ll. 39–44)

The transfiguration signals the rejection of the kind of concrete imagery that made up half of the tensions in *White Buildings* discussed earlier. "To Brooklyn Bridge" is the proem for the long poem to follow in that it teaches the reader not to expect the kind of physicality that is associated with the poet's former collection as well as with *The Waste Land.* Again, Crane describes his intentions in a letter: "The bridge in becoming a ship, a world, a woman, a tremendous harp (as it does finally) seems to really have a career."[55] The span of the bridge encompasses America, not just the individual experience of the poet who is subsumed within it. "To Brooklyn Bridge" is concerned centrally with the metaphysical and the abstract by contrast to the poems of *White Buildings* that merely vacillated in that direction. The figures are allowed to exist in *The Bridge* as specters and thus reveal the extent to which Crane managed to extend the implicit thematization that had been reserved primarily for instances of homosexual desire and of the Mother to include a greater range of images from the world around him.

The homoerotic and mother-erotic are figured in Merrill's poetry as images that often combine masculinity and femininity. Toward the end of the first book, "The Book of Ephraim," from the "x" section of the alphabetically organized epic *The Changing Light at Sandover*, Merrill's speaker looks at a painting by Giorgione called *La Tempesta.*[56] He tells us that x-rays of the painting reveal a "Nude arisen" from "flowing water which no longer fills / The eventual foreground" (p. 83). The lesson learned from this x-ray vision about the painting's life follows: "Images that hint / At meanings we had missed by simply looking." True to his words, Merrill's is a poetry that requires more than a surface "looking." Closer reading yields insight and understanding of the poem's meanings and allusions as well as insight into the poet himself. The speaker continues in the next verse stanza:

All of which lights up, as scholarship
Now and then does, a matter hitherto
Overpainted—the absence from these pages
Of my own mother. Because of course she's here
Throughout, the breath drawn after every line,
Essential to its making as to mine;   (pp. 83–84)

In this first book of his epic poem that is characterized by the poet's memories, he turns to the subject of his mother. Just when the reader thinks that Merrill is being forthright in his language and revelations, it becomes clear that he is punning on his revelation—and its absence—in order to joke about, and make comparisons between, the biological and biographical mother, and the "Mother" of his poems. His mother is present, he says, through an ineluctable umbilicus that joins mother and son together; she gave "breath" to him and remains a spiritual part of him. At the same time, she rarely makes an explicit appearance in his written work, and so it is a kind of untrue to say that she is "here / Throughout." Indeed, unlike with Crane and Bishop, for whom scholars have had more time to make characterizations and judgments on both their work as well as their lives, Merrill's death in February 1995 is beginning to allow enough critical distance of time to evaluate him and his considerable body of work. In the absence of a critical biography on Merrill, the sources for a discussion of Merrill's mother are from his memoir, *A Different Person* and from their lack of reference within the poems themselves.[57]

Merrill's mother in *A Different Person* reiterates the poet's observation in *The Book of Ephraim* about her conspicuous absence. While helping his mother box up articles and clippings to send to a library archive, she remarks: " '*The articles about you always tell who your father was,*' she said without petulance, '*but there's never any mention of me. It's as if you'd never had a mother.*' "[58] Merrill bristles in the narrative at her comment; certainly part of him wishes he did not have his mother. Merrill's mother, Hellen Ingram, like Crane's, views her son as a narcissistic extension of herself. Indeed, he explains at the beginning of the book that chronicles his years living in Europe at the beginning of the 1950s that he was "glad to be putting an ocean between [him] and his parents." He was especially glad to be away from his mother:

> My mother was ill that year with a gastric ulcer, and I knew why. Four years earlier, she and I had done things the other could not forgive. Since then, despite the rare hour when the old unconditional intimacy shone forth, each had felt a once adored and all-comforting presence slipping gradually, helplessly away.   (DP, 4)

The "things" that he had done are not clarified here, but later it becomes apparent that he acted upon and admitted to a homosexual love affair. His mother did not act with grace under this perceived pressure:

> *The theory in those days was that homosexuality was an illness, hence curable. At my mother's earnest wish I agreed to consult a doctor her doctor had recommended. My mother flatly dismissed the life I dream of living. "Society will not condone it," she more than once told me in her soft, reasonable voice(.)*   (DP, 89)

Merrill's mother is a southern belle from Florida; the poet often characterizes his mother in traditionally genteel, southern terms, "her soft, reasonable voice," that present a dramatic contrast with the derisive import of her comments. Like the tone of his poems, Merrill does not seem angry with his mother for her emotional treason, urging him toward secrecy; rather he adopts a tone of acceptance and, at times, of a bemused condescension at her bourgeois attitudes and social concerns.

Merrill's mother had always urged him to keep his sexuality a secret from his father. James was Charles Merrill's youngest son; Charles Merrill had two children from his first marriage. Merrill wrote that his father was cold and distant and often seemed more like a grandfather than a father to him. Charles Merrill also suffered from several heart attacks. Merrill's mother warned him not to tell his father for fear it "would kill him." Merrill, however, discovered that his father did in fact already know about his son's homosexuality; he had known since Merrill was in college at Amherst and having an affair with a fellow, male student named Kimon. When he confronted his mother about it, the narrative of parental control became deeply troubling:

> My father's reaction was appalling, my mother says, beyond anything I could imagine. Why, his first impulse, until she talked sense into him, was to have Kimon killed—"rubbed out" by Murder, Inc. (Surely Czar Lepke and his henchmen were all behind bars by 1945? The question goes unasked; I am listening in pity and terror.) At the very least, my father could have Kimon dismissed from Amherst—a scandal involving us all, my mother pointed out. (DP, pp. 150–151)

The story seems too bizarre to believe at face value. There is the initial question of Hellen Ingram's role, and whether she is lying about this in order to win the allegiances of her son. She is nonetheless a controlling and manipulative woman, whose honesty can only reinforce the poet's sense of his homosexuality as a destabilizing gesture for his parents' lives. The incident functions as an effort to represent familiar emotions as a narrative within a dramatic and received literary code. At the same time, the reader wonders about Merrill's creative hand in this narrative. The reference to "Czar Lepke" brings to mind Robert Lowell's "Memories of West Street and Lepke," where a fellow jailbird points out to the speaker "the T-shirted back / of *Murder Incorporated's* Czar Lepke(.)"[59] Lowell's poem is concerned with feeling out of time with one's era and community in the "tranquillized fifties." Perhaps the story is invented by the poet in order to reinforce his feelings of alienation from his parents. Merrill is not averse to such an "infinite mischief": indeed the relationship between art and life is a central question in Merrill's poetry and one that the poet plays with throughout his career. In an interview after the publication of *Nights and Days*, Merrill complicates the dynamics of life and art when he addresses the confessional mode: ". . . confessional poetry . . . is a literary convention like any other, the problem being to make it *sound* as if it were true. One can, of course, tell the truth, but I shouldn't think that would be necessary to give the illusion of a True Confession."[60] The reader is left to wonder here how the life signifies and how it is signified within the poems to create the "illusion" of a "James Merrill." Or how is Merrill distorted and what is being distorted?

Another friend and former lover of the poet is the subject of the title poem of Merrill's second book of poems, "The Country of a Thousand Years of Peace," an elegy dedicated to Hans Lodeizen. In *A Different Person* Merrill writes: "Hans was a graduate student at Amherst when we met in 1946. . . . True to form, I fell in love." Hans was a fellow poet and someone that Merrill looked up to for his sophistication and literary knowledge. The five quatrains of the poem are densely musical; rhymes are carried through from one stanza to the next. For example, "race" and "face" (ll. 3 and 6) give the poem a forward motion. The poem also moves from general images of death and awe to concrete images of Hans, dying of leukemia:

> Here they all come to die,
> Fluent therein as in a fourth tongue.
> But for a young man not yet of their race
> It was madness you should lie
>
> Blind in one eye, and fed
> By the blood of a scrubbed face;   (ll. 1–6)

The "Here" of the first line refers to the poem's title "The Country of a Thousand Years of Peace"; it is this "country" where "they all come to die" and where one is required to be "Fluent" in the language of death—a language similar to that of poetry because of its immortal, or recurring, space. The "But" of the third line serves not to counter the relevance of the first two to the speaker's friend; he is included within the "they." This is in part because of Hans's status as a fellow poet and therefore particularly well-versed in the language of recurring time.

The poet complicates the rhyme scheme of the quatrains in the middle stanzas of the poem. This complication reflects and intensifies the "madness(es)" of the poem; these are, chiefly, the repetition of the word "madness" in lines four and then seven. This "madness" is extended to place; the "city" is a "toy." The city is not named but clues, like "glittering neutrality," assure us that it is probably in Switzerland; in his memoir, Merrill confirms that Hans died in a hospital in Lausanne (DP, p. 46). Although the city is characterized by things that would seem to be positive, by "clock and chocolate and lake and cloud," they prove "less than you could bear." The speaker subverts the expectation of the phrase "more than you can bear" into "less," which serves to reinforce the degree of loss that is at stake. These devices all conspire to construct a world that is awry—not only because it allows for a gifted, young man to die but also because it allows for an unintelligible loss.

The concluding stanzas move away from the concreteness of the representation of Hans and of his hospital in Switzerland and toward an abstraction of language that produces a multiplicity of meanings for the poem's losses:

And makes me cry aloud
At the old masters of disease
Who dangling high above you on a hair
The sword that, never falling, kills

Would coax you still back from that starry land
Under the world, which no one sees
Without a death, its finish and sharp weight
Flashing in his own hand.

Grammatically, the "sword" is the "old masters of disease" that "dangl(es)"; it also introduces, as it simultaneously denies its introduction through a deferral, an eroticism between the speaker and the "young man." In the declarative statements, "Here they all come to die" and "that starry land," "here" and "that" are words that point to places that are familiar to the speaker. These statements are reminiscent of Yeats's "Sailing to Byzantium" that begins: "That is no country for old men."[61] When Yeats's poem is associated with Merrill's, his references are clarified. Merrill's "country" might be Yeats's "country that is no place for old men," and situated in the "artifice of eternity." This comparison also helps to open the poem up and explore its range of signification. The "they" of the first line inscribes a multiple purpose to this elegy; the loss that it chronicles is not specific to Merrill's friend but extends to include other losses, especially of the Mother. In this way, the blood that feeds the "young man," "fed / By the blood of a scrubbed face" (ll. 5–6), not only refers to the "scrubbed face" of the blood donor but also invokes the "blood" of the mother whose biological function is signified by her feeding her child.

"The Country of a Thousand Years of Peace" ends with an image of a "hand": "its [the sword's] finish and sharp weight / Flashing in his own hand" (ll. 19–20). While the "hand" in Crane almost always is a site of erotic potential, in Merrill's poems the "hand" traditionally combines potentiality for art (as the place where the poet holds his pen) and sexuality. The image of the "hand" is interesting because of the frequency with which it appears in the poems of Crane, Bishop, and Merrill; for example, the hand will return as a central image in Crane's "Voyages" and Merrill's "Between Us," both of which I discuss in the third chapter.

Merrill eventually came to sum up his poems—if not his entire oeuvre—as "chronicles of love and loss." "The Country of a Thousand Years of Peace" marks the beginning stages of the poet's "chronicles" that combine in significant ways "love" and "loss," revealing through their combination the interrelatedness of Merrill's homoeroticism and Mother-eroticism. These combined themes appear in poems from Merrill's middle work, such as in the poem "Days of 1935." "Days of 1935" appears in *Braving the Elements*, published in 1972, and is dedicated to the poet's mother. Merrill wrote a series of poems with the "Days of . . ." title, such as "Days of 1935," "Days of 1964," and "Days of 1971." Merrill's title is an allusion to the poems of C. P. Cavafy who also wrote a number of "Days of . . ." poems, such as "Days of 1908." Merrill included Cavafy among his favorite international writers partly because the two shared a love for Greece, where Merrill lived part of every year; at the same time, Merrill must have enjoyed the erotic and openly homosexual poetics that Cavafy exemplifies. For an example of the homoeroticism of C. P. Cavafy's poems, "Days of 1908" concludes as the poet says:

> Oh days of the summer of nineteen-hundred eight,
> your vision, exquisitely, was spared
> the view of that faded cinnamon suit.
> Your vision preserved him
> as he was when he undressed, when he flung off
> the unworthy clothes, and the mended underwear.
> And he'd be left completely nude; flawlessly beautiful; a marvel.
> His hair uncombed, springing back;
> his limbs slightly colored by the sun
> from his being naked in the morning at the baths, and at the
>     seashore.[62]

Like Cavafy, Merrill's "Days of . . ." poem plays with eroticizing an unlikely object. In "Days of 1935" the speaker imagines a scenario in which he is kidnapped. The kidnapping of the Lindbergh baby sent a wave of fear into the hearts of many wealthy Americans such as James Merrill's parents, who were afraid that their son might be kidnapped for ransom as well. In "Days of 1935," the speaker, who, like Merrill, is the son of a wealthy man, imagines a scenario in which he is kidnapped. The poem is composed of seventy-six quatrains (304 lines) with a rhyme of a-b-a-b, and it begins with the description of a liminal position that is partly a dream: "Ladder horned against moonlight / Window hoisted stealthily—/ That's what I'd steel myself at night / To see, or sleep to see." The speaker dreams, "sleeps to see," a fantasy that is both a wish and a fear:

> My parents were out partying,
> My nurse was old and deaf and slow.
> Way off in the servants' wing
> Cackled a radio.
>
> On the Lindbergh baby's small
> Cold features lay a spell, a swoon.
> It seemed entirely plausible
> For my turn to come soon,
>
> For a masked and crouching form
> Lithe as a tiger, light as moth,
> To glide towards me, clap a firm
> Hand across my mouth,
>
> Then sheer imagination ride
> Off with us in its old jalopy,
> Trailing bedclothes like a bride
> Timorous but happy.    (ll. 5–20)

The poem establishes the speaker's parents as distant and uncaring, and their behavior is contrasted with the attention that the speaker receives from the couple who kidnap him, "Floyd and Jean," and the figure of the maid at the end of the poem who is a mother-manqué. Here the speaker takes an aggressive posture against the parents who are "out partying" like teenagers and the other grown-ups, the "servants," who are busy in their own world. The "firm / Hand" of the kidnappers sets up the first in a series of contrasts between the kidnapping couple and the parents; the kidnappers have a stern hand that signals some interest in the child's welfare. When they take him away, he is joyous and happy to be rescued by them.

The kidnappers take the child to their "hovel," where his imagination indulges in a dramatic fantasy about his captors. The "hovel" to which they take him reinforces the domesticity of the scene: he is taken from one home to another. One appears to be a perversion of the other but which one is the perversion is unclear for the speaker. The domesticity of the scene reinforces the degree to which the dream is an attempt to erase and re-create the mother. Once he is safely in their hideout, the speaker describes the captors: "A lady out of *Silver Screen*, / Her careful rosebud chewing gum, / Seems to expect us, lets us in, / Nods her platinum // Spit curls deadpan" (ll. 29–33). He describes her as a wise-cracking, platinum blonde along the lines of a Jean Harlow character, highlighting her as a quasi-camp figure. Jean's "chewing gum" is "rosebud" which signals her as a pretty, young girl. At the same time, "rosebud" is a further Hollywood reference to Orsen Welles's "Citizen Kane," a narrative about another young boy who is separated from his mother. The poet's description of the man is less flippant: "The man's face / Rivets me, a lightning bolt. / Lean, sallow, lantern-jawed, he lays / Pistol and cartridge belt // Between us on the oilskin . . ." (ll. 37–41). He is like a cowboy; he is hypermasculine, "lean" and carrying a "pistol." The gun reinforces the extent of his masculinity and reminds the reader that the speaker's interest is sexually charged, like a "lightning bolt." The homoeroticism of this introduction is reinforced by the close of this first scene with the two kidnappers. The speaker has been biting Floyd who tells him to stop; the poet clarifies what he means: "Meaning my toothprints on his hand, / Indenture of a kiss" (ll. 51–52). This is an interesting moment because it establishes the Oedipal nature of the scenario that the speaker creates; he imbues Floyd with the ambivalence—the love and aggression—that is characteristic of a parent/child dynamic.

Indeed, this fantasy of a better parent contains a mock primal scene in which the poet imagines waking up to their sounds of lovemaking:

> One night I woke to hear the room
> Filled with crickets—no, bedsprings.
> My eyes dilated in the gloom,
> My ears made out things.
>
> Jean: The kid, he's still awake . . .
> Floyd: Time he learned . . . O baby . . . God . . .
> Their prone tango, for my sake,
> Grew intense and proud.   (ll. 121–128)

The speaker seems to construct himself in self-consciously naïve terms; he does not know what the sound is that wakes him and wonders if it is "crickets," which conveys the idea that the speaker has heretofore not been confronted with the reality of sex between his real parents. At the same time and in contrast to his naiveté, the speaker imagines himself a concern to Jean and Floyd during their intercourse; they talk about him and include him. Indeed, Floyd's response seems to say that their sexual activity is for the benefit and education of the speaker, "for [his] sake." Indeed, for the rest of his time with Jean and Floyd, the speaker remains the center of their attention: "Do you know any stories, Kid?" she asks him, and he is surprised and delighted, "I stared at her—*she* was the child!-" (ll. 141 and 145). The speaker then tells her fairy tales, as a parent would entertain an imaginative child, reversing once again his position with respect to his parents.

His fantasies crisscross in terms of his positionality and his relationship to his parents; at the beginning, he is the child, and here, he takes their place. As the narrative of the poem continues, Floyd returns to the speaker and Jean with the news that the speaker "will be home tomorrow." As they go to bed, the speaker's reversal becomes complete as he replaces Jean with himself in the primal scene with Floyd. Floyd and the poet sleep beside each other on the floor:

> Commenced a wary, mortal heat
> Run neck by nose. Small fingers felt,
> Sore point of all that wiry meat,
> A nipple's tender fault.
>
> Time stopped. His arm somnambulist
> Had circled me, warm, salt as blood.
> Mine was the future in his fist
> To get at if I could,
>
> While his heart beat like a drum
> And *Oh baby* faint and hoarse
> Echoed from within his dream . . .  (ll. 225–235)

The news that he will be going home is not met with happiness; rather, the speaker worries that perhaps he was not polite enough, that he had "failed" his substitute parents in some way. Reversals continue in this sexual description. It is Floyd's "arm" that is around the speaker; the descriptions are of Floyd's actions to him, whereas the speaker is acted upon, not acting himself.

The eroticism is cut short by daybreak and the descent of "G-men" to rescue an ambivalent speaker. From the "witness-box," their once attractive gaze is now "stupid, speechless." The change in the poet's view of Jean and Floyd from heroic and erotic rescuers to fallible and "empty" reminds the speaker of his own parents, and he wakes up from his dream into the caring arms of his "old nurse" (ll. 268–269). In the final eight stanzas of the poem the tone is different. The speaker no longer says "I"; now, he speaks of himself in the disassociation of the third person, "The Child" and "he." The poet's language reinforces the representation of life at home as dull and mundane: "The kitchen dado is of board / Painted like board." (ll. 275–276). The speaker's attention to the wall's "dado" is an attempt toward a world of multiple levels and meanings, signaled by the pun of "dado" and a child-like pronunciation of "dad." Life, however, seems to "mimic( ) the real"; reality is comprised of business and indifference (l. 278).

The close of the poem is sealed with a kiss that echoes the dreamed of kiss with Floyd: "She [his mother] kisses him sweet dreams, but who- / Floyd and Jean are gone- // Who will he dream of?" (ll. 299–301). The mother's empty kiss commingles in the poet's memory with that of Floyd—also "empty" now. Nonetheless the homoerotic and mother-erotic "kiss" combine in his imagination to produce an effect of lamentation that erases the flippancy of the poem's dream. This is underscored by the speaker's breaks in his language.

The combination of the homoerotic and the mother-erotic that appears in "Days of 1935" continues as an echo in its companion poem in *Braving the Elements*, "Days of 1971." "Days of 1971" is a series of ten linked sonnets in which the speaker addresses a "you" that is a former lover:

> Proust's Law (are you listening?) is twofold:
> (a) What least thing our self-love longs for most
> Others instinctively withhold;
>
> (b) Only when time has slain desire
> Is his wish granted to a smiling ghost
> Neither harmed nor warmed, now, by the fire. (ll. 37–42)

Homosexual love is in the language of the poem; however, the speaker yearns within that love for a more complete sense of love. For the speaker, "our self-love longs for most" what cannot be attained, although love is part of the elements that constitute the poet's world, along with "fire" or the Mother. In an article on *Braving the Elements*, J. D. McClatchy writes that Merrill:

> found his own *bonheur conjugal* in 1953 with David Jackson. Jackson could play the piano, write a story, dash-off a water-color; he was ebullient, daring, funny, irresistible. Over their years together, strains in

their relationship were sometimes apparent. But they stayed together—if, lately, at a certain distance from each other. It was as if Merrill were determined to keep for himself the kind of relationship his parents had thrown away. He was constant to his lovers, as well.[63]

The description of Merrill's relationship with David Jackson, whose presence figures centrally in *The Changing Light at Sandover* as "DJ," becomes a replacement for the Mother, as he does in Merrill's representation of their relationship. The "law" of love here is one in which the lover exists together with the "smiling ghost" of the Mother.

The specter of the Mother, textually implicit in these poems by Crane, Bishop, and Merrill, not only reinforces the centrality of the mother in the development of individuals as they relate to the outside world but also illustrates the degree to which associational meanings of poetic language to the poet's psychology are embedded in the rhetoric of poetry. Perspective, and its strategic manipulation in a poem, functions symbiotically with the alternation between revelation and concealment. Perspective limits the modes of revelation; it means for the reader to look at something in a particular, subjective way. Perspective forces a certain view, making it necessary for the reader to see the subject in a singular way. Because the poetry of Crane, Bishop, and Merrill is always simultaneously expressing as it is concealing, it engages the reader who wonders about this tension and who formulates questions based on it. These thematic shifts are reflected in the combination of representations of homoerotic and mother-erotic images that serve to foreground an ambivalence. The psychoanalytic paradigm underscores the ambivalent nature and destructive impulses that accompany the figure of the mother. Crane's, Bishop's, and Merrill's poems illustrate this reaction and extend it to characterize their feelings surrounding homosexual desire. The interpretation of rhetoric requires that the question, "what is behind this language?" be asked. It presupposes that there is something missing, or encoded, that there is some state of affairs that is being concealed and that should, and can, be revealed. The idiosyncratic styles of Crane, Bishop, and Merrill highlight the degree to which their poetic language acts as rhetoric, to express something else along with the impacted images and "associational meanings" of Crane, or the descriptive language of Bishop, or the mannerisms of Merrill.

# Coda: Literary Mothers

While in many of their poems Hart Crane, Elizabeth Bishop, and James Merrill align the homoerotic with the mother-erotic, the representation of the figure of the Mother in the poems discussed in this second chapter is not limited to a metaphorical or a biographical one. Crane, Bishop, and Merrill also inherit or acquire a Mother figure from their literary predecessors. T. S. Eliot's essay "Tradition and the Individual Talent," which first appeared in 1919, argues for the importance of a literary tradition and outlines what many twentieth-century poets feel is their relationship to their literary predecessors, one that involves, in Eliot's words, a "sacrifice" or "self-surrender" of the individual artist to a kind of historical continuum of literature.[1]

In "Tradition and the Individual Talent" Eliot makes the claim that "no poet, no artist of any art, has his complete meaning alone."[2] Indeed Hart Crane's poetic representation of a mother is acquired from Walt Whitman's, especially the figure of the mother that is constructed in the Sea Drift poems, "Out of the Cradle Endlessly Rocking" and "As I Ebb'd with the Ocean of Life." The maternal is represented in these poems through the image of the sea, which is both merging and obliterating. Despite a childhood that was often "restless and unhappy," Whitman was close to his mother, Louisa.[3] When she died in May of 1873, Whitman was devastated, and the poet's health, already in an ill state, turned worse; he suffered a stroke and a breakdown. Louisa Whitman's life was a difficult one, spent managing the care of an alcoholic husband as well as a house full of children—some of whom, like Walt's brother Eddy, required Louisa's constant attentions.

Diane Middlebrook characterizes the voice of the maternal sea in "As I Ebb'd with the Ocean of Life" and "Out of the Cradle Endlessly Rocking" as "a crier of loss" but, she writes, the speaker "also returns to her as to a mother from whom new life can be won."[4] Middlebrook elucidates Whitman's poetic project in these poems, pointing out the poet's belief that poetry derives from the knowledge of death, but she does not refer to the Mother's ambivalent position. The paradoxical coupling of death with birth—especially the "birth" of poetry—leads, for my discussion, to Crane's reinterpretation of Whitman's figure of the mother. The life-giving and death-containing elements of the maternal sea in Whitman's poems foreground her ambivalent status; she is both good and bad, positive/life and negative/death. The fact that Whitman's speakers do not seem to feel the maternal sea's death-containing element as negative but rather constructs it as a hostile factor serves to reinforce the sea's ambivalent position. The sea as a maternal figure does seem to frighten the speaker in "As I Ebb'd with the Ocean of Life." This is in part due to the fact that the speaker here does not present a past state of affairs from which the reader feels he has reached a state of equanimity. In addition, "As I Ebb'd" is fundamentally concerned with the speaker's crisis over artistic inspiration; this anxiety reinforces the disquieting force of the sea's image. Indeed, the speaker begins the third section of the poem: "You oceans both, I close with you," where "both" recalls not only the mother's two-fold purpose but also the two-fold nature of the mother that Melanie Klein describes in her characterization of the "good breast" and "bad breast."[5] As with Whitman, Klein also allows the two opposing sides— "good" and "bad"—to exist simultaneously as ambivalent objects in the mind of the infant.

The movement in the mind of the infant of the "good breast" and the "bad breast" into a unified, ambivalent object suggests an analogous movement that Freud describes in "The Uncanny." In this essay Freud examines the words "heimlich" or canny and familiar and "unheimlich" or uncanny, noting that "heimlich is a word the meaning of which develops towards an ambivalence until it finally coincides with its opposite, unheimlich."[6] In highlighting the degree to which two words that would appear to mean opposite things can mean the same thing, here "heimlich" and "unheimlich," Freud connects through the means of his analysis the words "ambivalence" and "uncanny." This gesture reiterates the alignment of Freudian interpretation and literary analysis. In fact, literary critics hold up Freud's essay "The Uncanny" as a defining moment for deconstructive readings. Barbara Johnson clarifies this deconstructive act and argues that the uncertainty of meaning engendered by "difference," because of the way that two dissimilar words can appear similar [heimlich and unheimlich] is a "problem for reading," whereby "reading proceeds by identifying and dismantling differences that cannot be identified." This kind of analysis is a "teasing out of warring forces of signification within a text."[7] I would argue that Johnson's "teasing out of warring" factions, which do not destroy the text, create a situation of ambivalence in meaning. The juxtaposition of "ambivalence" with "uncanny" cannot be a coincidence and serves to signify the uncanny nature—the dread of the unfamiliar—of ambivalence itself, a fear that comes from a resistance to allow two opposing structures, such as a "good breast" and a "bad breast," to remain together, without canceling each other out. Here, the difference between Freud's scientific theories and those of literary critical analysis appears to collapse.

If Hart Crane inherits Whitman's ambivalent figuration of the Mother, Elizabeth Bishop does not so much *inherit* Marianne Moore's representation of a Mother figure, but acquires Moore as a literary mother figure with whom she must do battle and then from whom she must declare her freedom.[8] The friendship and artistic influences between Marianne Moore and Elizabeth Bishop have been well documented by several critics.[9] On the cusp of her graduation from Vassar College in 1934, Bishop met Marianne Moore on a bench outside of the Reading Room of the New York Public Library. Having discovered that a librarian at Vassar was a friend of Marianne Moore, Bishop asked the librarian to arrange for the two women to meet. After Bishop graduated from college, she moved to New York and was able to visit frequently Moore and her mother at the apartment they shared in Brooklyn on Cumberland Street: the two poets soon became good friends. Bishop met Marianne Moore on March 16, 1934 and Bishop's mother died on May 29, just a couple of months later. The chronology of these two important events in Bishop's life are extraordinarily close and could lend itself to a structure of erasure and replacement. Nonetheless, the importance of Bishop's mother as a specter in her poems—as I have demonstrated in this second chapter—argues against the creation of such a narrative of replacement.

When Bishop met Moore she was already a fan of her work. Remarking upon Moore's book *Observations*, Bishop wonders: "Why had no one ever written about *things* in this clear and dazzling way before."[10] Soon after they became friends, Bishop started sending Moore drafts of her poems and short stories for her approval and suggestions. Moore became Bishop's mentor, offering the younger poet helpful advice and, more importantly, securing Bishop's first few choice publications. In the fall of 1940, Bishop sent Moore a draft of "The Roosters." Objecting to what she felt were the younger poet's indecencies, Moore retyped the poem to make it more polite (removing the phrase "water closet") and retitled the poem "The Cock." Moore's extensive revisions signaled an end to her poetic mothering and mentorship; Moore had overstepped her bounds and made

Bishop realize her own definable voice and poetic vision that was separate from Moore's. Bishop was so shocked by Moore's reworked version that she never sent Moore another poem, until it was a finished copy. Perhaps what Moore objected to in "The Roosters" was one of Bishop's early references to homoeroticism. Homoeroticism and violence are central to the poem and constitute what the roosters need to " 'Deny deny deny.' "

While not exactly a lesson in the diplomacy of restrained language, Moore's poem "Marriage" from 1935 offers Bishop a figuration of a Mother, both in terms of Moore's example in having written the poem and through the representation of the mother's role in the text. "Marriage" contains Moore's characteristic use of quotations within her poems. These quotations reinforce the degree to which Moore is examining or making direct reference to the world outside of her poems. The exteriorizing effort of Moore's quotations are in contrast to Bishop's interiorizing mode of her speakers that is characteristic of her poems, especially in "The Roosters." Indeed, "Marriage" is, like many of Bishop's poems, a rumination. This instance is a rumination on the subject of marriage; it begins in the language of examination:

> This institution,
> one should say enterprise
> out of respect for which
> one says one need not change one's mind
> about a thing one has believed in,
> requiring public promises
> of one's intention
> to fulfill a private obligation:[11]

Where Bishop's speakers manipulate the rumination into a spiritual examination and thereby turn to inward thoughts, Moore's speaker focuses outward throughout. The language here is formal; "marriage" is not an affair of romance or passion but is an "institution" that is an "obligation" on the part of the participants. The speaker uses the distancing pronoun, "one," and the "I" of the speaker does not appear until line nine. The speaker further eschews interiority when she says: "Psychology which explains everything / explains nothing, / and we are still in doubt" (ll. 18–20). The "doubt" derives from the speaker's refusal to examine the "psychological" or emotional workings of marriage; Moore's poem is a clinical and cold discussion of it.

The speaker considers the example of "Adam and Eve" (l. 9) for her discussion and in so doing presents a vision of marriage—or more

accurately a vision of the "impossibility" (l. 46) of marriage. The
speaker's vision of the "institution" is one in which the woman retains
a position of power: "this amalgamation which can never be more /
than an interesting impossibility" (ll. 45–46). Her interests lie on the
side of women and Eve, whom she finds attractive: "Eve: beautiful
woman— / I have seen her / when she was so handsome / she gave
me a start" (ll. 21–24). There is a homoerotic element between the
speaker and "Eve" that is complicated by the use of the masculinizing
adjective, "handsome." Indeed, insofar as Eve is the mother of
humanity, Moore's image combines the homoerotic and the mother-
erotic. As Bishop frequently does, Moore's speaker plays with expectations of gendered images. Certainly much of the power of the
poem for Bishop must come from the bravery with which Moore
presents views of an attraction for, and a dynamic of power with,
female figures.

Bishop wrote a memoir of Moore called, "Efforts of Affection:
A Memoir of Marianne Moore."[12] The title implies a continuity of
action; Bishop is making "efforts" toward "affection" for Moore,
which is to say she is continually trying in her "efforts" but not necessarily succeeding in them.[13] In the opening paragraph of "Effort of
Affection," Bishop explains that her title is a variation on the title of
Moore's poem "Efforts and Affection" and that Moore, in inscribing
the book to Bishop, crossed out the "and" and wrote "of." Bishop's
explanation does not prevent my own, despite the apparent contradiction. Rather, Moore's re-inscription might also signify her own
parallel feelings of ambivalence to Bishop and suggest a competition
between the two poets.

Bishop's title is reminiscent of Crane's "For the Marriage of
Faustus and Helen," where the "for" conveys the sense of a continuing
process toward something that is not met. There is no "marriage" in
the poem. Here, however, the "efforts" that are required toward
"affection" for Moore convey the sense of an ambivalence on the part
of Bishop. In her memoir, Bishop quotes briefly from a small number
of Moore's poems, and in particular includes a passage from
"Marriage"; she writes that the poem "transforms a justified sense of
injury into a work of art" and quotes the following lines:

> Unhelpful Hymen!
> a kind of overgrown cupid
> reduced to insignificance
> by the mechanical advertising
> parading as involuntary comment,

by that experiment of Adam's
with ways out but no way in—
the ritual of marriage . . .   (ll. 130–137)

Bishop interestingly chooses to foreground a poem with political
import out of all of Moore's work and discusses the poem as a
response to feminist critics who dismiss Moore's poems for their lack
of seriousness. The fact that "Marriage" is a kind of poem that Bishop
herself rarely writes—political and with overt homoerotic imagery—
but that Bishop nonetheless admires reflects the ambivalent relationship that the two women share as rival poets and sources of
inspiration.

Similar to Bishop's friendship with Marianne Moore, Bishop's
friendship with James Merrill, too, is well-documented. Merrill's poem
for Bishop, "The Victor Dog," is a manifestation of Merrill's
adoption of Bishop as a literary mother figure. "The Victor Dog" is
the penultimate poem in Merrill's 1972 collection *Braving the
Elements*. The book's dedication reads *"For my mother,"* yet his troubling relationship with his mother, Hellen Ingram Merrill, leads one
to wonder to which "mother" he might be referring. As I discuss earlier, Merrill's relationship with his mother is a complex and strained
one: "she and I had done things the other could not forgive," cen-
tering on his living as a homosexual against her urgent pleas for him
to suppress his desires.[14] The poems in *Braving the Elements* present
several maternal options—Kleo, the poet's maid in his home in
Greece in "After the Fire"; Jean, the archetypal Hollywood floozy
kidnapper in "Days of 1935"; the specter of the poet's mother in the
apartment blown up by student activists in "18 West 11th Street";
and, finally, Elizabeth Bishop to whom "The Victor Dog" is
addressed.

If Bishop acquires a notion of the mother as a self-sustaining and
self-sufficient, but nevertheless ambivalent individual from Moore's
"Marriage" on which to base her own conceptions of the representation of the mother, Merrill's poem thematizes the lessons in craft and
dedication that an artist can learn from Bishop, and in so doing,
elevates her as a maternal figure whom the speaker can admire. As mother
figure, Bishop, Merrill writes, appears to "refrain" from "judgment"
on the world around her favoring quiet, studious observation:

Bix to Buxtehude to Boulez,
The little white dog on the Victor label

> Listens long and hard as he is able.
> It's all in a day's work, whatever plays.
>
> From judgment, it would seem, he has refrained.
> He even listens earnestly to Bloch,
> Then builds a church upon acid rock.  (ll. 1–7)

Bishop, as the "little white dog," is praised for her ability to "listen()
long and hard." This is the uncompromised concentration of the
artist for whom "it's all in a day's work." The praise is reminiscent of
Robert Lowell's in his fourth poem from "Four Poems for Elizabeth
Bishop," where he asks of her: "Do / you still hang words in air,
ten years imperfect, / joke-letters, glued to cardboard posters, with
gaps / and empties for the unimagined phrase . . .?"[15] It is a familiar
compliment to Bishop, her ability to keep a poem for as long as
necessary—even "ten years"—until it is finished to the best of her
knowledge. Merrill also notes Bishop's tendency to keep overt psychological "judgments" out of her poems. This line at the same time
provides a contrast between this imagined, idealized mother figure
and his own mother whose lack of "refrained" judgment causes so
much narrative turmoil in *A Different Person*.

The "white dog" at first simply "listens," but then the speaker
qualifies and alters this, deciding that he is observing:

> *Does* he hear? I fancy he rather smells
> Those lemon-gold arpeggios in Ravel's
> "Les jets d'eau du palais de ceux qui s'aiment."
>
> He ponders the Schumann Concerto's tall willow hit
> By lightning, and stays put. When he surmises
> Through one of Bach's eternal boxwood mazes
> The oboe pungent as a bitch in heat,
>
> Or when the calypso decants its raw bay rum
> Or the moon in *Wozzeck* reddens ripe for murder,
> He doesn't sneeze or howl; just listens harder.  (ll. 10–19)

The internal question, "Does he hear?" and the assorted references
to European composers, "Bix," "Buxtehude," "Boulez," "Bloch,"
"Ravel," and "Schumann," and an opera, "Wozzeck," remind us that
we are distinctly in the world of a James Merrill poem—but one that
is describing the poetic project of Bishop that is characterized by her
patience and her observations. The close of the poem is self-
consciously in the domain of a discourse about poems: "Is there in

Victor's heart / No honey for the vanquished? Art is art. / The life it asks of us is a dog's life" (ll. 38–40). The meta-poetic gesture of the last lines secures the subtext of the poem in the fore-text; we are, as is so often the case with Merrill, speaking of "art" itself. Many of the sentiments that "The Victor Dog" praises are reiterated by Merrill in his comments about Bishop in an interview with J. D. McClatchy:

> It was *du coté de chez* Elizabeth, though, that I saw the daily life that took my fancy even more, with its kind of random, Chekhovian surface, open to trivia and funny surprises, or even painful ones, today a fit of weeping, tomorrow a picnic. I could see how close that life was to her poems, how much the life and the poems gave to one another. . . . Elizabeth had more of a talent for life—and for poetry— than anyone else I've known, and this has served me as an ideal.[16]

The "daily life" that Merrill admires is "a dog's life," quiet and mundane and perfectly given to opening itself up to the "honey" that comes from making art.

This final line of "The Victor Dog" is also reminiscent of another of Merrill's favorite poetic precursors, Rainer Maria Rilke. Rilke concludes his poem "Archaic Torso of Apollo" with the line: "for here there is no place / that does not see you. You must change your life."[17] Rilke's poem is about the poet's ability to imagine light and life in an otherwise darkened and lifeless "torso" and suggests the power of art. Rilke's line that connects life and art echoes within Merrill's, "The life it asks of us is a dog's life." In so doing, the line conveys the sense that "art" does "ask" the artist to change his life in significant and potentially disruptive ways. However it is a lesson to the artist to endure for his poetic achievements. Furthermore, Rilke exists behind many phrases and images in Merrill's work and provides the poet with a similar parental figure. If Bishop is the mother, then Rilke, together with Marcel Proust, combine to provide a father figure. Rilke often figures in Merrill's poems; Merrill revises the characteristic Rilkean question: who will hear me, if I cry or who will see me? This question begins Rilke's "Duino Elegies": "Who, if I cried out, would hear me among the angels' / hierarchies?"[18] Merrill's speakers revise this into the question, "how can I speak"; there are several examples of this, one of which is from "A Renewal" when the speaker says, "when next I speak." Merrill often revises Rilke's question into one that is applied to others. An example of this is the figure of Hans Lodeizen in the elegy "A Dedication"; the poet wonders how Hans can speak and be heard: "There are moments when speech is but a mouth pressed / Lightly and humbly against the angel's hand." The image of the lover's "mouth" proposes an alternative to the more common images of body parts, generally the hand, that the poet employs; the "mouth" conveys the sense of the lover's femininity because "mouth" recalls the womb. It is also a body part associated with the pleasure derived from the mother's breast. Merrill also figures his revision of Rilke's question in "An Urban Convalescence," where he writes: "The words she must have spoken, setting her face / To flutter like a veil, I cannot hear now, / Let alone understand" (ll. 35–37). The woman's words are unknowable, distorted like a face behind a veil.

James Merrill's poems lend themselves to this kind of analysis because his poems are based on literary favorites, as do the poems of Crane and Bishop by virtue of their densely allusive status. This discussion works in conjunction with my larger consideration of the figuration of the mother in this chapter in Crane, Bishop, and Merrill. Whereas my concern was previously to reveal the ways that poetic images combine the homoerotic with the mother-erotic, this additional exploration illustrates that when such representations occur they also serve to reify Crane, Bishop, and Merrill within the literary tradition in which they write because they are building upon figurations of the mother that they have acquired. Freud prepares for this type of analysis of the multiplicity of significations not only for the mother but also for the lover when he writes in a letter:

> I am accustoming myself to the idea of regarding every sexual act as a process in which four persons are involved. We shall have a lot to discuss about that.[19]

Freud's and Klein's theories on human development illustrate the presence and continued recollection of the figure of the Mother, the lover, and the self in psychic structures. The difference between the theories of human development they present and of literary critical analysis that had seemed significant grows uncertain as poems reveal these same structures of recollection as a feature of the always already writtenness of their tropes.

# CHAPTER 3

# BURNT MATCHES, OR THE
# ART OF LOVE

What is a poet writing about when he or she writes about love? Here is Wallace Stevens's possible response to this question:

> It is posed and it is posed
> But in nature it merely grows.
> Stones pose in the falling night;
> And beggars dropping to sleep,
> They pose themselves and their rags.
> . . .
> . . . In the way you speak
> You arrange, the thing is posed,
> What in nature merely grows.[1]

These lines from "Add This to Rhetoric" do not immediately seem to concern love, but they do provide insight into more general questions about the roles of rhetoric and thematics in poetry, a notion that is complicated by Emerson's idea that everything that is not natural is rhetorical.[2] Rhetoric is the opposite of nature. That which is rhetoric, "posed," is "arranged" and manipulated, whereas "nature merely grows," unabated. To write about love is to "pose" and to "arrange." Writing about love is a project that is removed from nature; there is thus the suggestion that writing about love involves something manipulated and implicitly is unsatisfying. James Merrill seems to have "Add This to Rhetoric" in mind when he writes about this distinction between rhetoric and nature in "A Renewal":

> Having used every subterfuge
> To shake you, lies, fatigue, or even that of passion,

> Now I see no way but a clean break.
> I add that I am willing to bear the guilt.
> 	. . .
> 	When next I speak
> Love buries itself in me, up to the hilt.[3]

If both of these quotations from Stevens and Merrill are metalinguistic commentaries, then the word "speak" in each context is representative of the discourse that characterizes the rhetoric of poetry; it is a language that is always doing something artificial, "posing" and creating "subterfuge." It is engaged in an "infinite mischief."

Noting that the rhetoric of poetry contains "subterfuges," it is easier to consider the various purposes of love poems. Love poems are especially useful in exploring the role of rhetoric in poetry because readers usually come to love poems with specific expectations—the assumption that the poem will describe a feeling of love for another person as a kind of objectification of that love. Love poems seem rarely to do just that.[4] Rather, they have ulterior motives; for example, they seek to persuade a lover into an erotic relationship, or they are implicitly involved in the description of another person in a similar way to the poems discussed in the previous chapter, which were shown to be concerned with the figures of the poet's lovers and their mothers.

The poems of Hart Crane, Elizabeth Bishop, and James Merrill that I discuss in this chapter are love poems, although they may not always appear to be explicitly engaged in the subject of a lover or of a love between the poet and his or her beloved. Love poems in Crane, Bishop, and most of Merrill's earlier collections require the reader to return to prior forms of this genre from the tradition of poetry. They require a return in order to fill in the blanks, to lay smooth the ambiguities of rhetoric that the poets put into place in order to obscure the dynamics of same-sex desire in which their love poems would necessarily engage.[5] In Plato's *Phaedrus* Socrates tells Phaedrus that human love is a recollection of divine beauty.[6] This return from a lover to divine beauty is significant because it illustrates the nature of citations, whereby one can trace the specter of the divine within the loved one.[7] Similarly, one can trace the specter of the figuration of the mother in the lover or of the poet's self within the figure of the lover. Indeed, like love narratives are cyclical. For instance, psychoanalysis produces an explanatory narrative that returns us to Freud, returns us to an action in order to create a meaning.[8] Like psychoanalysis—or within its framework—love returns us to a prior action, to the love of the mother. This return is also present in language, whereby love poems recall their earlier forms within the genre. Furthermore, this return is reminiscent of my discussion in the previous chapter of the figure of the Mother that Melanie Klein describes. Klein's theory that "anything that is felt to give out pleasure and satisfaction, in the physical or in the wider sense, can in the unconscious mind take the place of this ever-bountiful breast, and of the whole mother" equally presents a theory of a returning narrative that cites the relationship with the mother as a model within the present relationship.[9] In that chapter, however, my concern was with the ambivalent figuration of the Mother and of the lover in a series of poems of different subjects. My focus changes most notably, here, in the specificity of the kind of poem under consideration.

In this chapter, I continue to explore the connection between the rhetorical language that characterizes Crane, Bishop, and Merrill's poetry and how that language commingles with the explicit themati-zation of desire by focusing on examples of love poems. I look at a series of poems—Crane's "For the Marriage of Faustus and Helen" and "Voyages" sequence, and "The Tunnel"; Bishop's "Love Lies Sleeping," "Insomnia," "It is marvelous to wake up together," "The Shampoo," "Crusoe in England," and "One Art"; and Merrill's "Between Us," "Nightgown," "The Mad Scene," "Days of 1964," and "Clearing the Title"—and examine their use of doublings of images and words. The use of doublings reflects the function of the poem as a whole to repeat or cite love poems as a genre. In *Black Sun* Julia Kristeva examines doublings as they are featured in a poem by Gerard de Nerval and as they are concerned with melancholy. She writes: "melancholy persons settle the lost Thing or object within themselves, identifying with the loss's beneficial features on the one hand, with its maleficent ones on the other. This presents us with the first state of the self's doubling. . . ."[10] While Kristeva's conception concerns the melancholic subject, it works in parallel with my discussion of doubling in love and helps to show the presence of melancholic feelings within love. Through an analysis of individual poems that are concerned with the representation of the poet's love for another, often constructed as a gender neutral "you," I reflect upon the degree to which Crane, Bishop, and Merrill's poetics of love cites as it blurs traditional love poems.

As these poets make clear, love is a term of ambiguity. While it is also an elastic term, it is ambiguous for Crane, Bishop, and Merrill in that it does not always bear a resemblance to prior forms of love. Love seems to be a fundamental subject for rhetoric. The rhetoric of the

Shakespearean sonnets is to persuade. By contrast, the rhetoric of these poems is always engaged in a multiplicity of purpose that functions in part to deflect or to distract attention from the poet's discussion of homosexual erotics, which I discuss previously to be problematic for these three poets.

I intend to show how the rhetoric of Crane, Bishop, and Merrill's poetry creates a linguistic distance from the generic tradition of the love poem. Crane's highly impacted, rhetorical style has already been noted by other critics but not sufficiently clarified. Crane's purpose in this difficult style may be for a variety of reasons: the words to describe the feeling may be unavailable to the poet; this is the case with Crane as well as with Bishop and Merrill, when they attempt to write about their homosexuality as they must necessarily do in poems that are concerned with expressions of love. Lee Edelman, in his study *Transmemberment of the Song: Hart Crane's Anatomies of Rhetoric and Desire*, examines Crane's poems for their uses of catachresis. Edelman connects the Greek term, *katachresis*, to its Latin origin, *abusio*, and postulates catachresis as "a trope that substitutes the name of one thing for another that lacks a name of its own, the subversiveness of catachresis can be emblematized in the way it subverts the notion of figure itself by simultaneously bridging and collapsing the opposition between figural and literal naming." Catachresis is different from metaphor because when metaphor is used there is a term available, but, rather than using it, its meaning is transferred from one word or image to another for reasons that are contextually apparent. Catachresis is the rhetorical instance where the poet chooses an approximate term to represent something for which there is no other term available. Indeed, it is a perversion or misuse of language and serves to distort further the poet's revelations. According to the *Oxford English Dictionary* the definition of catachresis is "the improper use of words; abuse or perversion of a trope or metaphor."[11] Its "perversion" of language offers a linguistic contrast and/or connection to the genre of love. Catachresis functions as a device in the work of all three poets to stand in for painful emotions associated specifically here with expressions of love. Edelman notes this type of rhetoric within specific poems. His analysis concentrates on Crane's rhetorical practices at the expense of his thematics. In an effort to promote the simultaneous import and interrelated functions of rhetoric and thematics, I extend this notion to the individual poem itself. In the love poems of Crane, Bishop, and Merrill, catachresis characterizes the poem as a whole in that the poem itself becomes the name for "the love that dare not speak its name." Additionally, I connect catachresis with my psychoanalytic framework and argue that catachresis produces affect (love) through dissonance.[12] In this way, it is linked with catharsis, whereby the connection of otherwise dissonant figures produces immediate recognition, surprise, and delight.[13] The dissonance that catachresis highlights and its abuse and misuse of language makes it especially fitting for Crane, Bishop, and Merrill to use. Catachresis' inappropriate nature reflects the poets' position as outsiders to a normative, heterosexual status. Catachresis, then, may seem desirable precisely because it is a subversive rhetorical technique.

Crane's first of two long poems in *White Buildings* is "For the Marriage of Faustus and Helen." The word "marriage" in the title aligns the poem within the discourse of heterosexual romance. Why does Crane write a poem about marriage? The question of why Crane should concern himself with overt heterosexual themes should not be hastily dismissed. Given the values and climate of the early decades of the twentieth century, a definite social pressure to produce women as objects of desire, beauty, and virtue is not hard to imagine. Although Helen appears less an object of the speaker's desire, than as a symbol of an idealized, feminine beauty, this is not unlike the idealization of movie divas such as Bette Davis and Joan Crawford by contemporary gay men. These Hollywood divas, feminine ideals themselves, are less admired for their sexual attractiveness than for the power that such sexuality wields over the heterosexual man. These women use their beauty not simply for the sake of beauty but to intelligent means; they control and implement their attractiveness to attain what they want subtly but forcefully and unapologetically. Yet, "For the Marriage of Faustus and Helen" is a marriage poem where no marriage ever takes place, because, as the title announces, it is concerned with the preparation for a union but not the actual coming together. The "for" in the title could mean a dedication to marriage but then why pay homage to the event in a poem in which no marriage actually takes place? Thus, "for" seems to be saying "toward."

The title of the poem, specifically the word "marriage," works in opposition to the line of italicized prose: "*There is the world dimensional for / those untwisted by the love of things / irreconcilable...*" (ll. 16–18). Where "marriage" unifies people in love, the "love of things irreconcilable" counters this movement toward consanguinity. If the figures of Faustus and Helen represent a mythologized heterosexual desire, Crane and his repressed homosexual desire are characterized by a love that is fundamentally "irreconcilable." The poem is written in three parts. Each part confronts a general theme or idea;

for example, the first part concerns a problem of division that is ameliorated through the figure of Helen. In this first section, words like "stacked partitions," "memoranda," "stenographic," "stock quotations," "numbers," and "margins" (ll. 4–6, 9–10) are all representative of the world of business and the crowded, city life of New York. R. W. B. Lewis calls this the "wall street idiom" that presents the speaker with an increased possibility for homosexual desire within the predominantly male world of economic exchange.[14] The "numbers" represent the individual-less crowds of predominantly men; they are sources of potential love objects for the speaker. At the same time, they present the speaker with a chain of reflections of himself, or repetitions of like images.

Parts two and three of "For the Marriage of Faustus and Helen" are more vague and veer from a romantic narrative between a figure of Helen and of Faustus; rather, they are concerned with music, especially jazz, and humanity as an alternate remedy to social division. The first section of the poem opens with a description of a crowded city street that celebrates the world of business. The opening description moves into a supposition, "suppose some evening . . . ," and presents homoeroticism as a form of narcissism:

> . . . suppose some evening I forgot
> The fare and transfer, yet got by that way
> Without recall,—lost yet poised in traffic.
> Then I might find your eyes across an aisle,
> Still flickering with those prefigurations—
> Prodigal, yet uncontested now,
> Half-riant before the jerky window frame.    (ll. 19–25)

In these lines, the "eyes" that the speaker finds "across an aisle" smile at him; they seem to be his own eyes reflected within the "jerky window frame," though the speaker does not say "within" but "before" the window frame, so they are the speaker's reflected eyes or Faustus's. Otherwise, at this point in the poem, "your eyes" are ambiguous; they could be Faustus's or Helen's. It is not until line forty-three that the speaker says, "To you who turned away once, Helen," and establishes her as a stable figure within the poem. The repetition of the word "eye" (ll. 22, 48, and 51) reinforces the - importance of seeing—it is through seeing that the speaker "might find your eyes."

The poem's crisis comes from the speaker's sense of division from the world around him as well as from the lovers. The closure to the speaker's sense of division that is the teleological aim of "For the Marriage of Faustus and Helen" remains unattainable through the romantic means that the poet creates. The two figures are represented in isolation; each is in their "world which comes to each of us alone" (l. 50). Connection between the speaker and Helen exists through an act of vision, a desexualized space.

Closure is also the subject of Crane's long poem "Voyages," in which the speaker attempts to reconcile distances between himself and his lover. In "Voyages," Crane celebrates his love for Emil Opffer, who was a sailor. Although the poet extols his homosexual love within the poem's six parts, homosexuality remains textually obscure. This obscurity extends to Crane's biography, *Voyager*, where his relationship with Opffer is described in euphemistic terms; Crane's is a "heightened friendship" with Emil. Because Crane wrote to his friend, Waldo Frank: "there is nothing dirty in [his relation with Emil]," Unterrecker concludes that the relationship must have been characterized by "devotion," "understanding," and "platonic love."[15] In a letter to his mother, Crane writes in mid-November 1924 that he is "engaged in writing a series of six sea poems called 'Voyages' (they are also love poems)."[16] Though the poem is a "sea poem" and though this subject fittingly represents the milieu of his lover (Opffer was a sailor), it is interesting that Crane describes the poem's genre only parenthetically to his mother. Crane recognizes and denies that the poem's connection to the sea connects its themes with the Mother/maternal sea of Whitman.

While it seems redundant or, at best, simplistic to say, "Voyages" is a poem that *moves*: it is a poem that takes the reader on a voyage across a six-part narrative that chronicles six events in a relationship. Each stage in the sequence of six parts registers a different overriding emotion for the speaker. The "Voyages" sequence begins with a section that seems to confound the project of a celebration of love. The first part introduces a scene, children at play on the beach: "Bright striped urchins flay each other with sand" (l. 2). While the children, "urchins," are innocently at play, the speaker watches them and imagines addressing them: "could they hear me I would tell them" (l. 9). Why is it that the children at play cannot hear the speaker? Is he inaudible to them merely because of their own noisy play and of the crash of the waves: "And in answer to their treble interjections / The sun beats lightning on the waves, / The waves fold thunder on the sand()" (ll. 6–8)? While it might be that the natural world drowns out the speaker's voice preventing him from advising them, their inability to hear him also signifies the inevitability of the lesson they must learn;

it is a matter of course in psychosexual maturation. Thus, the speaker is asking: could the children understand, "hear," what I was saying, though they cannot understand him because his lesson is one that the children must live in order to come to know. The speaker's vocative, "O brilliant kids," is reminiscent of Thomas Gray's "Ode on a Distant Prospect of Eton College"; Crane's speaker wants to warn the children he sees. Gray's warning is to children who, "regardless of their doom, / The little victims play! / No sense have they of ills to come, / Nor care beyond today."[17] Crane's concern stems from a sexual ambivalence:

> O brilliant kids, frisk with your dog,
> Fondle your shells and sticks, bleached
> By time and the elements; but there is a line
> You must not cross nor ever trust beyond it
> Spry cordage of your bodies to caresses
> Too lichen-faithful from too wide a breast.
> The bottom of the sea is cruel.   (ll. 10–16)

The speaker's warning is to delineate what constitutes acceptable and unacceptable forms of love. The words "frisk" and "fondle" have definite sexual import, and the children's "shells and sticks" are vaginal and phallic images respectively. The "line" that must not be crossed is that of homosexual desire, for that is a kind of love that is anathema to the natural world depicted here. Homosexual desire, here an unacceptable form of desire, is contained within the language itself in the "O" of the vocative. The natural world threatens; the sun "beats lightening," and waves "fold thunder." As if these are not foreboding enough, the final line of the section, "The bottom of the sea is cruel," completes the picture of a vengeful world. Recalling the poem that precedes this one in the collection, "At Melville's Tomb" helps to explain further why the "bottom of the sea" is described as being "cruel." In "At Melville's Tomb," it is on the bottom of the sea that the "numbers" on the "dice of drowned men's bones" (l. 2) are obscured; that is to say, any messages or bits of information that the sailors might have had are lost, "scattered" and "obscured," by the indiscriminate erasures of the water. As is the case with Crane, Bishop's images of drowned persons are equally erotically charged.

  This reading of "Voyages I" follows from John Hollander's in which he claims Crane's poem is a transumption of Whitman's eleventh section of "Song of Myself."[18] Crane switches the positions of the speaker and the children—Crane's speaker is in the water and the children play on the shore, while Whitman's female persona remains on the shore, watching the "twenty-eight young men" frolic in the sea:[19]

> Where are you off to, lady? for I see you,
> You splash in the water there, yet stay stock still in your room.
>
> Dancing and laughing along the beach came the twenty-ninth bather,
> The rest did not see her, but she saw them and loved them.
>
> The beards of the young men glisten'd with wet, it ran from their
>        long hair,
> Little streams pass'd all over their bodies.
>
> An unseen hand also pass'd over their bodies,
> It descended tremblingly from their temples and ribs.
>
> The young men float on their backs, their white bellies bulge to
>        the sun, they do not ask who seizes fast to them,
> They do not know who puffs and declines with penchant and
>        bending arch,
> They do not think whom they souse with spray.   (ll. 206–216)

The eleventh section of "Song of Myself" is, according to the editors of the Norton edition, "audacious for its time and extraordinarily delicate in its sensitive recognition of loneliness and desire." The poem is, despite its "audaciousness," not concerned with judgments about modes of sexuality. Here, the Whitmanian speaker revels in the sexual excitement of the "wet" and unclothed "bodies." Unlike the speaker in "Voyages," the Whitmanian speaker is as unselfconscious as his bathers, who are too busy frolicking in the beach to consider questions outside of themselves or of the moment. The bathers "do not ask" (l. 214), "do not know" (l. 215), and "do not think" (l. 216), and no one seems to condemn them for basking in a state of ignorance. Indeed, the final declaration, "They do not think whom they souse with spray," is allowed to stand as a signifier of their carefree status and of the potential for sexual gratification in a way that Crane does not permit his own poem to indulge.

The rejection of " 'Voyages' " first section as an utterly dark image of a world that has created and contains the speaker and his lover is presupposed and thematized at the beginning of the second part of the poem, "-And yet. . . ." This transitional expression, technically conjunctive, serves to connect the thoughts of the first part with those of the second. At the same time, it functions to save the first section from a complete critical rejection as nonsensical. In this second part the sea that had been seen as dangerous still threatens to separate the lovers; however, the threat of the sea is lessened by its personification. The sea does not continue in its unabated cruelty; now its "demeanors motion well or ill" (l. 9). The prosopopoeia of the sea is female, "Her undinal vast belly," (l. 4), "her demeanors" (l. 9), "her tides" (l. 13); however, as the speaker continues, the figure of the sea becomes increasingly maternal, reiterating the combination of the figure of the lover with the Mother that was discussed in the previous chapter:

> In these poinsettia meadows of her tides,-
> Adagios of islands, O my Prodigal,
> Complete the dark confessions her veins spell.
>
> Mark how her turning shoulders wind the hours,
> And hasten while her penniless rich palms
> Pass superscription of bent foam and wave,-
> Hasten, while they are true,-sleep, death, desire,
> Close round one instant in one floating flower.
>
> Bind us in time, O Seasons clear, and awe.
> O minstrel galleons of Carib fire,
> Bequeath us to no earthly shore until
> Is answered in the vortex of our grave
> The seal's wide spindrift gaze toward paradise.   (ll. 13–25)

Again, Crane's speaker presents us with a message, a "confession," that he cannot know; it is "dark." The sea frustrates; its "veins" "spell" some "confession" that is not clear. As we read through this symphony of language, the rhetoric and images take over, assume control, and focus our attention; in this way, because of the distracting rhetoric, it is difficult to remember that the "us" in the twenty-first line is the speaker and his lover. Love poetry in its traditional form has not yet appeared in the poem. The language is characteristically dense in these lines; one notes the combination of punctuation—commas and dashes—that appear in lines thirteen, eighteen and nineteen, as if the impacted rhetoric requires a doubling of punctuation to handle its force. Like the vocatives that close the proem to *The Bridge*—"O harp and alter . . . ," or "O Sleepless as the river . . ."—the vocative here signals an entrance into a prayer-like discourse in which the speaker asks to be bound in time in a vainglorious attempt to supersede the need to "hasten" (ll. 17 and 19). The final lines secure this request; however, they seem to accomplish this with a surprising image of drowning: "Bequeath us to no earthly shore until / Is answered in the vortex of our grave / The seal's wide spindrift gaze toward paradise" (ll. 23–25). Like most of the poem, these lines resist the reader's attempt to paraphrase them into a satisfying narrative; nevertheless, the "vortex of our grave" is the bottom of the sea. We are at the same locale as the close of section one. The "wide . . . gaze" is an upward one—from the sea floor upward "toward paradise." This image of drowning together with the lover is an odd request, although it would serve the purpose of binding the poet and his lover together in the eternal space of death.

At the same time, the "spindrift gaze" is an evocative one. As is often noted with this poem in particular and Crane's poetry in general, Whitman and Melville exist behind the poet as influential literary forefathers. In the "Voyages" poems, it is the Whitman of "Out of the Cradle Endlessly Rocking" and "As I Ebb'd with the Ocean of Life" where death is a necessity for poetry and the Melville of *Moby Dick*. In the first chapter of *Moby Dick*, Ishmael explains why "almost every robust healthy boy with a robust healthy soul in him" desires to go to sea:

> And still deeper the meaning of that story of Narcissus, who because he could not grasp the tormenting, mild image he saw in the fountain, plunged into it and was drowned. But that same image, we ourselves see in all rivers and oceans.[20]

Ishmael's reason for going to sea is to answer a mythic call, "the story of Narcissus," for a person to return to a state of affairs that reminds him of his own individual narcissism. Crane's speaker in the "Voyages" provides a series of repetitions of the images that Ishmael describes here, especially of the figure of the drowned boy. In the light of this quotation from Melville, the "spindrift gaze" can be read not only as a "gaze" upward of a drowned man but also as a "gaze" into the "paradise" of his own reflection within the "spindrift."

Freud analyzes the role of narcissism in human development in among other places his essay "On Narcissism" from 1914. In this essay, he posits a developmental stage of narcissism, which he inserts between the infant's primitive autoeroticism and the child's object-love. Continuing from Freud's work, Julia Kristeva in *Tales of Love* confronts love, which she sees as reigning "between the two borders of *narcissism* and *idealization*."[21] The idea and importance of narcissism is central to this discussion of the poems of Crane, Bishop, and Merrill because of the way that the image of Narcissus is itself a repetition: the viewer seeing his or her reflection, his or her own image, and desiring it.

In opposition to the request in the second section of "Voyages" to be bound in time, this section of the poem—like the sequence as a whole—is concerned with movement. Indeed, the impacted language highlights the degree to which the poet's language is equally moving: the poet "packs" a great deal of meaning into a small space. The phrase "Adagios of islands" is explained in Crane's essay "General Aims and Theories": "the reference is to the motion of a boat through islands clustered thickly, the rhythm of the motion, etc." (p. 221). Crane continues in this essay to write counterintuitively that his phrase is the most direct expression: "And it seems a much more direct and creative statement than any more logical employment of words such as 'coasting slowly through the islands,' besides ushering in a whole world of music" (p. 221). As Crane's description of his intent makes clear, his use of rhetoric reflects the more general theme of movement in the poem; the poet's phrases are composed in order to move the reader through a rapid succession of images and connotations.

In the third section of "Voyages," the poet is no longer separated from his desired object, whose identity and gender is nonetheless concealed. The third part begins with an image of the sea as innocuous:

> Infinite consanguinity it bears-
> This tendered theme of you that light
> Retrieves from sea plains where the sky
> Resigns a breast that every wave enthrones;
> While ribboned water lanes I wind
> Are laved and scattered with no stroke
> Wide from your side, whereto this hour
> The sea lifts, also reliquary hands.   (ll. 1–8)

The sea no longer obscures but allows for an "infinite consanguinity," a closeness between the lovers. The sea becomes a nurturing figure, who "lifts reliquary hands" to embrace and to comfort rather than to destroy. In contrast to this is the recurring notion of scatteredness, of the sea as a figure capable of dissemination and, therefore, obscuring or making ambiguous the various readable texts that the poet puts forth or encounters. The word "wide" seems to function in conjunction with this. The fear of "too wide a breast" (I, l. 15) or of a "wide spindrift gaze" (II, l. 25) continue the notion of the sea's dangerous potential to create "widenesses" between the poet and the lover, which are situations where the potential to create and receive meaning from the world is lost.

The speaker counters this dangerous potential through a repetition of words. The symbol of the "hands" has a multitude of meanings here: "reliquary hands" and "your hands . . ." (ll. 8 and 19). As is the case in several poems by Crane, such as "Episode of Hands," the hands are both nurturing and erotic, the Mother and the beloved, metonymically referring to the bodies of the speaker and the beloved. Crane assigns the sexual space upon a desexualized one, a dismembered hand. Crane's hands are disconnected from any particular body part and exist solely as hands. They are relics of a dismemberment or castration, thereby reinforcing the anxiety with which the speaker presents his love. The hand is also the part of the body specifically associated with the creative act of writing. The dismemberment of the hand foregrounds it as a point of intersection between the body of the poet and the tools—paper, pen—of poetry.

The speaker continues to represent the "consanguinity" between the lover and him through the repetition of words:

> And so, admitted through black swollen gates
> That must arrest all distance otherwise,-
> Past whirling pillars and lithe pediments,
> Light wrestling there incessantly with light,
> Star kissing star through wave on wave unto
> Your body rocking!   (ll. 9–14)

These lines, laden with adjectives, convey the eroticism of this passage: "swollen gates," "whirling pillars," and "lithe pediments." Although these couplings of adjectives and nouns may appear to cancel each other out as oxymorons, they serve to enhance their meaning rather than negate it. The "pediments" that are "lithe" can be read as an allegory for the signification of words in Crane's poems: words are lithe, or flexible, in that they are able to include a series of meanings. These adjectives also convey the eroticism of the poem. The words, "light," "star," "wave," and "dawn" are all repeated on the same lines in which they first appear (ll. 12, 13, and 17). The repetition of the words creates a liminal space for the speaker in which to exist comfortably with his lover. The repetition also serves to reinforce the image of Narcissus and his reflection; the words are mirror images of themselves.

The fourth section of the poem presents several of the same tropes from the first three sections—repetition, fear of dissemination and unintelligibility. The first stanza of the poem concerns the speaker's consideration of a "spectrum" to show that there is no "greater love" than his. One of the "spectrums" he considers is "(from palms to the

severe / Chilled albatross's white immutability)" (ll. 4–5). This is a
curious image in part because of the imbalance of the comparison,
where "palms" seems a mundane point in comparison to "the severe
(c)hilled albatross's white immutability." Also, why is this statement
relegated to the parenthetical? The lines contain information that is
more central to the poem than its parenthetical status would indicate.
The word "immutability" stands out here as an unusual word; it is
awkward, even within the work of a poet who favors unconventional
words for his poems. One could make the same point with
"irrefragably" in line nine, except that it provides an internal rhyme
on the following line with "logically." In addition, Crane must also
have meant to refer to Coleridge's albatross that serves as a symbol of
guilt in "The Rime of the Ancient Mariner."[22] Why would the poet
include a symbol of guilt? Perhaps the poet feels guilt in response to
his desire for an immutable relationship with his love because such a
desire would, of course, be unnatural. The relationship exists in the
realm of time, in the shifting seascape he describes, where things
begin to change as the poem moves toward its close.

Much of the argument of this section of the poem is toward
an impossible permanence. In pursuit of this, the speaker considers
words themselves: "In signature of the incarnate word / The harbor
shoulders to resign in mingling / Mutual blood" (ll. 17–9). These
lines are Crane's reworking of his spiritualizing declaration describing
his excitement over his relationship with Emil Opffer, "I have seen the
Word made flesh." The word incarnate means to invest something
with human form. The "incarnate word" functions in the opposite
way from permanence. To give a "word" a human form would make
it subject to mortality. The phrase is reminiscent of Stevens's "pink
and white carnations," especially as the phrase foreshadows the "petalled
word" of Crane's final section. The carnations, like the "petals," carry
the hint of eroticism in their connection to flesh, "carnal," in "The
Poems of Our Climate" from Stevens's 1942 collection *Parts of a
World*.[23] The Stevensian speaker says of his carnations that "one
desires / so much more than that," as if the carnations were more
than enough eroticism. By contrast the Cranean speaker really does
want more; he wants a hyperbolic excess in language that will rival the
extent of emotion for the lover.[24] Thus, his final couplet, "In this
expectant, still exclaim receive / The secret oar and petals of all love"
(ll. 24–25), jokingly underestimates the force of his "exclaim" by
calling it "expectant" and "still," for while these adjectives may be
accurate in their description of the tone, they do not characterize
the force of the poet's language. The explicit nature of the final line's

sexual imagery foregrounds the degree to which the speaker's "exclaim" contains much more than its "still" tone.

In the fifth section of "Voyages," the "cables of our sleep" establish the connection between intelligible communication—"cables"—and states of unintelligibility characterized by dreams. These "cables" are "swiftly filed"; they are as uselessly cryptic as the "scattered chapter" and the "livid hieroglyphs" of "At Melville's Tomb." The "cables" as well as the "smile" are nonetheless means of communication; the cables are useless in themselves, and the smile is described as "frozen" and "trackless." After the "smile," there is a break in the line with an ellipsis; the ellipsis appears to encode an opaque message between the two. The "smile" embodies an awkwardness of homosexuality and acknowledges through a glance, the discursive basis for the gay exchange, the cruise. The question that follows the ellipsis, "What words / Can strangle this deaf moonlight?" (ll. 8–9), is ironic; no words are necessary because the glancing smile was encoded with words that were unsaid and are unsayable. The moonlight is charged with secret signification; it is "deaf" and therefore not able, even perhaps resistant, to understand the words of the poet. The verb "strangle" is interesting here, for even if the "moonlight" cannot hear, the words are prevented from speaking by being "strangled." Words themselves destroy the relationship by their inability to communicate.

The poet's language intensifies as nature posits a "tidal wedge" that forever distances the poet from his lover:

> The cables of our sleep so swiftly filed,
> Already hang, shred ends from remembered stars.
> One frozen, trackless smile . . . What words
> Can strangle this deaf moonlight? For we
>
> Are overtaken. Now no cry, no sword
> Can fasten or deflect this tidal wedge,
> Slow tyranny of moonlight, moonlight loved
> And changed . . . "There's
>
> Nothing like this in the world," you say,
> Knowing I cannot touch your hand and look
> Too, into that godless cleft of sky
> Where nothing turns but dead sands flashing.   (ll. 6–16)

There has been a drastic change in sentiment between the fifth section and the third. Where the speaker once asked, "Permit me voyage, love, into your hands . . . ," he now says, "I cannot touch your hand." Unable to hear, the moonlight is resistant to the "cry" of the poet;

neither the physical "sword" nor the linguistic "cry" can reduce the distance that separates the speaker from his lover. The "tyranny of moonlight" lies in its resistance to the lovers' communicability. The moonlight had provided for love but now provides a "change()." Without the connection of the hands, the sense of mutual understanding that reached beyond the limits of speech is lost. The speaker now says: "No, / In all the argosy of your bright hair I dreamed / Nothing so flagless as this piracy" (ll. 18–20). The metonym of the "bright hair" for the lover and its association with an "argosy" break down the lover and transform his figuration into the broken one the speaker feared. The "argosy," a large fleet of ships, will sail away from the speaker; the word "piracy" adds an invidious note to the ship imagery; they are damaging, even virulent, attacking his love and causing the intelligibility that is "flagless." In these lines, the speaker describes the state of affairs that he seems to have foreseen and feared: despite the large amount of potentially intelligible text, the "argosy" of "bright hair," the "hair" remains unintelligible, "flagless," because of outside interference. The word "piracy" conveys the sense that the poet's text of "incarnate word(s)" are not merely lost to him but stolen.

In the story of a love affair that is described in the "Voyages" sequence, the fifth section provides the climax, the destruction of the relationship through the lovers' separation. By the end of the section, the speaker moves into a position of equanimity involving the crisis; he seems to have achieved an acceptance of his status: "Draw in your head, alone and too tall here. / . . . Draw in your head and sleep the long way home" (ll. 22 and 25). "Draw in your head" from where? Perhaps he draws himself away from the image of travel in order to go home. The idea of excessiveness remains the only troubling aspect for the speaker, who is "too tall" and whose home is a "long" way off. As I have discussed throughout this work, in most of Crane's poetry, excess engenders an anxiety in the poet. Where there is too much space, too much of something—a body part or a distance—the poet characteristically renders the distance something to be overcome reluctantly. The exception to this is perhaps in "My Grandmother's Love Letters," where the question becomes one of there being sufficient space for the spiritual and linguistic texts the grandmother provides: "There is even room enough / For the letters of my mother's mother, / Elizabeth" (ll. 5–7). Excess, "room enough," encapsulates the poet's expansive feelings for his grandmother, who is herself characterized in excessive or repetitive terms, "mother's mother."

The tone of equanimity that ends the fifth section prepares the reader for its continuation in the final, sixth section. There is no

longer the presence of a lover, a "you," and in its place there is only
the natural world, the sea. The tone and style of the poem fittingly
ends the *White Buildings* collection and looks forward to *The Bridge*
in part because of the way Crane's speaker displaces and projects his
lover's image onto the world around him:

> O rivers mingling toward the sky
> And harbor of the phoenix' breast-
> My eyes pressed black against the prow,
> -Thy derelict and blinded guest
>
> Waiting, afire, what name, unspoke,
> I cannot claim: let thy waves rear
> More savage than the death of kings,
> Some splintered garlands for the seer.   (ll. 9–16)

While the sea remains a source of awe, it is far from the medium of
"infinite consanguinity" that the poet celebrated in the third section.
The sea is now, "Where icy and bright dungeons lift / Of swimmers
their lost morning eyes, / And ocean rivers, churning, shift / Green
borders under stranger skies" (l. 1–4). The third line, like the thirteenth
line, "Waiting, afire, what name, unspoke," is heavily broken up with
commas. These caesuras create unusually choppy diction in Crane's
poems and betoken the poet's emotions of loss. The poet, nonetheless, acknowledges the texts he treasures in the "beating leagues" that
the "shell secretes"; there is a play on words here with "secretes" that
conveys the sense of "secrets" as well. The interplay of secretes/secrets
recalls the dangerous power of the sea that characterizes it in the
beginning of the poem and in "At Melville's Tomb."

The poem ends with a final quatrain that exemplifies the poet's
shift in affect:

> The imaged Word, it is, that holds
> Hushed willows anchored in its glow.
> It is the unbetrayable reply
> Whose accent no farewell can know.   (ll. 29–32)

All that the poet has left is the "imaged Word," which is interestingly
not the "*imagined* Word." The "Word," capitalized, is an autonomous
presence; this idea is reinforced by the difference between "imaged"
and "imagined." Where "image" implies a separation from the poet,
"imagined" would have given the poet some agency. The "reply" is
"unbetrayable" because the natural forces that were threats to the

intelligibility of the world are no longer threatening. Also, the distance between the poet and the lover is no longer a question; the "reply" is "unbetrayable" simply because there is nothing to betray.

Crane began to write his "Voyages" poems in 1921 and did not finish them until 1926, although portions were first published in the winter of 1923 and the spring of 1926. Some of the expressions of homosexual love within the poem cause Crane anxiety, which he expresses in a letter to his mother, written in December 1923:

> . . . I want to save you as much suffering from Life's obstacles as can be done without hypocrisy, silliness or sentimentality. You may have taken me on faith for some things, because I don't know whether it is possible for all people to understand certain ardours that I have, and perhaps there is no special reason why you, as my mother, should understand that side of me any better than most people. As I have said, I am perfectly willing to be misunderstood, but I don't want to put up any subterfuges before *your* understanding of me if I can help it.[25]

Crane interestingly admits that he is "willing to be misunderstood" about his "certain ardours," in particular his affair with Opffer. Nonetheless, Crane is compelled to write about his experiences with, and love for, Opffer—in decidedly veiled terms and images. In this light, it becomes clear that what Crane is attempting to do with his rhetorical pyrotechnics in "Voyages" is achieve a rhetorical extension of language, whereby the poem as a whole serves as an expression of his "certain ardours" in a way that was otherwise inexpressible to Crane. "Voyages" functions as a catachresis to express the homosexual love that he was not able to admit publicly. Furthermore, "For the Marriage of Faustus and Helen," in its movement toward closure and completeness that is never actually achieved, attempts to make this same catachrestic extension; the poem fails, however, to extend its rhetoric beyond the heterosexual scope of the "marriage," although it points toward something unsaid in the poem through the notion of what is "irreconcilable."

If the thematization of love does not succeed in surviving or bridging the expansive journeys in each of the six sections of "Voyages," Crane returns to the subject of love in the poems of *The Bridge* to establish love as a rhetoric of connection. Langdon Hammer writes that readers need to recognize *The Bridge* not only "as a poem, as numerous critics have observed, but to recognize it as a poem in its purely 'material' (or linguistic) presence."[26] *The Bridge* is composed of a proem "To Brooklyn Bridge," and poem in eight parts: "Ave Maria,"

"Powhatan's Daughter," "Cutty Sark," "Cape Hatteras," "Three Songs," "Quaker Hill," "The Tunnel," and "Atlantis." Crane first conceived of his epic in 1923 and said that he could write it in a year; however, the process of writing the poems proved to be more taxing than he had assumed. With long periods of inactivity, Crane took almost seven years to complete *The Bridge*.

Critics do not generally read the poems in this collection as love poems. The poems do, however, celebrate and conjoin Crane's vision of a democratic country, his poetics, and his sexuality. As a love poem, the poems of *The Bridge* offer a dark and unsatisfying representation. For example, "Cutty Sark," which Crane began writing in mid-1926 and finished in September 1929, opens with the description of a lone man:

> I met a man in South Street, tall-
> a nervous shark tooth swung on his chain.
> His eyes pressed through green glass
> -green glasses, or bar lights made them
> so-
>    shine-
>       GREEN-
>          eyes-
> stepped out-forgot to look at you
> or left you several blocks away-   (ll. 1–10)

The description of this man is decidedly odd. He is "tall" but has a "nervous shark tooth" on a chain. The "shark('s) tooth" raises questions: is the man a "shark" out to get someone? is he dangerous? is this a sexual meeting in which the shark-man is hungry for the speaker? The poet alleviates the man's potential threat by breaking his description across several lines (l. 5–8); this is a reversal of "At Melville's Tomb." In that poem, where the sea was the agent of scattering, the poet is now scattering. There is another, similar depiction of love in "The Tunnel." Crane began working on "The Tunnel" around the same time that he began "Cutty Sark" in 1926; however, he finished "The Tunnel" in July 1929, several months earlier than "Cutty Sark." "The Tunnel" is one hundred and thirty-eight lines long and has a frame structure to it. The poem opens:

> Performances, assortments, resumes-
> Up Times Square to Columbus Circle lights
> Channel the congresses, nightly sessions,
> Refractions of the thousand theatres, faces-
> Mysterious kitchens. . . . You shall search them all.

> Someday you'll learn each famous sight
> And watch the curtain lift in hell's despite;
> You'll find the garden in the third act dead,
> Finger your knees—and wish yourself in bed
> With tabloid crime-sheets perched in easy sight.   (ll. 1–10)

The poet speaks of a general interest in the expanse of the city before him. This is not the city of the "wall street idiom" that characterizes the opening of "For the Marriage of Faustus and Helen"; these "congresses" of faces are intriguing in their theatricality. The "kitchens" are "mysterious," not because they are frightening but because they are unknown. The speaker is curious about his surroundings. Even the details of the "kitchens" will become known, once he "search(es) them all." When that is done and the city with its various entertainments such as the theater become commonplace, then the poet tells the "you" that he will become accustomed to its excitements. Yet, despite the fascination and interest in the city, the speaker is alienated from it. This sentiment does not appear to be changed by the end of the poem:

> O my City, I have driven under,
> Tossed from the coil of ticking towers . . . . Tomorrow,
> And to be. . . . Here by the River that is East-
> Here at the waters' edge the hands drop memory;
> Shadowless in that abyss they accounting lie.
> How far away the star has pooled the sea—
> Or shall the hands be drawn away, to die?
> Kiss of our agony Thou gatherest,
> > O Hand of Fire
> > > gatherest—   (ll. 129–138)

If the poem ended with the question, the last lines 132–135, with an a-b-a-b rhyme, might sound like a typical Yeatsian question at the end of the poem. The final three scattered and broken lines, however, affirm them as Crane's. The speaker knows the city now; he has "driven" around it, but nonetheless it still appears to be alienated from him. The repetition of "gatherest" is a last appeal for a connection that is sustaining.

In the middle portion of "The Tunnel," there is a crisis for the poet. He writes: "The phonographs of hades in the brain / Are tunnels that re-wind themselves, and love / A burnt match skating in a urinal—" (ll. 58–60). Although Lee Edelman in his study of catachrestic extensions in Crane does not discuss "The Tunnel," the rhetorical dislocations of meaning here are representative of the kind of language Edelman posits as catachrestic. The image of "love" as a "burnt match skating" works in multiple ways. The "burnt match" is foremost a traditional view of love; like the "moth" and the "flame" in "Legend," love is often characterized by its ability to entice and to burn. The potential for love to burn is a deconstructive moment because the image contains both the idea of pleasure and its antithesis, pain, for the lover. The negativity of the later half of the image, "skating in a urinal," would seem to bring the burning closer to its painful signification. The image of the "burnt match" that is "skating in a urinal" is one of dirt—both in terms of the used match that is being tossed into the "urinal" and of the "urinal" itself. The dissonant images produce an ambivalent affect. It is important to recall, however, that the "urinal" is also the site of gay male sexual cruising.[27] Crane's letters and biography make clear that he favored going to such places for casual sexual encounters, especially with sailors. In this way, "urinal" becomes a site of ambivalence. Its potential positive and sexually exciting connotations are enhanced by the word "skating," which conveys a sense of play that would describe the ethos of the men's room cruise. The instability of signification of the image of "love" here signals the use of catachresis, whereby the image of "love" as a "burnt match skating in a urinal" is meant to extend itself from a traditional, heterosexual notion of normative, reproductive sexuality to this depiction of homosexual and pleasurably "dirty" sexuality.

In Bishop's poetry more than Crane's or Merrill's, it is hardest to find explicit love poems. Several poems from *North & South*, such as "Love Lies Sleeping," were written while Bishop was in love with her friend Louise Crane. In the years after Bishop graduated from Vassar College in 1934, Bishop and Louise Crane became lovers. They traveled extensively together in Europe and together bought a house in Key West in 1938. Despite this, many critics who write about Bishop's love poetry, such as Lorrie Goldensohn, Marilyn Lombardi, and Margaret Dickie, focus their attentions on Bishop's unpublished poems and fragments to find the poet's discussions of love.[28] Bishop's reticence to open up was absolute. From her casual admission to her best friend Frani Blough, "I guess I should tell you that Mother died a week ago today," to her ambiguous explanations of her Brazilian lover, Lota, as "my hostess," to friends, Bishop remained true to her love of "closets, closets, and more closets."[29] An example of Bishop's reticence in love is her letter to Robert Lowell in response to his letter in which he admits his love for her. Lowell recalls spending a day together with

Bishop in Stonington, Maine in 1948,[30] and of the love that he felt for her that went unacknowledged: "I assumed that it would be a matter of time before I proposed and I half believed you would accept. . . . But asking you is the might-have-been for me, the one towering change, the other life that might have been had."[31] Lowell's letter was written on August 15 at the close of an American vacation Bishop was on with Lota. Bishop waited months before replying in mid-December. Her letter, written over several days, makes no explicit reference to his declaration. She thanks him for gifts and complains frequently about her "letter writing blocks," the fact that she "can't seem to say the right things," and that she wishes she were more "articulate." Her letter does contain her initial responses to Lowell's manuscript of poems *Life Studies*, an important book in which Lowell secures the confessional mode of poetry. Perhaps the strong degree to which Lowell writes himself into his poems is sufficient for her to "have" him around. Bishop admitted that she had considered marrying Lowell because she would have liked to have children but worried that given their two histories with mental illness that it was not ultimately a good idea. She appears to be thinking of this impossibility when she writes: "the whole phenomenon of your quick recovery and simultaneous productivity seems to me in looking back to be the real marvel of my summer" (p. 347).

Bishop's second collection of poetry contains nineteen poems and is named after the first poem, *A Cold Spring*. Bishop's poem "Insomnia" offers an expression of love in equally veiled terms to her letter. While "Insomnia" is reminiscent of a favorite state in Bishop's early poems—the hypnagogic, or the moment just before or after sleep—the poem lacks the characteristic nonsensicality of the *North & South* poems. The poem's title functions to situate the action of the poem; the speaker is awake at night and daydreams as she stares at a reflection in "the bureau mirror." "Insomnia" begins as a rumination on perspective but ends in a vision of a desired state of affairs:

> The moon in the bureau mirror
> looks out a million miles
> (and perhaps with pride, at herself,
> but she never, never smiles)
> far and away beyond sleep, or
> perhaps she's a daytime sleeper.
>
> By the Universe deserted,
> *she*'d tell it to go to hell,
> and she'd find a body of water,

or a mirror, on which to dwell.
So wrap up care in a cobweb
and drop it down the well

into that world inverted
where left is always right,
where the shadows are really the body,
where we stay awake all night,
where the heavens are shallow as the sea
is now deep, and you love me.

The "inverted world" that the speaker envisions is reminiscent of the world in the third section of Crane's "Voyages," where the speaker asks, "Permit me, love, voyage into your hands. . . ." We are in a place where the sea is deep, and that depth somehow allows for the "you" to love the speaker. The poem is peopled with feminine figures. Following a traditional literary trope, the moon is female: "she." The moon, who "never, never smiles," is Bishop's revision of this traditional trope of the moon that is virginal; Bishop's moon is serious, not chaste. The subtle inclusion of a plural pronoun, "we," "where we stay awake all night," foregrounds the potential sexual content in the speaker's desire for sleep and her bed. The line, "where we stay awake all night," makes the "insomnia" of the poet better; it is as if it is okay to be awake all night as long as the speaker is not awake alone. The speaker in Bishop's poems is often not alone in her bed, for example, "draw us into daylight in our beds" in "Love Lies Sleeping," or "As we lie down to sleep the world turns half away . . ." in "Sleeping Standing Up." The speaker in "Insomnia" is playful. She is joking with her reader when she says that the moon "never, never smiles." When the speaker says that the moon would "dwell" her attentions on either "a body of water" or "a mirror," it becomes clear that the speaker and the moon are aligned.

What is the function of the "mirror" in the poem? The poet, like the moon, is "dwell(ing)" on a "mirror," as well as perhaps the "body" of the last line's "you." If, however, the speaker and the moon are aligned, then the speaker is looking at a reflection of herself. The love that she envisions is one that seems based in a narcissistic reflection; yet it is one that allows for a same-sex eroticism. This is the state of affairs that the speaker says will permit the "you" to love her. At the same time, if, as Barbara Johnson theorizes, "femininity is that from which women are always in danger of deviating," then the speaker's reflection of femininity is an ideal one, although the speaker herself is lacking.[32] In this way, the reflected image of the moon in the mirror serves to question and to strengthen the poet's own femininity.

The speaker in "Insomnia" who is "beyond sleep" is reminiscent of "It is marvelous to wake up together," a Bishop poem that Lorrie Goldensohn uncovered in 1987 among Bishop's papers in Brazil. The poem is untitled, and its date of composition remains uncertain. It is assumed that the poem is nonetheless completed but abandoned because of its overt homosexuality. Interestingly enough, Hart Crane too left many poems that more centrally deal with homoeroticism uncollected or unpublished. For example, "C 33" was published in 1916 but was never collected. Also, his poems "Meditation," "Episode of Hands," and "The Visible The Untrue" are unpublished and/or incomplete works and are engaged centrally in homoerotic themes that are conveyed through Crane's favored trope of the hand.

"It is marvelous to wake up together" is composed of three stanzas of eight lines each and reads:

> It is marvelous to wake up together
> At the same minute; marvelous to hear
> The rain begin suddenly all over the roof,
> To feel the air suddenly clear
> As if electricity had passed through it
> From a black mesh of wires in the sky.
> All over the roof rain hisses,
> And below, the light falling of kisses.     (ll. 1–8)[33]

An electrical storm while the poet was in Key West is the inspiration for this poem that is often cited as an example of Bishop's more explicit love poetry. Interestingly, there are no qualifications on the other person with whom the speaker is waking up in bed. The importance of the "kisses" between the speaker and her lover is drowned out by the image of the falling rain; the "rain" and "kisses" are "falling," and there is an electrical excitement to both. At the same time, the "light falling of kisses," because the object is still unidentified, shows the speaker and her lover enacting the downpour. Repetitions of words such as "marvelous," "suddenly," and "rain," together with sounds, especially "hisses" and "kisses," create an interiority to the poem, a liminal space that is continued in the second stanza through the use of gerunds: "coming," "moving," "prickling," "lightning," and "frightening." These words create a sense of continuing action, of being on the threshold of action, out of which the poet attempts to move in the concluding stanza:

> An electrical storm is coming or moving away;
> It is the prickling air that wakes us up.

If lightning struck the house now, it would run
From the four blue china balls on top
Down the roof and down the rods all around us,
And we imagine dreamily
How the whole house caught in a birdcage of lightning
Would be quite delightful rather than frightening;

And from the same simplified point of view
Of night and lying flat on one's back
All things might change, equally easily,
Since always to warn us there are these black
Electrical wires dangling. Without surprise
The world might change to something quite different,
As the air changes or the lightning comes without our blinking
Change as our kisses are changing without our thinking.    (ll. 9–24)

The final line of the poem has a hint of sadness to it because of the
sense of "change." It raises questions about the poet and the lover;
why are their "kisses" "changing"? The sadness comes from the fact
that the "change" might signify the end to the relationship; the "kisses"
are not the same signals of love that they once were. "Change" here
seems also to be the continuity of time in a less dangerous way—
everything is always changing, without our knowing it. Also, there is
a change because the kisses began lightly and are now more passionate.
The change serves to carry the speaker and her lover out of the liminal
space created by the repetition of words and into one in which the two
can regularly share "kisses" without the threat of the natural world
and its frightening weather.

The use of the word "kisses" in "It is marvelous to wake up
together" serves as a stabilizing force in the poem's hermeneutics.
"It is marvelous to wake up together" provides a striking contrast to
"The Shampoo," which is the final poem of the collection *A Cold
Spring*. "The Shampoo" is an interesting departure for Bishop. Firstly,
it is the closest thing to a love poem between two women that she
has published. The rhetoric is much less ambiguous here than in
"Insomnia," and it is without the nonsense tones that are the under-
current of the *North & South* poems that thematize Bishop's mounting
love for Louise Crane. The explicitness of "The Shampoo" explains its
anomalous publishing history. The poem was published in *The New
Republic* in July of 1955 after having been sent to, and been rejected
by, a number of leading magazines. Bishop never had trouble placing
poems before. In the very beginning of her career, Marianne Moore
helped her place them. In 1947 after the successful publication of

*North & South*, Bishop signed a "first-read" contract with *The New Yorker*, which meant that they would have first option on her poems.[34] As a result, most of Bishop's poems appeared in *The New Yorker*. The rejection of "The Shampoo" by *The New Yorker* and *Poetry* is seen as discomforted acknowledgment of the poem's lesbian eroticism.[35] In a letter to Pearl Kazin, Bishop writes: "Here is the little poem ["The Shampoo"] Mrs. White couldn't understand. I have changed three words, though, since she returned it."[36] Mrs. White was the poetry editor of *The New Yorker* at the time; perhaps Bishop's tendency to render her eroticism ambiguous in her poems was what made the poem not understandable. The problems that Bishop had placing "The Shampoo" in a journal and her decision not to publish "It is marvelous to wake up together" interestingly follow the argument on the literary history of lesbianism put forth by Terry Castle. In *The Apparitional Lesbian* Castle calls the literary history of lesbianism one of "de-realization"; she writes that there is a tradition of anti-lesbian writing in which "women who desire other women repeatedly find themselves vaporized by metaphor and translated into empty fictional spaces."[37] Castle's ideas recall Bishop's figurations of the moon as insubstantial and dream-like. Castle examines fiction of the eighteenth, nineteenth and early twentieth centuries, and so she is not considering the same period as when Bishop was writing. While it is pointless to fault Bishop, as some critics do, for her veiled expression of homosexual love or for her refusal to acknowledge her homosexuality, it is striking that Bishop continues to represent lesbian love in the same terms that had characterized its depiction in less socially accepting times.

Held up to be clearly about a love between two women, "The Shampoo" opens with a startling image of contrasts, "still explosions":

> The still explosions on the rocks,
> the lichens, grow
> by spreading, gray, concentric shocks.
> They have arranged
> to meet the rings around the moon, although
> within our memories they have not changed.   (ll. 1–6)

The word "still" in the first line functions as an adjective, describing the kind of "explosions." They are unusual "explosions" in that they are hushed and stationary—probably more silent than motionless because they are "spreading." The "still(ness)" of the "explosions" might also lie in their continuity, as in they are "still" going on. As in

"Insomnia," the "moon" is a central image, invoking a feminine figuration. The "explosions" are compared to "lichens," which are "any of various small plants composed of a particular fungus and a particular algae growing in an intimate symbiotic association and forming a dual plant, commonly adhering in colored patches to rock, wood etc."[38] Given the title of the poem, the reader comes to understand that the "explosions" are bits of shampoo suds that fall onto rocks. The suds on the rocks are compared to lichens, centrally, in order to foreground the idea of the "intimate symbiotic" relationship between the speaker and the person whose hair she is washing. The descriptive language of the first three lines grows more dream-like and spiritual: "They have arranged / to meet the rings around the moon. . . ." The movement of Bishop's speaker not only in "The Shampoo" but also in the other poems discussed here is toward an interiority that is often signaled by the "moon," "memory," and "sleeping." Bishop's movement seems to reflect that of Klein's when she composes her own theories in contrast to Freud's. As Judith Hughes clarifies:

> The "object relation" that Klein, in contrast to Freud, postulated as existing "from the beginning of post-natal life"—"a relation to the mother (although focusing primarily on her breast)" which was "imbued with . . . love, hatred, phantasies, anxieties, and defenses"— was not simply a relation to an external object. . . . Klein meant something more than internal thoughts about external objects(.)[39]

Klein's "internal objects" (e.g., the moon, hair, the mother) function like a lover does; both are internalized, imagined to be inside the person.[40] As Hughes explains, Klein "was concentrating . . . on how one thought about an inner world." Bishop's ambivalent phantasies about love and the mother reveal the poet's construction of her "inner world." It is, of course, the business of the poet to illustrate her imagination through language, but this is a project, narratology, to which Klein merely aspires.[41] Bishop's dream-like tone throughout these poems reinforces the degree to which these "internal objects" are not concrete but metaphors of relationships to others.

In contrast to the dreamy tone of the poem, Bishop writes in a fairly rigid form. The poem is composed of three stanzas; each stanza is six lines with a rhyme scheme of a-b-a-c-b-c. While the rhyme scheme is consistent in the second stanza, the poet struggles within the confines of the rhyme and uses off-rhymes, reflecting the nontraditional subject matter (for Bishop's oeuvre) of the poem:

> And since the heavens will attend
> as long on us,
> you've been, dear friend,
> precipitate and pragmatical;
> and look what happens. For Time is
> nothing if not amenable.
>
> The shooting stars in your black hair
> in bright formation
> are flocking where,
> so straight, so soon?
> —Come, let me wash it in this big tin basin,
> battered and shiny like the moon.     (ll. 7–18)

The celestial imagery of "The Shampoo" with its "stars" and "moons" highlights the degree to which Bishop searches for a space in which to feel comfortable with her sexuality. This was also the case in "Insomnia," where the "inverted world" of the mirror provided a nonrealistic space in which lesbian desire could comfortably exist. This search is carried over into the realm of time as well. Why is it that "Time" is "nothing if not amenable" (ll. 11–12)? The idea of time is also inherent in the first stanza, when the poet says that "within our memories they have not changed." Presumably the "they" refers to the "concentric shocks"— the same "they" as the one in line four. The use of the poet's collective voice, "our memories," leaves her out of the poem. The "our" is the poet and the "you," who the speaker addresses; nonetheless, there is an absence of a subject self, an "I." Yet, this "our" functions more than just to conjoin the poet and the "you"; it is reminiscent of the "we" of "At the Fishhouses": "it is like what we imagine knowledge to be: . . . since / our knowledge is historical, flowing, and flown" (ll. 78 and 83). "At the Fishhouses" appears in the same collection and so can be used to gain insight into the nature of this collective voice. In "At the Fishhouses," the "we" reinforces the poet's sense of alienation from herself, highlighting the complete lack of affect within the poem as a whole, as was illustrated in my discussion of this poem in the previous chapter. When she does write, "it is like what *we* imagine knowledge to be" (italics mine), the "we" is a substitute for, or projection of, the poet; it constitutes an insistence on her perspective. If the "our" in "The Shampoo" functions in the same way, then "our memories" can also simply be the poet's. This reading illustrates the degree to which "The Shampoo" occupies a position of both a love poem as well as a poem about the self.

If catachresis is "a rhetorical figure that violates the authority of proper naming," then is it possible to see "Insomnia" and "The Shampoo" as catachrestic poems?[42] Both "Insomnia" and "The Shampoo" extend the meaning of the poetic language within them in order to represent, ultimately, a love between two women. In so doing, these poems extend language to express—and simultaneously to conceal—the expression of this love. Like "The Shampoo" and "Insomnia," poems from Bishop's later work, such as "Crusoe in England," function in a similar way to express a feeling of love for which there is no suitable term available; however, in the case of "Crusoe in England" this love is concomitant with loss.

"Crusoe in England" is a companion love poem to "The Shampoo"; both are addressed to Lota de Macedo Soares, and both reveal images of doublings that recall a lover from a position of loss. One hundred and eighty-two lines long, "Crusoe in England," was completed in 1971 and first appeared in *The New Yorker*; Bishop includes it in *Geography III*. The poem, as Harold Bloom points out, is a dramatic monologue in the mode of Robert Browning. Bishop displaces herself, here, onto a male speaker, "Crusoe." The poem reimagines Defoe's "Crusoe" in which the speaker occupies an ambivalent position with respect to the island he both longs for and despises: "But my poor old island's still / un-rediscovered, un-renamable. / None of the books has ever got it right" (ll. 8–10). A central feature and problem of the island is the speaker's burden of naming. The poem's burden of naming underscores Bishop's own burden in these poems to name a love that is beyond her scope to name. The speaker's longing involves the island's status as "un-renamable," one in which signifiers remain separate from signifieds to exist in a liminal position as images subject to interpretation and without specific meaning. This liminality is reinforced by repetitions of words, such as "giant," "rollers," "closing," and "glittering" (ll. 20, 21, 24, 25, 26, and 27).

The burden of naming, the fear of "registering their flora, / their fauna, their geography," produces the speaker's freedom to revise the landscape around her through personification (ll. 140–141). In this way, "[his] island" is populated by the "parched throats" of the volcano craters and the waterspouts' "heads in the cloud, their feet in moving patches" (ll. 32 and 49). The personification of the geography around the speaker is combined with images of sadness, such as the "turtles" that are "hissing like teakettles" (ll. 36–37). The turtles' "hissing" is sinister: unheimlich and heimlich. The "teakettles" are an image from "Sestina," which conveys Bishop's longing for her childhood home in

Great Village and for her absent mother whose memory combines with this place. The speaker tries to battle loneliness by communing with the personified landscape: "with my legs dangling down familiarly / over a crater's edge, I told myself / 'Pity should begin at home' " (ll. 61–63). The poet, however, acknowledges the limits of the metaphors of volcanoes and waterspouts as companions: "Beautiful, yes, but not much company" (l. 54). The recognition of the limits of language, here, functions to reinforce the speaker's sense of loneliness and loss.

The speaker combines a representation of loss and loneliness with an image of the Mother through the trope of drinking. Finding a "kind of berry," the speaker makes a "home-brew" out of it: "I'd drink / the awful, fizzy, stinging stuff / that went straight to my head" (ll. 79–81). Imbuing Crusoe with attributes from Bishop's own life, the speaker drinks homemade alcohol. The "home-brew" reduces the speaker's defenses and strikes associations in his mind: "Home-made, home-made! But aren't we all?" (l. 85). The alcohol permits the speaker to allude to a source of his loss: "we" are "home-made" in the sense of being produced from the Mother. The reference to the Mother is interestingly combined with a trope of drinking that recalls the nourishment that the Mother provides (her milk and her breast) and its resulting comfort and pleasure. The trope also reinscribes the ambivalence with which the mother engenders the child's love and hate—this hate can often be figured as a desire to internalize, or eat, the Mother.[43]

The sense of loss overpowers the speaker such that his solitude is unbearable; this figuration provides a striking contrast to the poet's desire for solitude that is most notably present in "The End of March." Here, books offer no solace; the speaker cannot just read because the act would remind him that he wants a companion to whom he can read: "I tried / reciting to my iris-beds / 'They flash upon that inward eye, / which is the bliss . . .' The bliss of what?" (ll. 94–97). The problem of isolation, here, represses the speaker's memory of his quotation from William Wordsworth, whereby he cannot recall the "bliss of solitude."

The poet continues on the theme of solitude but introduces a series of disturbing images that represent the speaker's isolation and his concatenated emotions of anger and aggression. For example, the speaker again tries to personify things; this time animals:

> The goats were white, so were the gulls,
> and both too tame, or else they thought

I was a goat, too, or a gull.
*Baa, baa, baa* and *shriek, shriek, shriek,*
*baa . . . shriek . . . baa . . .* I still can't shake
them from my ears; they're hurting now.
The questioning shrieks, the equivocal replies
over a ground of hissing rain
and hissing, ambulating turtles
got on my nerves. (ll. 101–110)

The attempt to personify the "goats," "gulls," and "turtles" is achieved by giving them speech; however, their utterances—questions, "equivocal replies" and "hissing"—prove to be more irritating to the speaker than comforting. These types of utterances seem like paranoid projections on the part of the speaker who is afraid that the "goats" are excessively ambiguous and therefore are, like the unnamed things on the island, a threat to, and an anxiety of, the lack of stable signification. Indeed, the speaker tries to change his environment and thereby the set of meanings before him: "I got so tired of the very colors! / One day I dyed a baby goat bright red / with my red berries, just to see / something a little different. / so then his mother wouldn't recognize him" (ll. 124–128). The poet's act from boredom is an aggressive one in that he symbolically kills, "dye(s)," the goat. This symbolic act is highlighted not only by the play on "dye"/die but also by the choice of color, "red," which makes the goat appear bloody. The connection with the goat's "mother" reinforces the degree to which the speaker is thinking of his own mother and his aggression and love for her.

The poet's aggression for, and sadness over, the goat arises from its unnerving tendency toward "unequivocal replies"; this aggression appears even in the speaker's unconscious, where dreams reveal further connections between images of the Mother and of violence:[44]

Dreams were the worst. Of course I dreamed of food
and love, but they were pleasant rather
than otherwise. But then I'd dream of things
like slitting a baby's throat, mistaking it
for a baby goat. (ll. 129–133)

The dream of "food" and "love" is a dream of the Mother, the primal source of nourishment and affection. The dream, however, solidifies the wish first established when the speaker "dyes" his goat red. Thus, "dye" also suggests the pun prevalent in English Renaissance poetry, where dying means sexual gratification.[45]

The dynamics change in the next verse stanza with the sudden appearance of "Friday": "Friday was nice. / Friday was nice and we were friends" (ll. 145–146). Friday comes from nowhere; his appearance is unexplained and unexamined in the poem. This gives the impression that he is a projection on the part of an unreliable speaker—a projection of a double image, a reflection to provide some companionship. Friday's entrance does shift the poem from the domestication of the island to a domesticity, as the speaker and Friday become "friends."

There is a proto-sexual relationship between Friday and Crusoe in which the figure of Friday functions like the "proto-dream-house" of "The End of March" as a principal fantasy of fulfillment and erotic desire. The speaker says of Friday: "If only he had been a woman! / I wanted to propagate my kind, and so did he, I think, poor boy," then, ". . . he had a pretty body" (ll. 147–149, 152). The lament that Friday is not a woman works less to lament the sexual nature of their relationship and more to remind the reader of Bishop's switch with respect to the speaker's gender. The speaker and Friday have a sexual relationship; the speaker's lament is specifically about the desire to "propagate," a desire that would certainly solve the speaker's problem of isolation. The sexual relationship between Crusoe and Friday fore-grounds the fact that the loss is not only one of the Mother but also one of the loved object, Friday.

As suddenly as Friday appears, the two are removed from the island: "then one day they came and took us off" (l. 153). Speaking now from the position of "another island," Crusoe's loss centers on objects associated with the island, "lumber," and the "knife" that "reeked with meaning." These objects had gained meaning because of their rarity for Crusoe; now, there are many knives, and each has little significance. This change seems to require another renaming. As the poem concludes, the speaker considers his former possessions from the island: "the parasol that took me such a time / remembering the way the ribs should go" (ll. 176–177). The word "ribs" recalls Milton's *Paradise Lost*, where the "ribs" of Adam were important because, out of Adam's rib, God produces Eve. Adam and Eve, like Crusoe, have the burden of naming the world around them and of propagating their kind. At the same time, the sex that produces Eve is a same-sex one between Milton's Adam and God that reflects the kind between Crusoe and Friday.

The poem ends: "How can anyone want such things? / —And Friday, my dear Friday, died of measles / seventeen years ago come March" (ll. 180–182). This final question is the central one of the poem: "how can anyone want" the island that produced nothing but misery and isolation? How can the speaker want Friday and the Mother when they are ambivalent figures?

Because of Bishop's use of conversational language that is reflective of everyday speech in poems like "Crusoe in England," the language establishes an expectation of clarity that the poem then resists. Bishop's speakers in "Insomnia," "It is marvelous . . . ," and "The Shampoo" refuse to impose any kind of analyses, self-critical or otherwise, onto the poems. At the same time, they are equally resistant to gender characterizations. For example, Bishop displaces her own gender in order to assume a male voice in "Crusoe in England." While the male voice seems to reinforce dominant ideologies that see the aggressive acts of Crusoe as specifically masculine, the aggressive nature of the poem is undercut by concomitant themes of love, melancholia, and loss. To expect the poet to create generalizations about gender difference in love poems is to assume, traditionally, that the love poem is concerned with heterosexual love; in this way, female poets are expected to produce a representation of femininity (coy and submissive) that is in contrast with the (presumably male) lover. "The Shampoo," for example, produces a speaker whose primary characteristic is observation, specifically the observation of shampoo in her lover's hair. This act of observation aligns the speaker with a masculine gaze. Bishop's speakers subvert such expectations primarily through observation and skepticism.[46]

Like "The Shampoo" and "Crusoe in England," "One Art" straddles the fence of definition of its subject matter; it is a love poem, but it is one that addresses the self as much as a lover in order to reflect upon a series of losses. "One Art" appears in Bishop's final collection of poems from 1976, *Geography III*. There are only ten poems in the book: "In the Waiting Room," "Crusoe in England," "Night City," "The Moose," "12 O'clock News," "Poem," "One Art," "The End of March," "Objects & Apparitions," and "Five Flights Up." Each of the poems deals with recalling the "places" of childhood memories in order to remember their innocence. In this way, the poems contain an innate sadness and sense of loss.

The emotional qualities of "One Art" are not immediately apparent because they are often subsumed within the tone of the poem's play with words. "One Art" is a villanelle. Like the sestina, it is a complicated and traditional verse form that creates a stitching of words. Villanelles consist of five tercets and a quatrain; the rhyme scheme for the tercets is a-b-a and the quatrain is a-b-a-a. The first line is repeated as the final line of the second and fourth stanzas, whereas the third line provides the repetition for the final line of the third and fifth stanzas. The opposite of rhyme is repetition, not off-rhyme or blank verse; repetition occupies a central position in the poem. It reinforces the doubling images that have characterized Bishop's love poems. The repetition reflects the repetition of gender in same-sex love and allows for the discussion of lesbian love. The poem begins with a catalogue of lost things:

> The art of losing isn't hard to master;
> so many things seem filled with the intent
> to be lost that their loss is no disaster.
>
> Lose something every day. Accept the fluster
> of lost door keys, the hour badly spent.
> The art of losing isn't hard to master.
>
> Then practice losing farther, losing faster:
> places, and names, and where it was you meant
> to travel. None of these will bring disaster.    (ll. 1–9)

The title, "One Art," is a condensed version of "The Art of Losing Things."[47] Yet, the title also can be read as an *ars poetica* for Bishop's work.[48] Some critics read this poem as a lesson in losing things; this reading, however, is too literal and underestimates the emotional power of the final stanzas as well as the figurative purpose of the beginning stanzas:

> I lost two cities, lovely ones. And, vaster,
> some realms I owned, two rivers, a continent.
> I miss them, but it wasn't a disaster.
>
> —Even losing you (the joking voice, a gesture
> I love) I shan't have lied. It's evident
> the art of losing's not too hard to master
> Though it may look like (*Write* it!) like disaster.    (ll. 13–19)

With the admission that the poet "miss(es)" what she has lost, the emotional subtext of the poem becomes increasingly more central. The emotional core of the poem raises questions about the speaker, concerning her self-deprecating view in which her misfortunes in life are an "art" in "losing" things. The final quatrain discusses a "you," who is a loved one; the speaker says, "I shan't have lied," calling into question what is the lie. The lie seems to be that "loss is no disaster" but it also refers to the flippant and inconsequential list of things lost: "keys," "names," "a watch." These things are associated with great meaning, the "mother's watch" for the Mother. They are also diversions from the larger loss of the "you." The imperative, "write it," is hidden behind parentheses that signal the poet's ambivalence about her project of writing about loss in general. Yet the poet's pun, write / right, shows how "[writing about] it" can right or correct it at least for poetry. Barbara Page notes that often Bishop's drafts argue for the opposite of what the final poem seems to be saying. Early drafts of "One Art" are more forthcoming about the series of painful losses in the poet's life. The final lines of the poem might seem to be saying that "losing" is "not too hard to master," but this means the opposite. She is really saying that it is "too hard," and it "may look like . . . disaster" precisely because it is disastrous.

   It is possible, however, to read the speaker of "One Art" as not being self-deprecating when she calls her misfortunes an "art." Rather, the speaker can also be striving for transcendence, righting it by writing it. As an "art" the problem of loss can be transformative, or it can fall under the advice of "The Victor Dog": "Art is art. / The life it asks of us is a dog's life." James Merrill's poem that is written to Bishop reminds her of the heavy price in labor that art requires; as "art," however, the burden of work appears palatable to Bishop's sense of the requirements of poetry.

James Merrill's fourth collection of poems *Nights and Days* appeared in 1966 and owes a debt to Bishop's *A Cold Spring*. Most notably, both are short works. Bishop's *A Cold Spring* was never published as a separate volume; it was combined with the *North & South* poems and released as *Poems: North & South—A Cold Spring*. Nonetheless, like Bishop's collection of roughly twenty poems many of which are concerned with various forms and degrees of love, Merrill's *Nights and Days*, for which the poet won the first of two National Book Awards, contains twenty poems that are engaged in a discussion of different kinds of love: romantic, maternal, and maternal-substitutes. As the title suggests, the poems have an intimate quality, establishing a poetic voice that seems to be revealing intimate aspects of the speaker's everyday life—these are thoughts and experiences that are characteristic or representative of the general "nights" and "days" of the poet's life. The poet, however, is not without his wit and sense of humor that makes its presence felt even in the elegy "Annie Hill's Grave," "Necropolis is a nice place to visit; / One would not want to live there all year round." This deadpan tone is a strategic fiction of the poems. Indeed, in an interview about this book, Merrill says that confessional poetry is a literary convention; the problem is to make the poem's confession sound as if it were true. Whether or not the poet is presenting the actual facts of his experience is irrelevant, but he must give the "illusion of a True Confession."[49] Except for the long poem, "The Thousand and Second Night," the poems of *Nights and Days* are short and intimate in their tonality. "Nightgown," a poem of two quatrains, a-b-b-a, opens the collection and provides an adept introduction to the poems that follow:

> A cold so keen,
> My speech unfurls tonight
> As from the chattering teeth
> Of a sewing-machine.
> Whom words appear to warm,
> Dear heart, wear mine. Come forth
> Wound in their flimsy white
> And give it form.   (ll. 1–8)

While the language here is resolutely Merrill's, the image in the second half of the first quatrain of the "chattering teeth" that sound like a "sewing-machine" is a kind of Bishopian, observation-based metaphor. The poem is interesting in its comparison of "words" to the "flimsy white" of the "nightgown"; "words" clothe. Yet, the "flimsy" nature of the "words" renders them ghost-like; the speech is a specter—a shadow for something behind it or ephemeral and time-bound. "Nightgown" also prepares the reader for the tonal quality and intimacy of the poems that follow; for example, the address "Dear heart" establishes a familiarity with the reader, and it also sets up an allusion to Crane's work through the pun, "heart"/Hart. The notion that "words"—those of the poet—possess a materiality, a "form," is extended throughout *Nights and Days*, for instance in the image of the face. This notion also recalls lines from Crane's work, his "incarnate word" and "word made flesh." For Merrill, faces are sites of interest and information, and they appear in "Annie Hill's Grave": "And as the brief snail-trace / Of her withdrawal dries upon our faces / The silence drums into her upturned face." Here they are a site of comparison between the tear-strewn "faces" of the mourners and the "face" of the woman who stares up at the living world.

The face is the central trope of "Between Us," an intriguing poem in Merrill's work because of its commingling of several themes, yet it is characteristically fanciful and oddly witty. "Between Us" is a love poem; however, what secures it within this genre is the speaker's reflections on the "you('s)" face while they are in bed together:

> A . . . face? There
> It lies on the pillow by
> Your turned head's tangled graying hair:

Another—like a shrunken head, too small!
My eyes in dread
Shut. Open. It is there,

Waxen, inhuman. Small.
The taut crease of the mouth shifts. It
Seems to smile,
Chin up in the wan light. Elsewhere
I have known what it was, this thing, known
The blind eye-slit
And knuckle-sharp cheekbone—

Ah. And again do.
Not a face. A hand, seen queerly. Mine.
Deliver me, I breathe
Watching it unclench with a soft moan
And reach for you.    (ll. 1–8)

"Between Us" takes place in a similar moment to Bishop's "Love Lies Sleeping" and "Insomnia," the period just around waking up, and, as in those Bishop poems, subtle signs define the poem as a love poem. Whereas Bishop provides clues that an otherwise crepuscular moment of reflection is based in love because she includes the word, "love," Merrill does not explicitly mention love here. The speaker is awakened and, in his state of being half-awake, is not sure if he is seeing a second face, "A . . . face?" (l. 1). The poet sets the poem while he is in bed with someone else; the face of the other "lies on the pillow" beside the speaker. Same-sex eroticism is conveyed if the reader takes the speaker's "I" to be the gender of the poet. Except in the case of Bishop's "Crusoe in England" where the speaker specifies his gender, the gender of the speaker is generally assumed to be the poet's.

The speaker believes that he sees a second head; this one is "shrunken" but presumably has the same "tangled graying hair" as that of the head of the "you," because the speaker cannot tell the two apart. The image of the second head is an interesting complication to the trope of the reflection that has been discussed in this chapter, because, here, the poet offers a repetition of a lover's image, but the image is "shrunken" and "inhuman."

Most of the space of this otherwise short poem of three stanzas of six lines each is devoted to the question of this face. The speaker finds the second face scary; it is "like a shrunken head" and is "inhuman." After he allows his imagination to run wild, as it were, the speaker realizes that he "(has) known" this object; he recognizes its "knuckle" as his own "hand." The speaker's misperception / misrecognition of his hand as a small face that lies beside the "you" next to him in bed seems, at first, to be a harmless rumination on an understandable, dreamlike situation. The final lines of the poem, however, secure its erotic import: "Deliver me, I breathe / Watching it unclench with a soft moan / And reach for you." The "soft moan" and "unclench(ing)" provide sexual overtones to the scene. The declarative, "Deliver me," is reminiscent of those that appear in Crane's "Voyages" sequence, especially "Permit me voyage, love, into your hands." Comparison to Crane is also helpful to clarify the import of the misperceived "hand." As is the case with Crane, the hand in Merrill's poetry is a recurring image that is often used to foreground an erotic potential within a desexualized context. Perhaps this is reinforced by the witty use of the word "queerly"; the hand is "seen queerly" because it is an erotic site on the body. At the same time, the "hand" is also the agent of the writer's work. In this way, the poem resists a stable position in terms of its subject because the poem suggests a desire to connect with a creative agency as well through the act of writing, symbolized through the "hand." The poem ends with a tender moment between the speaker and the "you," his lover; this reinscribes the poem within the love genre to which it aspires.

In "James Merrill's Masks of Eros, Masques of Love," Eric Murphy Selinger considers the question of love poetry in Merrill's work. He writes: "Merrill is hardly the first poet to have rebelled against the love poem's claim to be an object of desire, the poet and his words the only true and lasting pair."[50] This observation points toward the degree to which Merrill, by contrast to Crane and Bishop, uses the rhetoric of the love poem not only to create poetic language but also to comment on the way rhetoric functions in poems to instruct the reader about the manifold significations of love.

The last two poems of *Nights and Days*, "The Mad Scene" and "Days of 1964," weave discussions of romantic love with maternal love. "The Mad Scene" is a dream poem that recalls the first poem of the collection through the "sheets" of the laundry that are like the "flimsy white" material of "The Nightgown." "The Mad Scene" opens: "Again last night I dreamed the dream called Laundry. / In it, the sheets and towels of a life we were going to share" (ll. 1–2). The sheets of laundry are spectral figures, recalling the figures of lovers and the Mother. Set in Greece, "Days of 1964" is another poem in Merrill's series that reflects upon a particular set of days as a nostalgic idealization of that time.[51] Words such as "hospital" and "sun-cured" connote sickness and convey the sense that there is, or was, something wrong, as was the case with "An Urban Convalescence" where there was a creative malady troubling the speaker. The poem opens with lines that in essence provide a description of the "neighborhood":

> Across the street that led to the center of town
> A steep hill kept one company part way,
> Or could be climbed in twenty minutes
> For some literally breathtaking views,
> Framed by umbrella pines, of city and sea.
> Underfoot, cyclamen, autumn crocus grew
> Spangled as with fine sweat among the relics
> Of good times had by all. If not Olympus,
> An out-of-earshot, year-round hillside revel.     (ll. 4–12)

The second verse stanza introduces "Kyria Kleo who cleaned for us [the speaker and his lover]" (l. 14).[52] "Kyria Kleo" is endearing: she "wore brown, was fat, past fifty," and, more significantly, she embodies a kind of unconditional, maternal love: "How she loved / You, me, loved us all, the bird, the cat! / I think now she *was* love" (ll. 18–20). It is through the description of Kyria Kleo's affection for the speaker that the reader comes to understand who the "us" that Kleo cleans for is; the "us" is comprised of the speaker and the "you" of the poem.

While "Days of 1964" recalls and complicates the discussion in the previous chapter about the interrelated figurations of the lover and the Mother, the poem does not so much conflate the two kinds of love as it compares them. The love of "Kyria Kleo" allows for the contemplation of the love for the "you." The "you" comes up in contrast to the cleaning woman initially in the lines, "How she loved / You, me," and later:

> I paid her generously, I dare say.
> Love makes one generous. Look at us. We'd known
> Each other so briefly that instead of sleeping
> We lay whole nights, open, in the lamplight,
> And gazed, or traded stories.     (ll. 25–29)

The economic images here recall Stevens's line, "Money is a kind of poetry," and introduce the meta-poetic nature of the poet's words.[53] The commodification of love, the speaker's generosity, turns to the artifice of love, when the speaker describes seeing Kyria Kleo downtown with her face "painted / Clown-white" (ll. 38–39). Again, her appearance functions as a catalyst for the poet toward his disquisition on love and art, which he speaks of as "illusion." The final verse stanza's tone shifts from that of the beginning. The speaker is less concerned with place than with the nature of the love between him and the "you" and the question of whether their love was an "illusion":

> I had gone so long without loving,
> I hardly knew what I was thinking.
> Where I hid my face, your touch, quick, merciful,
> Blindfolded me. A god breathed from my lips.
> If that was illusion, I wanted it to last long;
> To dwell, for its daily pittance, with us there,
> Cleaning and watering, sighing with love or pain.     (ll. 59–65)

Merrill argues for a commingling of art and love in his poetry. Love is elastic; it can contain the "heights" of pleasure as well as those of "degradation." These final lines of the speaker's ruminations move from "love or pain," a choice, to "pain and love" (ll. 65 and 74). The degree to which Kyria Kleo is a device that engenders thoughts about the lover erases her as a character; she becomes more of a symbol than a figure. Like Yeats's swans, she seems to have written under her, "another emblem there."[54]

"Clearing the Title" is another example of a love poem from much later in Merrill's career. "Clearing the Title" appears in *Late Settings* which was published in 1985; it is 152 lines long; there are nineteen stanzas of eight lines each. The poem is dedicated to Merrill's lover, David Jackson, "for DJ," and creates the appearance of a forthright revelation about the speaker's surprise and coming to terms with Jackson's purchase of a house in Key West. "Clearing the Title" functions as a revision and a subversion of a traditional love poem in that what usually binds a couple together—a house—does not work in this way; rather, it is art that joins the poet with his lover. The poem's subversion is a theme that opens the poem. It appears in the poem through a contrasted state of affairs between revision and stasis:

> Because the wind has changed, because I guess
> My poem (what to call it though?) is finished,
> Because the golden genie chafes within
> His smudged-glass bottle and, god help us, you
> Have chosen, sight unseen, this tropic rendezvous
> Where tourist, outcast and in-groupie gather
> Island by island, linked together,
> Causeways bridging the vast shallowness—     (ll. 1–8)

The poem begins with a list of things, "because . . . ," that seem to be reasons for the poem's creation; they describe a newness. The reason for the list, however, is unclear because the speaker does not finish his thought; he interrupts himself with the recognition that the "you" has "chosen" this place. Through the course of the opening lines—as well as the title's clue—the reader learns that the "you" has bought a house in Key West, Florida:

> The appalling truth now bores
> Into my brain: you've *bought* a house
> And pass, en route to it, the peeling white
> Five-story skyscraper in which "our" title
> Is being cleared!   (ll. 33–37)

The reader expects the purchase of the "house" to be good news. This house is defined by negation and associated with negative terms: "appalling" and "bores." It is not wanted. Also, it is not domestic or associated with domesticity because it does not act as an image that conjoins the speaker with the "you."

Indeed the unwanted house conveys the sense that the speaker and his lover are out of sorts. This idea is reinforced by the description of Key West: "What's left of nature here? Those trees five thousand tin / Roofs, like little mirrors in distress,/ Would flash up from if the sun were out . . ." (ll. 12–14). Also, the lover is out of sorts: "such a mistake—past fifty and behaving / As if hope sprang eternal" (ll. 17–18). These images of dissatisfaction are combined with language that is disjointed, interrupted by internal questions and dashes that convey the speaker's sense of rupture from his lover.

The instances of rupture, however, are in contrast to the poet's language, as he begins to come to terms with the possibility of living in this house in Key West. The poet's pronouns that had reinforced his division from the "you" when he spoke of the house now seem to work to conjoin the two. The potential for doubling is thus revised to conflation. For example, the speaker says: "(But can you picture *living* here? Expect / *Me* to swelter, year by sunset year" (ll. 42–43). Here, where the poet says, "can you picture," the "you" means both "I" as well as "you"; the speaker has conflated the two personas. Then, in the seventh and eighth stanzas, the poet continues to conflate, as he speaks of a "we" and figures them as "two old bent trees" or as a couple "waiting companionably for kingdom come" (ll. 51, 56, 63, and 64).

What produces this shift from a representation of the troubled relationship between the speaker and his lover to one in which they are conjoined is not the purchase of the house but rather the creation of poetry. The poet writes:

> *Our* poem now. It's signed JM, but grew
> From life together, grain by coral grain.
> Building on it, we let the life cloud over . . .     (ll. 97–99)

The shift in representation has extended itself to the "poem"; the opening of "Clearing the Title" refers to the speaker's poem, "My poem . . . is finished," (l. 2). His poem is revised to "*Our* poem"; its change is reinforced by the italicization of "our." The "poem" to which the speaker refers is *Changing Light at Sandover* in which "JM" along with his lover, "DJ," figure as central characters. Their love, their former separateness, has been revised into art, specifically the poem that each has a hand in producing.[55] Kristeva notes the power of art, when she writes that the "imagination is a discourse of transference— of love."[56] Love in connection with the imagination's work, art, therefore has the power to "cure" the separateness of the speaker from his lover. The poem's closing lines reinforce the import of the connection that "our poem" produces: "—although tonight we trust no real / Conclusions will be reached—float higher yet, / Juggled slowly by the changing light" (ll. 150–152). The final phrase's reiteration of the "poem's" title, "the changing light," highlights its function as the figurative house that contains the speaker and his lover in a state that is "companionable" in a way that the Key West house could not be.[57]

The image of the house also remains a considerably ambivalent one for the speaker because of the literary ancestral specters associated with "Key West." The poem notes that "the Wilburs live downstreet," referring to the poet Richard Wilbur (l. 79). The poem does not explicitly register the large number of poets and writers associated with Key West, including Elizabeth Bishop, who owned a house there for a number of years, Hart Crane, Ernest Hemingway, Tennessee Williams, and Truman Capote. Merrill's ambivalence toward the Key West house aligns him with Stevens's representation of the "girl" who sings beyond the place of the sea in his "The Idea of Order at Key West."[58] In Merrill's poem, the literary significance of Key West undercuts the speaker's shock about it and foregrounds the importance of literature and art in the poem. The failure of the poet's imagination to be able to "picture *living*" in Key West threatens to destroy the poem; in the end, though, poetry is restorative and allows for the poem's conclusion.

"Clearing the Title" is a reluctant love poem, or it can be read as one because of the poem's "less is more" presentation of domesticity and affect. This "less is more" tone is made into a theme in Merrill's short, six line poem, "Her Craft":

> Elizabeth Bishop—swan boat or
> Amazon steamer? Neither: a Dream Boat.
> Among topheavy wrecks, she stays afloat.
> Mine's this white hanky waving from the shore
> —In lieu of the requested "essay." (Faute
> De pire, if I may say so. Less is more.)[59]

Always generous and eloquently deferential to Bishop, Merrill's "less is more" represents the rhetorical project of Crane, Bishop, and Merrill's poems on love. In order to keep "certain ardours" out of the public discourse of the poem, Crane, Bishop, and Merrill employ their rhetorical prowess to conceal homosexuality. Unable not to write about such a central concern, these three poets write about love following the "less is more" dictum. Crane, Bishop, and Merrill exhibit a homosexual anxiety that is figured in their love poems by a dislocation with, or rupturing of, images of the self, or of a lover, into itself and its mirror image. In this way, the love poems present a repetition or doubling that is reminiscent of the image of Narcissus gazing at his own reflection—an image, which is central to a psychoanalytic understanding of love. Rhetoric in these poems is a doubling of images that creates a destabilizing gesture within them such that they are often unrecognizable as poems about love.

# AFTERWORD

$T$oward the end of his memoir, James Merrill addresses the significance of the trope of the closet and postulates on its importance to the artist:

> To the artist a closet is quite useful as it once was to the homosexual: what John Hollander calls, in the lingo of spy thrillers, a cover life, allowing us to get on with our true work as secret agents for the mother tongue—a phrase itself grown ineffably off-color, thanks to Wystan. (DP, 230)

"Wystan" is Wystan Auden, who Merrill is about to meet in Athens in 1965. Merrill claims to have kept a distance from Auden—perhaps both the man as well as the poetry, although Merrill's own poems might suggest otherwise—precisely because of Auden's openness about his homosexuality—a forthrightness that Merrill found uncomfortable.[1] The discomfort is present in Merrill's choice of words, such as "true work." Merrill is writing about both life and art here; when he describes his discomfort, he reveals that the rhetoric of his poems functions, in part, to distance overt homosexuality from his work. The phrase "mother tongue" is an interesting choice; Merrill foregrounds it, he says, in terms of its relation to Auden. The phrase is also intriguing, however, in the context of this discussion and in particular to the considerations of the figure of the Mother as extrapolated upon in the second chapter.

At first glance Merrill's assertion that the "closet is quite useful" to the artist appears politically unaware or outdated. Merrill's comment begs the question in what ways might a symbol of homosexual oppression, "the closet," be "useful?" Bishop "believed in closets, closets, and more closets" to avoid personal revelations and would agree with Merrill, despite the different contexts of their closets here.[2] The trope of the closet presents the artist with a preexisting and sustaining metaphor for gender and sexual identity—one that can be utilized freely by anyone willing to claim it. In this way, the elasticity of the closet, its ability to encompass and represent persons across boundaries of race, class, or gender, functions like catachresis to speak for and to represent individuals for whom there are no other forms of representation. The closet can be "quite useful" precisely in the way that it provides the artist with a preexisting metaphor into which he or she can construct his or her own web of images. The closet is a starting point, the lack of which can lead to purely mundane, material revelations.

Crane, Bishop, and Merrill's poetry rhetorically distorts identity to conceal and reveal ambivalence for the Mother and lovers, but in so doing their poetry reconceives identity as a distorting concept. Their poetry takes the notion that homosexuality is constructed and extends it, pointing out that identity in general is a construct. Crane, Bishop, and Merrill use rhetoric to distort revelations of love and hate for the mother because of social taboos against them and for the lover because of social and personal anxiety about homosexuality. This gives rise to questions about categories of identity and what it means to be in love. In this way, their poetry opens up questions about the nature of love, desire, and identity. Each is reconfigured because each is shifting, unstable, and ambivalent.

The rhetorical gestures and thematic representations of identity, love, sexuality, and figurations of mothers in Hart Crane, Elizabeth Bishop, and James Merrill extend beyond them and can be found in the work of other American poets. While my discussion of Crane, Bishop, and Merrill reveals a homosexual anxiety within their poems that engenders a rhetoric of ambiguity in which to closet troubling emotions, more contemporary poets who embody their legacies, such as Frank Bidart, Henri Cole, and Mark Doty, do not reveal so much a homosexual anxiety as a more generalized sexual anxiety.[3] This shift is in great part due to the explicit place of homosexuality within the poetry. Frank Bidart, for example, a friend of Bishop's and one of her literary executors, writes poems that are indebted a great deal to her style as well as Merrill's. Like Merrill, Bidart takes a discreet, yet open, attitude toward homosexuality. Bidart's play with punctuation, such as combinations of commas and dashes or dashes and semi-colons, recall Crane's subjective use of punctuation as a component part of the poem. In Bidart's poems, including "The War of Vaslav Nijinsky" and "The First Hour of the Night," punctuation functions as a dialect of the monologist's consciousness. In poems such as "To the Dead," punctuation serves to convey meaning and a sense of force to language that can only be controlled by punctuation used in tandem: "There is a NIGHT within the NIGHT,-(.)"[4] The comma and dash combine to convey the speaker's discomfort with the characteristic shift in his poetry between confession and detachment from the confession.

Bidart's sequence of fourteen poems collected as *Music Like Dirt* confronts what Bidart says is "the human need to make," and the poems in the sequence can be read as elegies for makers—various artists, musicians, actors—of the twentieth century as well as an elegy for the twentieth century itself. In the opening poem, "For the Twentieth Century" he makes this backward glance at the now-past century clear: "Therefore you and I and Mozart / Must thank the Twentieth Century."[5] In its focus on making, however, Bidart reworks Merrill's ideas about the difficulty of art and importance of it that he includes most notably in "The Victor Dog." In Bidart's final poem in the sequence "Lament For the Makers" the speaker builds upon Merrill's ideas and wonders about the rewards such sacrifices for art bestow upon the maker of art:

*Many creatures must*
*make, but only one must seek*

*within itself what to make*[6]

For the speaker, seeking "within" is its reward and involves the distinctly human need or tendency to be introspective and reflective. Yet, the poem suggests that this human need to search "within itself what to make" is an uncanny one, and the poet seems at times to have ambivalent feelings about the process. Still, it is this going "within" that brings the poem to its conclusion: "Teach me, masters who by making were / remade, your art" (ll. 15–16). The reward for making is an internal one; it is being "remade" which is interestingly a continuation of the act of making. Though not explicitly mentioned, Crane, Bishop, and Merrill loom as spectral "masters" from whom the poet wants to be taught his and their art.

Like Frank Bidart, Henri Cole is a poet interested in learning lessons from his literary tradition. Henri Cole's collection *The Visible Man* is concerned with a quest for, and a centrality of, a self that is unabashedly and clearly homosexual and takes its title and epigraph from Hart Crane's incomplete poem "The Visible The Untrue." The epigraph is taken from the first few lines of Crane's poem: "Yes, I being / the terrible puppet of my dreams, shall / lavish this on you."[7] Crane's title, "The Visible The Untrue," appears to be missing a word; one wants to complete it, add a word between "visible" and "the" in a way that reflects the addition needed to connect Crane's dedication, "to E.O.," to Emil Opffer—the lover from "Voyages." Cole's poems do not require this work; he begins in a more sexually "visible" position.

There is also much of Bishop and Merrill in Cole's collection: the exploration of common things and everyday events, infused with fresh images and language, in pursuit of understanding the world's and the poet's fear, hatred, love, and wonder. For example, the speaker in "Black Mane" offers a vision of wisdom that is harsh and combative: "When your body sorrows into his, / it is as if a bolt is pushed into place, / metal hitting metal, like wisdom" (pp. 49–50). Or, in "The Blue Grotto," Cole's speaker says:

> I sat up, as in a coffin
> after three hundred lovers.
> Starboard, an oar-blade splashed
> emeralds against valedictory black.
> Once again, description
> unemotional shorthand
> for sublimated wisdom,
> fails to conjure what we felt;
> the poem yearns for something more.   (ll. 15–23)

These lines could almost be a praise of, and response to, Bishop's poems, where "description" reigns as a kind of "unemotional shorthand" for the poet. Here, Cole departs from Bishop because he feels his "poem yearns for . . . more." In case, however, the reader was unclear that we are in the realm of Bishop, Cole's speaker sees "a serpentine thing" in the water that is "grasping at" them; the creature is reminiscent of the seal in "At the Fishhouses." "The Blue Grotto" seems to have "At the Fishhouses" behind it as a poem of self-reflection, meditation and loss; however, where Bishop's poem exhibits a surprising absence of affect, Cole's speaker tries to move beyond the "unemotional shorthand" into the self. Indeed to reiterate these points, Cole's opening poem, "Arte Povera," questions the complacency of poetry's rhetoric of descriptions:

> How pleased I was and defiant because
> a dry basin meant the end of description & rhyme,
> which had nursed and embalmed me at once.
> Language was more than a baroque wall-fountain.   (ll. 5–8)

The "description & rhyme," the learned behavior in rhetorical modes from Crane, Bishop, and Merrill, was a "nurse" but, at the same time, they were their tools. Poetic influences are, at once, helpful and unhelpful, necessary and unnecessary.

Cole's speaker achieves this gaze into selfhood in his sequence of fourteen sonnets, entitled "Apollo," that end his collection.[8] Here, he looks into himself at the same time as he explores the world around him: "For a moment, / I was the eye through which the universe / beheld itself, like God." The poet's "eye" gazes into himself with a great deal of honesty, as in his ninth section:

> All I want is to trust a man with plain
> unshaken faith. Because I was not loved,
> I cannot love.
>
>     . . .
>
>     You, with your unfalse nature
> and silver arrows, won't you take my wrist.
> Speak to me. My words are sounds
> and sounds are not what I feel. Make me a man.

The confluence of desire, self-hatred, and sexuality is constructed without coyness or material explicitness.

Similarly, many of Mark Doty's poems have Crane, Bishop, and Merrill behind them, especially his books *My Alexandria* and *Atlantis.* The poems in these two books successfully create an aesthetic where homosexuality exists and are chiefly concerned with elegiac poems commemorating the AIDS-related death of the poet's lover, Wally. Though highly influenced by these poetic forbearers, Doty's poems never fail to be authentic and contemporary and stand out for their genuine sense of humor and play. In *My Alexandria,* for example, the opening poem "Demolition" recreates the scene of Merrill's "An Urban Convalescence." By its title, "Days of 1981" refers to Merrill's "Days of . . ." series. The proximity of "Demolition" to "Days of 1981" in the collection invokes Merrill; then Doty proceeds to write beyond Merrill through the materiality with which homosexuality appears in the poems.[9] Similarly, "At the Boatyard," from *Atlantis* also returns to the scene of Bishop's "At the Fishhouses"; Doty's speaker is engaged with an observation of beauty in order to create a homosexual aesthetic vision; here he concentrates on the colors of the "boarder / between worlds" that is the boatyard.[10] The poet invokes Bishop when he too sees a creature in the water:

> And some days,
>
> only when I am not looking,
> a slick brother head

watches from between the lapping,
mirror waves. He is whiskered,
placid, and keeps his distance,
lone ambassador

The "brother head" repeats Bishop's seal but in a way that secures, or "seals" the "seals" masculinity—a homosexual erotic figure with whom the poet can engage in "total immersion" in the safety of the creature's complete otherness.

Bishop, as Crane and Merrill would certainly have agreed, felt that poets should constantly read other poets and understood that a talented poet should write beyond the shadow of influence. The work and the advice present challenges to future poets, as in her poem "The Bight" where she sums up her project of poetry: "All the untidy activity continues, / awful but cheerful."

# NOTES

## INTRODUCTION

1. The publication of Ted Hughes, *Birthday Letters*, New York: Farrar, Straus and Giroux, 1998, was also heralded by a series of articles in the popular press, including one on the front page of *The New York Times* entitled, "In Poetry, Ted Hughes Breaks His Silence on Sylvia Plath," Sarah Lyall, January 19, 1998. See also A. Alvarez, "Your Story, My Story," in *The New Yorker*. February 2, 1998. Katha Pollitt, "Peering Into the Bell Jar," *The New York Times Book Review*. March 1, 1998. See also Janet Malcolm, *The Silent Woman: Sylvia Plath and Ted Hughes*, New York: Alfred Knopf, 1994.

2. Is it possible to read *Ariel* without the biography of Plath behind it for "explanation"? This reductive gesture seems to do violence to the poem because it demands a rigidity of meaning of otherwise unstable and multiple significations.

3. Boris Tomashevsky as quoted in Marjorie Perloff, *The Poetic Art of Robert Lowell*, Ithaca: Cornell University Press, 1973, 80.

4. I use "identification," "association," and "recognition" interchangeably. It should be noted that in psychoanalytic discourse the terms are not the same; identification signifies a recognition that is introjected, whereas an association is an external recognition.

5. Here, as throughout my discussion, I use the term "rhetoric" primarily to mean the language of poetry and to distinguish it from other forms of language and discourse. The language of poetry is produced when the rules of grammar are subject to the rules of the line of the poem.

6. Thomas Yingling provides a model for how to decode implicit instances of homosexual desire in Hart Crane's poetry. *Hart Crane and the Homosexual Text*, Chicago: University of Chicago Press, 1990. See also Eve Sedgwick, *Between Men: English Literature and Male Homosocial Desire*, New York: Columbia University Press, 1985.

## 1   CHRYSALIS UNBOUND: POEMS OF ORIGIN AND INITIATION

1. For a thorough discussion of identification and the way it functions in literary and psychoanalytic structures, see Diana Fuss, *Identification Papers*, New York: Routledge, 1995. While I am not concerned here

with an exploration of the politics of identifications as Fuss is, she cogently explains the ways in which identification produces self-recognition.

2. See "Three Essays on the Theory of Sexuality" and "Female Sexuality," in *The Freud Reader*, ed. Peter Gay, New York: W.W. Norton & Company, 1989. In "Female Sexuality" Freud tries to understand the development of sexuality, specifically in women. Freud attempts to posit normative female sexual development in a dynamic like the one he establishes for males, namely an Oedipus Complex, whereby a male's attachment to the opposite sex, the mother, leads the child into masculine development. This structure does not follow in the same way for women. Because Freud can only theorize the female via the male, he must reluctantly accept here that there is no neat parallelism between male and female sexual development.

3. These architectural spaces that are rhetorically constructed at a point in which language fails to convey an emotional accuracy approach the function of catachresis that I discuss in the third chapter. Catachresis, similarly, is a word that is used to approximate the meaning for a word for which no other single term exists. For example, the word "leg" as in "the legs of a table."

4. I use here a specifically psychoanalytic conception of identification. There has been some significant work done on the notion of identification in the study of cinematic texts. Here, identification can refer to the psychoanalytic notion as well as an Aristotelian concept of catharsis. In the discourse of film theory, identification means, as Murray Smith explains, responses, and in particular emotional responses, of spectators to fictional characters. At its most imagistic, this criticism sees identification as a kind of bondage. This helps me to make clear my own use of identification to mean a process not only of a sympathy and empathy but also, more specifically, a process of internalization. See Murray Smith, *Engaging Characters: Fiction, Emotion, and the Cinema*, Oxford: Clarendon Press, 1995.

5. Julia Kristeva, *Black Sun: Depression and Melancholia*, trans. Leon Roudiez, New York: Columbia University Press, 1989, 33–68.

6. Ann Douglas in a section called "Dismembering the Mother," employs a structure of repudiation and identification to discuss the similarities between Crane's and Ernest Hemingway's childhoods and mothers in *Terrible Honesty: Mongrel Manhattan in the 1920s*, New York: Noonday, 1995, 225–232.

7. Diana Fuss, *Identification Papers*, 5.

8. For a discussion of the normative status of heterosexuality, see Adrienne Rich, "Compulsory Heterosexuality and Lesbian Existence," in *Adrienne Rich's Poetry and Prose*, ed. Barbara Gelpi and Albert Gelpi, New York: W.W. Norton & Company, 1975, 203–224. Also for a discussion on the closet, see Eve Kosofsky Sedgwick, *Epistemology of the Closet*.

9. While Michel Foucault in *The History of Sexuality, vol. I*, argues that the confession transforms sex into discourse, Judith Butler extends his idea to say that the closet is a discursive space. *Gender Trouble*, New York: Routledge, 1990.

10. Evidence of homosexual status proves to be a surprisingly difficult endeavor. See *The Noel Coward Diaries*, ed. Graham Payn and Sheridan Morley, Boston: Little, Brown, 1982. The diaries of Coward and other public figures, such as Vaslav Nijinsky, where the public image/reputation is of a homosexual identity who had relationships with men, is in contrast to the representation of the self in the diaries where little or no textual instances exist other than references to their respective lovers' names. *The Diary of Vaslav Nijinsky*, ed. Joan Acocella, New York: Farrar, Straus and Giroux, 1999.

11. Sandra Gilbert, "Rituals of Inititation in Whitman and Dickinson," in *Walt Whitman of Mickle Street*, ed. Geoffrey Sill, Knoxville: The University of Tennessee Press, 1994, 169–170.

12. Ibid., 171.

13. Walt Whitman, *Leaves of Grass*, New York: W.W. Norton & Company, 1973, 246–253, lines 1–8. All references to Whitman are to this edition and will hereafter be cited parenthetically within the text.

14. Julia Kristeva discusses in depth the relationships between language and loss in her examination of melancholia, where she describes "loss" in connection with "negation" and "language." The lost object for Kristeva can be recovered through language; by discussing loss, the object can be invigorated and recovered. Conversely, by remaining silent, the object remains lost. Kristeva, however, describes psychic structures around loss, where here loss serves a fundamental poetic function. *Black Sun: Depression and Melancholia*, trans. Leon Roudiez, New York: Columbia University Press, 1989, 33–55.

15. Sigmund Freud, *Group Psychology and the Analysis of the Ego*, trans. and ed. James Strachey, New York: W.W. Norton, 1959, 39.

16. Phillip Brian Harper, *Framing the Margins*, New York: Oxford University Press, 1994, 203–204, n. 9.

17. Many of the "costs" involved with identification for Butler are also bound within the dynamics of politics with which she is concerned. Judith Butler, *Bodies That Matter*, New York: Routledge, 1993, 126.

18. James Merrill's memoir discusses his problematic sexual identity and the turmoil he experienced with his homosexuality. See *A Different Person*, New York: Knopf, 1993.

19. For a further discussion on the history of this poem, see Hart Crane, *O My Land, My Friends: The Selected Letters of Hart Crane*, ed. Langdon Hammer and Brom Weber, New York: Four Walls Eight Windows, 1997.

20. Hart Crane, *The Poems of Hart Crane*, ed. Marc Simon, New York: Liveright Publishing, 1986, 160–161, lines 1–4. All references to

Crane's poetry are to this edition and will hereafter be cited parenthetically within the text as line numbers.

21. The order in which the subject identifies and repudiates has meaning in the psychoanalytic context. Time factors into this dynamic to illustrate whether the subject identifies first and then repudiates or vice versa. This difference is not apparent in the context of poems; temporal difference does not factor here because there is not a subject but a literary text. This reinforces the difference between the developmental and literary of the psychoanalytic projects at hand.

22. Thomas Yingling, *Hart Crane and the Homosexual Text: New Thresholds, New Anatomies*, Chicago: University of Chicago Press, 1990, 182.

23. Kristeva, *Black Sun*, 11 and 140–172.

24. Crane, "At Melville's Tomb," 33.

25. Langdon Hammer confirms this when he writes that these images are, "decipherable but complexly encoded, complexly burdened parts of an inaccessible self, the fragments of a mutilated—because unrepresentable—whole." See Langdon Hammer, *Hart Crane & Allen Tate: Janus-Faced Modernism*, Princeton, New Jersey: Princeton University Press, 1993, 154.

26. Hammer implies the connected nature of sexual, creative, and personal identities, but he does not place them within an ambivalent structure when he writes: "['The Broken Tower'] describes the disseminative violence that Crane's poems, from the beginning, participate in and celebrate. For Crane, the entrance into poetry is imagined as a breaking or scattering of the whole of his desire, ambition, identity; it is a passage into a structure that is, paradoxically, destructuring." Ibid.

27. Freud replaces his libidinal and egoistic drives with those of life and death in "Beyond the Pleasure Principle," *The Freud Reader*, 594–625. Freud also addresses Eros and aggression and the contradictions in society as individuals strive for pleasure in his *Civilization and Its Discontents*, trans. James Strachey, New York: W.W. Norton, 1961.

28. *O My Land, My Friends: The Selected Letters of Hart Crane*, ed. Langdon Hammer and Brom Weber, New York: Four Walls Eight Windows, 1997, 454–457.

29. While Hammer theorizes Crane's images of rupture, he does not explain their function fully. When Kristeva writes about dialogue in the course of her discussion of melancholia, she affirms the importance of "phrases and sentences, according to the secondary processes of grammar and logic" because "language is a translation." In this way, disruptions in grammar and logic of language signify a speaking subject's emotional crisis. *Black Sun*, 40–42. Despite the fact that Kristeva here offers prescriptions to analysts, her ideas point out the degree to which the rhythms of discourse reflect emotional states and help me to read Crane's breaks as revelatory of his poetic crisis.

30. Lee Edelman notes that there is a "feminizing" here "through the connotation of 'slip' as a female undergarment in opposition to the

earlier 'jacket' [masculine] of stone." See *Transmemberment of Song: Hart Crane's Anatomies of Rhetoric and Desire*, Stanford: Stanford University Press, 1987, 270–271.

31. Crane's visionary poetics, here, works its way into the poems of Elizabeth Bishop; see her "The Unbeliever," where the figure of the gull represents the visionary tradition of poets, like Crane. *The Complete Poems*, New York: Farrar, Straus and Giroux, 1979, 22.

32. Lee Edelman writes of these final lines: "the ejaculatory scattering of this erotic 'shower' is performed under the aegis of the male and female both." Edelman correctly notes a combination of gendered images here but does not connect the "shower" to the religious themes of the poem.

33. It is interesting to note the frequency with which Crane attempts to define a space to house the emotions of his poems in *White Buildings*. For example, the repetition of "enough" in "My Grandmother's Love Letters." See also his long poems in the collection "For the Marriage of Fautus and Helen" and "Voyages," both of which I discuss in the third chapter.

34. Langdon Hammer points out that the imagery of ruptures begins in the title of "Repose of Rivers": "The poem's alliterative title introduces antithetical terms, linking stasis and motion, the singular and the plural, in anticipation of the oxymoronic figures that dominate the poem." Hammer, 167.

35. Harold Bloom and Robert Martin as quoted in Yingling, *Hart Crane and the Homosexual Text*, 139.

36. Cf. *Black Sun*, 40–42.

37. Elizabeth Bishop, "In the Waiting Room," in *Geography III*, New York: Noonday Press, 1988, 3, lines 1–7. Hereafter Bishop's poems will be cited parenthetically within the text as line numbers.

38. Images of asphyxiation and of drowned women often appear in Bishop's poetry. For example, see my discussions of "At the Fishhouses" and "The End of March." Bishop suffered from asthma, so she knew first hand the intense fear that results from the threat of a loss of oxygen.

39. See *The Selected Melanie Klein*, especially 181.

40. This recalls Fuss's idea that identification "produces self-recognition," and her connection between identifying and metaphor, which she calls the process of replacing "the one for the other." *Identification Papers*, 5.

41. See Bishop's letter to Frank Bidart in *One Art*, ed. Robert Giroux, New York: Farrar, Straus and Giroux, 1994, 545–546, where she writes that she went "to the library to look up that issue of the *National Geographic*." See also David Kalstone, *Becoming a Poet*, 245–246 and Bishop's discussion of the "infinite mischief" that comes from the "mixture of fact and fiction," *One Art*, 241, in Robert Lowell's poems based on personal letters.

42. James Joyce, *A Portrait of the Artist as a Young Man*, New York: Penguin Books, 1944, 15–16.

43. David Kalstone, *Becoming a Poet: Elizabeth Bishop with Marianne Moore and Robert Lowell*, New York: Noonday Press, 1989, 244–245.

44. Bishop writes to Dr Anny Baumann: "I've just sold *The New Yorker* the first poem I have been able to finish in over three years [In the Waiting Room]" on June 17, 1970. Bishop, *One Art*, ed. Robert Giroux, 528.

45. Jacques Lacan, "The Mirror Stage," in *Ecrits: A Selection*, trans. Alan Sheridan, New York: W.W. Norton, 1977, 1–7.

46. The work of Louis Althusser provides concrete examples of "recognition" in order to illustrate that we are "always already subjects" (172), and therefore Bishop here is confirming her status as a "concrete, individual, distinguishable and (naturally) irreplaceable subjects" (173). Louis Althusser, "Ideology and Ideological State Apparatuses (Notes toward an Investigation)" in *Lenin and Philosophy and Other Essays*, trans. Ben Brewster, New York: Monthly Review Press, 1971, 170–177. Althusser points out that "ideology hails or interpellates individuals as subjects"; in the course of a subject's identification there is first an unconscious, ideological recognition or "interpellation." Althusser is concerned with "recognition" and "ideology" in a political context and so his project is fundamentally different from mine; however, his exploration of "recognition" would be a fruitful place for further inquiry.

47. James Merrill, "Afterwords," in *Becoming a Poet*, New York: Noonday, 1989, 252.

48. Melanie Klein, "The Psycho-analytic Play Technique," in *Selected Melanie Klein*, ed. Juliet Mitchell, New York: The Free Press, 1986, 50–51.

49. Samuel Taylor Coleridge, "Frost at Midnight," in *Selected Poetry and Prose of Coleridge*, ed. Donald Stauffer, New York: Random House, 1951, 62–64.

50. Wallace Stevens, "The Sun This March," in *Wallace Stevens: The Collected Poems*, New York: Vintage Books, 1990, 133–134.

51. This aggressive act of violence highlights the speaker's masculine identity. The double displacement of the image of the speaker as a child whom he does not at first recognize foregrounds the speaker's guilt over his aggressive act against his parents. Cf. Melanie Klein on the combination of guilt and aggression with respect to the parent. *Love, Hate and Reparation*, 70–71 and 85.

52. Frederic Jameson defines postmodernism as being characterized by, among other things, a depthlessness of subject matter. See his *Postmodernism: Or, The Cultural Logic of Late Capitalism*, Durham: Duke University Press, 1991, especially 1–54.

53. Merrill writes most notably of this address in the poem titled, "18 West 11th Street," collected in *Braving the Elements*.

54. J. D. McClatchy, "On *Water Street*," in *James Merrill: Essays in Criticism*, ed. David Lehman and Charles Berger, Ithaca: Cornell University Press, 1983.

## 2 Anatomy of a Mother

1. Hart Crane, "A Letter to Harriet Monroe," in *Hart Crane: The Collected Poems & Selected Letters and Prose*, ed. Brom Weber, New York: Liveright Publishing 1966, 234–240. Lee Edelman, in a reading of Crane's rhetorical dynamics, embraces descriptions of Crane's poems as obscure because he sees such comments as aligning the poems within the rhetorical structures they occupy. *Transmemberment of Song: Hart Crane's Anatomies of Rhetoric and Desire*, Stanford: Stanford University Press, 1987.

2. As quoted in Brett Millier, *Elizabeth Bishop: Life and the Memory of It*, Berkeley: University of California Press, 1993, 184.

3. In my discussion of the Mother, I differentiate between the biographical "mother" and the mother that is both the biographical and the figurative one, the "Mother," through the use of a capital letter.

4. For a discussion of "disseminative violence" in Crane's poetry, see Langdon Hammer, *Hart Crane & Allen Tate: Janus-Faced Modernism*, Princeton: Princeton University Press, 1993, 154.

5. Sigmund Freud, *The Ego and the Id*, in *The Freud Reader*, ed. Peter Gay, New York: W.W. Norton & Company, 1989, 638.

6. Melanie Klein, "Love, Guilt and Reparation," in *Love, Hate and Reparation*, New York: Norton, 1964, 58–59. For a detailed discussion of the figure of the mother, this essay, and Klein's work in general, see Carolyn Dever, *Death and the Mother from Dickens to Freud: Victorian Fictions and the Anxiety of Origins*, New York: Cambridge University Press, 1998.

7. In his essay "Femininity" (1932), Freud asserts the importance of gender categories when he writes: "When you meet a human being, the first distinction you make is 'male or female?' and you are accustomed to make the distinction with unhesitating certainty." Freud, however, does not decode the significations contained within these highly loaded, often overdetermined, terms, "male" and "female." *Sigmund Freud: The Standard Edition*, vol. XXII, trans. James Strachey, London: The Hogarth Press, 1961, 112–135.

8. "Love, Guilt and Reparation," 105.

9. Leo Bersani in *The Freudian Body* points out self-contradictory theory and moments of theoretical collapse in Freud's work. Using a deconstructive model, he calls for a reading of Freud's texts as works of art in order to save them from dismissals and charges against their scientific validity. New York: Columbia University Press, 1986.

10. *O My Land, My Friends*, ed. Langdom Hammer and Brom Weber, New York: Four Walls Eight Windows, 1997, 52–53.

11. Hart Crane, "Modern Poetry," in *Hart Crane The Complete Poems & Selected Letters and Prose*, ed. Brom Weber, New York: Liveright Publishing Corp., 1966, 261.

12. Ibid., 262.

13. Hart Crane, "Modern Poetry," in *Hart Crane The Complete Poems &* *Selected Letters and Prose*, 261. See also John Irwin's "Hart Crane's 'Logic of Metaphor,' " in *Critical essays on Hart Crane*, ed. David Clark, Boston: G.K. Hall, 1982, 210–212. Edelman also address Crane's "logic of metaphor." He argues that Crane misleadingly characterizes his poetic practice as a "logic of metaphor" and rewords it as an "ideology of catachresis." Edelman, 8. I engage more fully with catachresis in Crane as well as in Bishop and Merrill in the third chapter.

14. Crane, "A Letter to Harriet Monroe," 234.

15. As I note later in my discussion of Merrill's work, there is a difference between explicit discussion of love for a man and mere references to him within a poem.

16. For an account of gay male life and its social reception in New York before World War II, see George Chauncey, *Gay New York*, New York: HarperCollins, 1994.

17. Eve Kosofsky Sedgwick explores the importance of the homo/ hetero-sexual definition in Western thought, which she sees as an exacerbated cultural site over the issue of whether it is of interest to a minority or whether the binary definition of sexualities is an issue that cuts across every agency and subjectivity in the culture. Sedgwick assumes that the relations of the closet—the relations of the known and unknown, explicit and inexplicit around homosexual and hetero-sexual definitions—have the potential for being revealing about speech acts more generally. I contend that the relation of the explicit and implicit with regard to the closet produces a tension in language that can be revealed here through rhetorical analysis. See *Epistemology of the Closet*, Berkeley: University of California Press, 1990.

18. Eve Kosofsky Sedgwick notes the rhetorical figuration of the closet, which she discusses as a performative speech act, when she writes:

> But, in the vicinity of the closet, even what *counts* as a speech act is problematized on a perfectly routine basis. "Closetedness" itself is a performance initiated as such by the speech act of a silence—not a particular silence, but a silence that accrues particularity by fits and starts, in relation to the discourse that surrounds and differentially constitutes it. (*Epistemology*, 3)

19. Jacques Lacan, "The Mirror Stage as formative of the function of the I," in *Ecrits: A Selection*, trans. Alan Sheridan, New York: W.W. Norton, 1977, 1–7.

20. Ann Douglass, *Terrible Honesty: Mongrel Manhattan in the 1920s*, New York: Noonday Press, 1995, 228. For a reading of homosexual desire in Crane's poetry see also Thomas Yingling, *Hart Crane and the Homosexual Text*, Chicago: University of Chicago Press, 1990.

21. *O My Land*, 50.

22. "Love, Guilt and Reparation," 102–103.

23. *O My Land*, 305.

24. Ann Douglass, *Terrible Honesty: Mongrel Manhattan in the 1920s*, New York: Noonday Press, 1995.

25. Hart Crane, *O My Land, My Friends: The Selected Letters of Hart Crane*, ed. Langdom Hammer and Brom Weber, New York: Four Walls Eight Windows, 1997, 3.

26. Grace Crane insists here on her view of Crane as a narcissistic extension of herself.

27. Bishop's observations and descriptions of details have been compared to those of a painter's by some critics like David Kalstone and Meyer Shapiro. Bishop painted a number of watercolors with an equally detailed eye that is reminiscent of Vermeer. At the same time, her detail recalls the work of one of Bishop's favorite artists, Joseph Cornell, whose box collages have a quasi-scientific feel in which objects are arranged as a three-dimensional still life under glass. See *Exchanging Hats: Elizabeth Bishop's Paintings*, ed. William Benton, New York: Farrar, Straus and Giroux, 1996. See also Bishop's translation of Octavio Paz's poem "Objects & Apparitions," in *Geography III* that is dedicated to Cornell.

28. Elizabeth Bishop, *One Art: Letters*, selected and ed. Robert Giroux, New York: Farrar, Straus and Giroux, 1994, 561–562.

29. For a discussion of the role of truthfulness in Bishop's work, see Lee Edelman, "The Geography of Gender: Elizabeth Bishop's 'In the Waiting Room,' " in *Contemporary Literature*, 26.2, 1985, 179–196.

30. Ibid.

31. Michel Foucault, *The History of Sexuality, Volume One: An Introduction*, trans. Robert Hurley, New York: Vintage Books, 1978, 58–59.

32. Frank Bidart, "Elizabeth Bishop," *The Threepenny Review*, no. 58 (Summer 1994), 6–7.

33. Barbara Johnson, *The Feminist Difference*, Cambridge: Harvard University Press, 1998, 123.

34. Victoria Harrison, *Elizabeth Bishop's Poetics of Intimacy*, New York: Cambridge University press, 1993, 20.

35. Anne Colwell, *Inscrutable Houses: Metaphors of the Body in the Poems of Elizabeth Bishop*, Tuscaloosa: University of Alabama Press, 1997, 74.

36. Klein, 104.

37. Judith Hughes explains that Klein held a "long-cherished intention: 'to write a full case study of a child's analysis . . .' When one reads Klein's *Narrative of a Child Analysis*, it quickly becomes apparent that her title is a misnomer: there is no story whatsoever." *Reshaping the Psychoanalytic Domain*, Berkeley: University of California Press, 1989, 76. Klein's prioritizing of *interpretation* over *narrative* reinforces her distance from the literary in favor of metalinguistic commentary. Whereas Freud works within and against the literary (Cf. Fuss, *Identification Papers*, 5), Klein seeks to circumscribe it.

38. Lorrie Goldensohn notes that the poem's "contracted bodies on the map are . . . conspicuously touchable" and that Bishop "treats space in this poem as if it were both space and the ideation of space." Her two-fold description of space and its alteration reinforces my argument on the manipulation of perspective. *Elizabeth Bishop: The Biography of a Poetry*, New York: Columbia University, 1992, 105.

39. Brett Millier makes clear Bishop's poetic practice of portraying "a mind thinking rather than reposing." See Millier, *Elizabeth Bishop: Life and the Memory of It*, Berkeley: University of California Press, 1993, 77.

40. Harrison, 45.

41. Goldensohn, 109–110.

42. Diana Fuss argues that there are blurred boarders between inside/heterosexuality and outside/homosexuality and that the homosexual is a specter that crosses these boarders. She figures the ghosting of the homosexual as the simultaneous appearance and disappearance into the closet. *Inside/out: Lesbian Theories, Gay Theories*, New York: Routledge, 1991. See also Terry Castle, *The Apparitional Lesbian*, New York: Columbia University Press, 1993.

43. Qtd. in Millier, 79–80.

44. The extent to which the sestina is a highly traditional poetic form, often associated with Sir Philip Sidney's double sestina "Ye Goatherd Gods," aligns Bishop's poems in this form with an attempt to forge a connection with the patriarchal lineage of poetry in English. According to a glossary of versification, "The sestina, the most complicated of the verse forms initiated by the twelfth century wandering singers known as troubadours, is composed of six stanzas of six lines each, followed by an envoy, or concluding stanza, that incorporates lines or words used before: in this case the *words* (instead of *rhymes*) end each line" *The Norton Anthology of Poetry*, third edition, New York: W.W. Norton, 1983, 1418.

45. Helen Vendler's discussion of the "inscrutable house" (l. 39) in Bishop's second sestina, "Sestina," helps me to understand the poet's need to subsume the maternal as food in "A Miracle," when Vendler claims that for Bishop's speakers, "nothing is more enigmatic than the heart of the domestic scene." "Domestication, Domesticity, and the Otherworldly," in *Elizabeth Bishop and Her Art*, Ann Arbor: University of Michigan Press, 1983, 33.

46. For a discussion of introjection as it is associated with cannibalism (a literalizing of the desire to ingest the mother) and Roman Catholic communion, see Freud, *Totem and Taboo*, trans. James Strachey, New York: W.W. Norton & Company, 1950. See also Kristeva, *Black Sun*.

47. George Herbert, "The Collar," in *The English Poems of George Herbert*, ed. C. A. Patrides. London: J.M. Dent and Sons, 1974, 161–162.

48. David Bromwich, "Elizabeth Bishop's Dream Houses," in *Raritan*, Summer 1984, 77–94.

49. Ian Parker, *Psychoanalytic Culture: Psychoanalytic Discourse in Western Society*, London: Sage Publications, 1997, 90.

50. Mitchell, 28.

51. Millier, 267.

52. For examples of this, see Bishop's poems in which the speaker is reluctant to participate in an awakened world around her, such as "The Man-Moth" and the "Sleeping" poems.

53. The absence of religious faith and of religion's potential for redemption in Bishop's poems supports this reading.

54. *Letters*, 259.

55. *Letters*, 227.

56. James Merrill, *The Changing Light at Sandover*, New York: Alfred A. Knopf, 1982.

57. Merrill's poems that are comparable to father–son narratives like "The Broken Home" can, thus, be read as inherently concerned with the mother through her noticeable absence or lack of reference to the speaker's sense of domestic spaces.

58. James Merrill, *A Different Person*, New York: Alfred A. Knopf, 1993, 169. Hereafter, I will refer to this text parenthetically as DP and the page number. The use of italics here is Merrill's. Throughout his memoir, Merrill distinguishes between the person he was at the time of the narrative's action—predominantly 1950s—and the person he is as he is writing primarily through the use of italics.

59. Robert Lowell, "Memories of West Street and Lepke," in *Life Studies*, New York: Farrar, Straus and Giroux, 1959.

60. "An Interview with Donald Sheehan," in *Recitative: Prose by James Merrill*, San Francisco: North Point Press, 1986, 24.

61. William Butler Yeats, "Sailing to Byzantium," in *The Collected Works of W.B. Yeats*, vol. I, ed. Richard Finneran, New York: Macmillan Publishing, 1989, 193–194, line one.

62. Cavafy, "Days of 1908," lines 22–31, trans. Daniel Mendelsohn, *The Hudson Review*, volume L, no. 1 (Spring 1997). For a translation of Cavafy's complete poems, see *The Complete Poems of Cavafy*, trans. Rae Dalven, New York: Harcourt Brace & Co., 1976.

63. J. D. McClatchy, "Braving the Elements," in *Critical Essays on James Merrill*, ed. Guy Rotella, New York: G.K. Hall, 1996, 236.

## CODA: LITERARY MOTHERS

1. T. S. Eliot, "Tradition and the Individual Talent," in *The Norton Anthology of Modern and Contemporary Poetry*, ed. Jahan Ramazan et al., New York: Norton, 2003, 941–947.

2. Ibid.

3. Justin Kaplan, *Walt Whitman: A Life*, New York: Simon and Schuster, 1980, 62.

4. Diane Middlebrook provides helpful readings of the figure of the maternal in these two poems. See her *Walt Whitman and Wallace Stevens*, Ithaca: Cornell University Press, 1974, 96–98. There is a difference between the figuration of the mother as "maternal" and as the "Mother." The maternal connotes motherly attributes such as nurturer and ambivalence, whereas the figuration of the Mother incorporates the multiplicity of significations that I have been describing, combining the maternal as well as the specter of the mother.

5. Melanie Klein, "The Psycho-Analytic Play Technique," in *The Selected Melanie Klein*, ed. Juliet Mitchell, New York: The Free Press, 1986, 50–54.

6. Sigmund Freud, "The Uncanny," in *Sigmund Freud: Collected Papers*, vol. 4, trans. Alix Strachey, New York: Basic Books, 1959, 368–407.

7. Barbara Johnson, *The Critical Difference: Essays in the Contemporary Rhetoric of Reading*, Baltimore: Johns Hopkins University Press, 1980.

8. I take this notion of one poet doing battle with another and breaking free to find her own poetic voice from Harold Bloom, *The Anxiety of Influence: A Theory of Poetry*, New York: Oxford University Press, 1973.

9. The best and most thorough discussion of Bishop's relationships—both social as well as creative—is by David Kalstone in his *Becoming a Poet: Elizabeth Bishop with Marianne Moore and Robert Lowell*, New York: Noonday Press, 1989. See also Brett Millier, *Elizabeth Bishop*, Berkeley: The University of California Press, 1993. Joanne Feit Diehl, *Elizabeth Bishop and Marianne Moore: The Psychodynamics of Creativity*, Princeton: Princeton University Press, 1993.

10. Elizabeth Bishop's reflection is quoted from David Kaltone, *Becoming a Poet*, 9.

11. Marianne Moore, "Marriage," in *The Norton Anthology of Literature by Women*, ed. Sandra Gilbert and Susan Gubar, New York: W.W. Norton & Company, 1985, 1502–1509, lines 1–8. All references to this poem are to this edition and will hereafter be cited in the text by line numbers.

12. Elizabeth Bishop, "Efforts of Affection: A Memoir of Marianne Moore," in *The Collected Prose*, ed. Robert Giroux, New York: Farrar, Straus and Giroux, 1984, 121–156.

13. In the opening paragraph of "Effort of Affection," Bishop explains that her title is a variation on the title of Moore's poem "Efforts and Affection" and that Moore, in inscribing the book to Bishop, crossed out the "and" and wrote "of." Bishop's explanation does not prevent my own, despite the apparent contradiction. Rather, Moore's reinscription might also signify her own parallel feelings of ambivalence to Bishop.

14. James Merrill, *A Different Person*, New York: Alfred A. Knopf, 1993, 4.
15. Robert Lowell, *Notebook*, New York: Noonday, 1970, 234–236.
16. James Merrill, "An Interview with J. D. McClatchy," in *Recitative: Prose by James Merrill*, ed. J. D. McClatchy, San Francisco: North Point Press, 1986, 62–83.
17. Rainer Maria Rilke, "Archaic Torso of Apollo," in *The Selected Poems of Rainer Maria Rilke*, trans. Stephen Mitchell, New York: Vintage Books, 1989, lines 13–14.
18. Rilke, "The Duino Elegies—The First Elegy," Ibid., 151.
19. Sigmund Freud, *Letters*, as quoted in Lawrence Durrell, *Justine*, New York: E.P. Dutton & Co., 1957, epigraph.

## 3  BURNT MATCHES, OR THE ART OF LOVE

1. Wallace Stevens, "Add This to Rhetoric," in *Wallace Stevens: The Collected Poems*, New York: Vintage Books, 1982, 198–199, lines 1–5 and 10–12.
2. Emerson as quoted by Harold Bloom in *Wallace Stevens: The Poems of Our Climate*, Ithaca: Cornell University Press, 1976, 143.
3. James Merrill, "A Renewal," in *The Country of a Thousand Years of Peace*, New York: Atheneum, 1983, 15.
4. Consider, for example, the diverse import of love poems, such as Rilke's "Orpheus. Eurydice. Hermes." Here, the archetypal lovers, Orpheus and Eurydice, are each isolated, and when Orpheus finally recovers Eurydice in the underworld, she does not understand or recognize him. *The Selected Poems of Rainer Maria Rilke*, trans. Stephen Mitchell, New York: Vintage Books, 1982, 48–53. See also Anne Sexton, *Love Poems*, Boston: Houghton Mifflin, 1969.
5. Allen Grossman explains how poems allude to the "authentic speech" they seek to represent. "Authentic speech is speech that proceeds from the reputed source; and the reputed source of speech is always general humanity." He seems to postulate an idea of poetry along the lines of a Derridian notion of citationality, whereby poetic language is always "alluding" to a prior speech. See Allen Grossman with Mark Halliday, *The Sighted Singer: Two Works on Poetry for Readers and Writers*, Baltimore: Johns Hopkins University Press, 1992, 85–88.
6. Plato, *Phaedrus and Letters VII and VII*, trans. Walter Hamilton, New York: Penguin Classics, 1973.
7. While still the language of poetry, I complicate my notion of rhetoric and base my ideas on it and the citationality of language on the following works. Antony Easthope argues for a "poetic discourse" which I revise and refer to simply as "rhetoric" in *Poetry As Discourse*. New York: Methuen, 1983. Stanley Fish, "Rhetoric," in *Critical Terms for Literary Study*, ed. Frank Lentricchia and Thomas McLaughlin, Chicago: The University of Chicago Press, 1987.

Jacques Derrida writes: "Could a performative [statement] succeed if its formulation did not repeat a 'coded' or iterable utterance . . . if it were not identifiable in some way as a 'citation'?" in "Signature Event Context," in *A Derrida Reader: Between the Blinds*, ed. Peggy Kamuf, New York: Columbia University Press, 1991. Judith Butler continues to explore the nature of the citation of performative language in "Critically Queer," in *Bodies That Matter*, New York: Routledge, 1993, esp. 224–234. While Derrida and Butler confine their analyses to performative statements, such as "I pronounce you man and wife" in the marriage ceremony, I extend their ideas to examine a citation within genres of poetry.

8. Lee Edelman, "Return to Freud." A paper delivered at the 1998 MLA Convention in a session called "Queer Counternarrative Pressures in Film."

9. "Love, Guilt and Reparation," 102–103.

10. Julia Kristeva, *Black Sun: Depression and Melancholia*, trans. Leon Roudiez, New York: Columbia University Press, 1989, 166–167.

11. *Oxford English Dictionary*, second edition, Oxford: Clarendon Press, 1989.

12. For an explanation of catachresis and the production of affect, see Karen McKinnon, "Catachresis and the Identity of Opposites: Alexandria as Transitional Object in Lawrence Durrell's *Justine*." An unpublished M.A. thesis, CUNY Graduate Center, 1992.

13. Catharsis is not only "the purification of emotions by vicarious experience (drama)" but also has a psychological meaning as "the process of relieving an abnormal excitement by re-establishing the association of the emotion with the memory or idea of the event which was the first cause of it, and of eliminating it by abreaction," *Oxford English Dictionary*. See also Aristotle on catharsis and metaphor, *Poetics*, trans. Richard Janko, Cambridge: Hackett Publishing Co., 1987.

14. R. W. B. Lewis, *The Poetry of Hart Crane: A Critical Study*, Princeton: Princeton University Press, 1967, 93; see also his chapter on "For the Marriage of Faustus and Helen," for an explanatory reading, 80–119.

15. Unterecker, 354–356 and 360–364.

16. *O My Land, My Friends*, 198.

17. Thomas Gray, "Ode on a Distant Prospect of Eton College," in *The poems of Thomas Gray, William Collins, Oliver Goldsmith*, ed. Roger Lonsdale, New York: Longman Group Limited, 1969, 54–63, lines 51–54.

18. John Hollander, *The Figure of Echo*, Berkeley: University of California Press, 1981, 123.

19. Walt Whitman, "Song of Myself," in *Leaves of Grass*, New York: W.W. Norton, 1973, 38–39.

20. Herman Melville, *Moby Dick, or The Whale*, New York: Penguin Classics Books, 1988, 5.

21. Julia Kristeva, *Tales of Love*, trans. Leon Roudiez, New York: Columbia University Press, 1987, 6. My discussion of the Mother as both an extension of the self and an idealized figure suggests that the distance between narcissism and idealization is not always distinct.

22. Samuel Taylor Coleridge, "The Rime of the Ancient Mariner," in *Selected Poetry and Prose of Coleridge*, ed. Donald A. Stauffer, New York: The Modern Library College Edition, 1951, 6–24.

23. Wallace Stevens, "The Poems of Our Climate," in *The Collected Poems*, New York: Vintage Books, 1982.

24. Leo Bersani aptly notes the ability of love to blur the identity of the artist and provides an implicit reason for Crane's excitement in, and need for, love: "Art resembles love in that both the lover and the artist go outside themselves; they lose themselves in others." "Artists in Love," *Literature and Psychoanalysis*, ed. Edith Kurzweil and William Phillips, New York: Columbia University Press, 1983, 348.

25. *O My Land*, 173–175.

26. Hammer, 182.

27. For a discussion of gay male cruising in New York City, see George Chauncey, *Gay New York*.

28. Margaret Dickie begins her discussion of Bishop's love poems with a summary of critical views on Bishop's lack of poems that deal explicitly with love. Dickie, nonetheless, devotes a considerable amount of attention to uncollected poems. See Dickie, *Stein, Bishop, & Rich: Lyrics of Love, War, & Place*, Chapel Hill: The University of North Carolina Press, 1997, 82–103. Lorrie Goldensohn writes that "there are really only a handful [of poems] that talk about love," in *Elizabeth Bishop*, New York: Columbia University Press, 1992, 29. There is an anxiety on the part of some critics that Bishop should have written more love poems, especially poems that deal with expressions of lesbian love. This desire, however, approaches the misconception that because Bishop is a woman poet, she should write about traditionally feminine subjects like love. Of course, writing "openly" about lesbian love would for many mid-twentieth-century readers undermine the traditional expectations of the love poem.

29. *One Art*, 24; "Elizabeth Bishop," 6.

30. Lowell has written about this day with Bishop most notably in his poem "Water," which opens the collection *For the Union Dead*. This collection also includes "The Scream," a poem Lowell creates out of Bishop's short story "In the Village." While he acknowledges her influence on "The Scream," he makes no dedication before "Water." See, *Life Studies and For the Union Dead*, New York: Noonday Press, 1956. Lowell later reworked "Water" into the first of his sonnets "Four Poems for Elizabeth Bishop" under the title, "Water 1948." These poems are from Lowell's later poems when he reworked letters and conversations into sonnets. *Notebook*, New York: Farrar, Straus and Giroux, 1967, 234–235.

31. *One Art*, 344–346.
32. Barbara Johnson, *The Feminist Difference*, Cambridge: Harvard University Press, 1998, 102.
33. Goldensohn, 27–28. There seems to be some discrepancies among the versions of this poem. When compared with the text reprinted in Millier's biography (177), she alternates between "marvellous" in line one and "marvelous" in line two, whereas Goldensohn consistently writes "marvellous." Also, Goldensohn writes line four, "To feel the air clear," whereas Millier's version reads, "To feel the air suddenly clear." I have used Millier's version of this line because it is consistent with Bishop's tendency toward repetition. Bishop rarely capitalizes the first word of each line, as she does here; she does occasionally do this in poems like "The Burglar of Babylon," and many of her early poems that were written between 1927 and 1934. See "Poems Written in Youth," section in Bishop's *Complete Poems*.
34. *One Art*, 241.
35. Millier, 247–248.
36. *One Art*, 241.
37. Terry Castle, *The Apparitional Lesbian*, New York: Columbia University Press, 1993, 34–45.
38. Webster's New World Dictionary, third edition, ed. Victoria Neufelt, New York: Simon and Schuster, 1988.
39. Judith Hughes, *Reshaping the Psychoanalytic Domain: The Work of Melanie Klein, W.R.D. Fairbairn, and W.D. Winnicott*, Berkeley: University of California Press, 1989, 59–61.
40. For a further discussion of the paradox of love, wherein the poet searches outside the self for someone to invade or invade the self, see Bersani "Artists in Love," 348–349.
41. Hughes, 76. See my chapter two, n. 38.
42. *Transmemberment*, 197–198.
43. See Julia Kristeva for her explanations of "cannibalism" and "cannibalistic solitude" as they manifest themselves with respect to the mother and to depression. *Black Sun*, 71–79. Also, Freud, *Totem and Taboo*, trans. James Strachey, New York: W.W. Norton, 1950.
44. Kristeva writes: "mourning conceals an aggressiveness toward the lost object." Bishop's speaker seems to follow the structures of aggression and ambivalence that Kristeva describes. For more on aggression and its connections with language and the melancholic subject, see Julia Kristeva, *Black Sun*, 11.
45. Cf. e.g., John Donne, "The Cannonization," *John Donne's Poetry*, ed. Arthur L. Clements, New York: W.W. Norton & Company, 1992, 8.
46. Helen Vendler, *Music*, 370. Barbara Johnson points out many important differences between male and female literature in *The Feminist Difference*, Cambridge: Harvard University Press, 1998.

47. Brett Millier provides an interesting discussion of the seventeen available drafts of "One Art" and how Bishop worked her poem into its final form, see 507–512.

48. In this way, Bishop's "One Art" is similar in nature to the meta-poem "Jordan (I)" by her beloved George Herbert, in which the poet expresses his fondness for the plain over the artful. George Herbert, *The English Poems of George Herbert*, ed. C. A. Patrides, London: J.M. Dent and Sons, 1974, 75.

49. See the interview with James Merrill in "Contemporary Literature," 9 (Winter, 1968), 1–2, For a discussion of the conventions of the "confessional" mode of poetry, see Marjorie G. Perloff, *The Poetic Art of Robert Lowell*, Ithaca: Cornell University Press, 1973. In the third chapter of this work, Perloff explores the conventions of the "confessional" by examining the poems in Lowell's *Life Studies* collection from 1959, poems that thematize the poet's troubled marriage, patrician family history, and manic depressive episodes into brutally frank and intimate-seeming poems.

50. Eric Murphy Selinger, "James Merrill's Masks of Eros, Masques of Love," in *Critical Essays on James Merrill*, ed. Guy Rotella, New York: G.K. Hall and Co., 1996, 145–174.

51. Cf. my discussion of "Days of 1935" and "Days of 1971" in chapter two. See also Merrill, "Days of 1941 and '44" in *Late Settings*, New York: Atheneum, 1985, 23–25.

52. Kleo, also written as Kyria Clio, was "JM and DJ's cleaning lady in Athens"; Clio is also the Greek muse of history. She appears in several of Merrill's poems. See Robert Polito, *A Reader's Guide to James Merrill's The Changing Light at Sandover*, Ann Arbor: The University of Michigan Press, 1994, 43.

53. Wallace Stevens's dictum is quoted in a discussion about Hermes's function within Merrill's work by Stephen Yenser in "Metamorphoses," in *Poetry: James Merrill, A Memorial Issue*, September 1995.

54. W. B. Yeats, "Coole and Ballylee, 1931," in *William Butler Yeats: Selected Poems and Three Plays*, ed. M. L. Rosenthal, New York: Collier Books, 1962.

55. Eric Selinger suggests my point when he writes of this poem: "The art of love is an *art* at last." "James Merrill's Masks of Eros, Masques of Love," 170.

56. Julia Kristeva, *Tales of Love*, trans. Leon Roudiez, New York: Columbia University Press, 1987, 379–383.

57. For a comparison of an early poem in which the poet combines the themes of love and art, see Merrill, "The Broken Bowl," from *First Poems* (1951).

58. Stevens, "The Idea of Order at Key West," 128.

59. James Merrill, "Her Craft," in *Elizabeth Bishop and Her Art*, ed. Lloyd Schwartz and Sybil Estess, Ann Arbor: The University of Michigan Press, 1983, 241.

## AFTERWORD

1. Auden is present in Merrill's poems primarily as a stylistic influence. Auden's poetry teaches Merrill to use a formal and symbolic verse, written in conversational language.
2. "Elizabeth Bishop," 6.
3. I do not mean to suggest that the legacies of Crane, Bishop, and Merrill can only be inherited by gay male poets. While my considerations could consider female poets, such as May Swenson and Louise Gluck, Bidart, Cole, and Doty are especially obvious choices because of their explicit reworking of these poetic forbears.
4. Frank Bidart, "To the Dead," in *In the Western Night: Collected Poems 1965–1990*, New York: Farrar, Straus and Giroux, 1990, 3.
5. Frank Bidart. "For the Twentieth Century," in *Music Like Dirt*, Louisville: Sarabande Books, 2002, lines 13–14.
6. Bidart, "Lament For the Makers" (l. 2–4), ibid.
7. Henri Cole, *The Visible Man*, New York: Alfred A. Knopf, 1998.
8. While the immediate influences for "Apollo" are Stevens' "aspectual lyrics" and Keats' "Odes," the poems of *The Visible Man* when read together reveal that there is much derived from Bishop's and Merrill's surfaces and mannerisms.
9. Mark Doty, "Demolition" and "Days of 1981," in *My Alexandria*, Chicago: University of Illinois Press, 1993, 1–3 and 7–10.
10. Mark Doty, "At the Boatyard," *Atlantis*, New York: HarperPerennial, 1995, 29–31.

# BIBLIOGRAPHY

Althusser, Louis. *Lenin and Philosophy and Other Essays.* Trans. Ben Brewster. New York: Monthly Review Press, 1971.

Aristotle. *Poetics.* Trans. Richard Janko. Cambridge: Hackett Publishing, 1987.

Ashbery, John. *Selected Poems.* New York: Penguin Books, 1985.

Auden, W. H. *Selected Poems.* Ed. Edward Mendelson. New York: Vintage Books, 1976.

Barthes, Roland. "The Death of the Author." *The Rustle of Language.* Trans. Richard Howard. Berkeley: The University of California Press, 1989.

Bersani, Leo. "Artists in Love." *Literature and Psychoanalysis.* Ed. Edith Kurzweil and William Phillips. New York: Columbia University Press, 1983.

———. *The Freudian Body.* New York: Columbia University Press, 1986.

Berthoff, Warner. *Hart Crane: A Re-Introduction.* Minneapolis: University of Minnesota Press, 1989.

Bidart, Frank. "Elizabeth Bishop." *The Threepenny Review,* no. 58 (Summer 1994).

———. *In the Western Night: Collected Poems 1965–1990.* New York: Farrar, Straus and Giroux, 1990.

———. *Music Like Dirt.* Louisville: Sarabande Books Quarternote Chapbook Series, 2002.

Bishop, Elizabeth. *The Collected Prose.* New York: Farrar, Straus and Giroux, 1984.

———. *The Complete Poems 1927–1979.* New York: Farrar, Straus and Giroux, 1983.

———. *Exchanging Hats: Elizabeth Bishop's Paintings.* Ed. William Benton. New York: Farrar, Straus and Giroux, 1996.

———. *Geography III.* New York, Farrar, Straus and Giroux, 1984.

———. *One Art: Letters.* Selected and edited by Robert Giroux. New York, Farrar, Straus and Giroux, 1993.

Bloom, Harold. *The Anxiety of Influence.* New York: Oxford University Press, 1973.

———, ed. *Modern Critical Views: Elizabeth Bishop.* New York: Chelsea House Publishers, 1985.

———. *Wallace Stevens: The Poems of Our Climate.* Ithaca: Cornell University Press, 1976.

Bromwich, David. "Elizabeth Bishop's Dream-Houses." *Raritan,* 4 (Summer 1984: 77–94).

Butler, Judith. *Gender Trouble: Feminism and the Subversion of Identity.* New York: Routledge, 1990.

———. *Bodies that Matter.* New York: Routledge, 1994.

Castle, Terry. *The Apparitional Lesbian: Female Homosexuality and Modern Culture.* New York: Columbia University Press, 1993.

Cavafy, C. P. *The Complete Poems of Cavafy.* Trans. Rae Dalven. New York: Harcourt Brace & Co., 1976.

———. "Days of 1908." Trans. Daniel Mendelsohn. *The Hudson Review*, vol. L, no. I (Summer 1997).

Chauncey, George. *Gay New York.* New York: HarperCollins, 1994.

Clark, David, ed. *Critical Essays on Hart Crane.* Boston: G.K. Hall and Co., 1982.

———. *The Merrill Studies in The Bridge.* Columbus: Charles E. Merrill Publishing Co., 1970.

Cole, Henri. *The Look of Things.* New York: Alfred A. Knopf, 1995.

———. *The Visible Man.* New York: Alfred A. Knopf, 1998.

———. *The Zoo Wheel of Knowledge.* New York: Alfred A. Knopf, 1989.

Coleridge, Samuel Taylor. *Selected Poetry and Prose of Coleridge.* Ed. Donald Stauffer. New York: The Modern Library College Edition, 1951.

Colomina, Beatriz, ed. *Sexuality and Space: Princeton Papers on Architecture.* Princeton: Princeton Architectural Press, 1992.

Colwell, Anne. *Inscrutable Houses.* Tuscaloosa: University of Alabama Press, 1997.

Crane, Hart. *The Complete Poems and Selected Letters and Prose.* Ed. Brom Weber. New York: Liveright, 1966.

———. *O My Land, My Friends: The Selected Letters of Hart Crane.* Ed. Langdon Hammer and Brom Weber. New York: Four Walls Eight Windows, 1997.

———. *The Poems of Hart Crane.* Ed. Marc Simon. New York: Liveright, 1986.

De Lauretis, Theresa. *Technologies of Gender: Essays on Theory, Film, and Fiction.* Bloomington: Indiana University Press, 1987.

Derrida, Jacques. "Signature Event Context." *A Derrida Reader: Between the Blinds.* Ed. Peggy Kamuf. New York: Columbia University Press, 1991.

Dever, Carolyn. *Death and the Mother from Dickens to Freud.* New York: Cambridge University Press, 1998.

Dickie, Margaret. *Stein, Bishop, & Rich: Lyrics of Love, War, & Place.* Chapel Hill: The University of North Carolina Press, 1997.

Diehl, Joanne Feit. *Elizabeth Bishop and Marianne Moore: The Psychodynamics of Creativity.* Princeton: Princeton University Press, 1993.

Donne, John. *John Donne's Poetry.* Ed. Arthur Clements. New York: W.W. Norton, 1992.

Doty, Mark. *Atlantis: Poems.* New York: HarperPerennial, 1995.

———. *My Alexandria.* Chicago: University of Illinois Press, 1993.

Douglas, Ann. *Terrible Honesty: Mongrel Manhattan in the 1920s.* New York, Farrar, Straus and Giroux, 1995.

Durrell, Lawrence. *Justine*. New York: E.P. Dutton and Co., 1957.

Easthope, Antony. *Poetry As Discourse*. New York: Methuen, 1983.

Edelman, Lee. "The Geography of Gender: Elizabeth Bishop's 'In the Waiting Room.' " *Elizabeth Bishop: Geography of Gender*. Ed. Marilyn May Lombardi. Charlottesville: University Press of Virginia, 1993.

———. *Transmemberment of Song: Hart Crane's Anatomies of Rhetoric and Desire*. Stanford: Stanford University Press, 1987.

Eliot, T. S. *The Complete Poems and Plays*. New York: Harcourt, Brace, Jovanovich, 1980.

———. "Tradition and the Individual Talent." *The Norton Anthology of Modern and Contemporary Poetry*. Third edition. New York: Norton, 2003.

Foucault, Michel. *The History of Sexuality, Vol. I*. Trans. Robert Hurley. New York: Vintage, 1980.

———. "What is an Author?" *The Foucault Reader*. Ed. Paul Rabinow. New York: Pantheon, 1984.

Freud, Sigmund. *The Ego and the Id*. New York: W.W. Norton, 1961.

———. *The Freud Reader*. Ed. Peter Gay. New York: W.W. Norton, 1989.

———. *Group Psychology and the Analysis of the Ego*. Ed. James Strachey. New York: W.W. Norton, 1959.

———. *On Dreams*. Trans. James Strachey. New York: W.W. Norton, 1952.

———. *Sigmund Freud: The Standard Edition*, vol. XXII. Trans. James Strachey. London: The Hogarth Press, 1961.

———. *Totem and Taboo*. Trans. James Strachey. New York: W.W. Norton, 1950.

Fuss, Diana. *Identification Papers*. New York: Routledge, 1995.

———, ed. *Inside/out*. New York: Routledge, 1991.

Garber, Marjorie. *Vested Interests: Cross-Dressing and Cultural Anxiety*. New York: HarperPerennial, 1993.

Gilbert, Sandra. "Rituals of Initiation in Whitman and Dickinson." *Walt Whitman of Mickle Street*. Ed. Geoffrey Sill. Knoxville: University of Tennessee Press, 1994.

Gilbert, Sandra and Susan Gubar, ed. *The Norton Anthology of Literature by Women*. New York: W.W. Norton, 1985.

Goldensohn, Lorrie. *Elizabeth Bishop: The Biography of a Poetry*. New York: Columbia University Press, 1992.

Gray, Thomas. *The Poems of Thomas Gray, William Collins, Oliver Goldsmith*. Ed. Roger Lonsdale. New York: Longman Group Limited, 1969.

Grossman, Allen and Mark Halliday. *The Sighted Singer: Two Works on Poetry for Readers and Writers*. Baltimore: Johns Hopkins University Press, 1992.

Hammer, Langdon. *Hart Crane and Allen Tate: Janus-Faced Modernism*. Princeton: Princeton University Press, 1993.

Harper, Phillip Brian. *Framing the Margins*. New York: Oxford University Press, 1994.

Harrison, Victoria. *Elizabeth Bishop's Poetics of Intimacy*. New York: Cambridge University Press, 1993.

Herbert, George. *The English Poems of George Herbert*. Ed. C.A. Patrides. London: J.M. Dent and Sons, 1974.

Hollander, John. *The Figure of the Echo*. Berkeley, University of California Press, 1981.

Hughes, Judith. *Reshaping the Psychoanalytic Domain: The Work of Melanie Klein, W.R.D. Fairbairn, and W.D. Winnicott*. Berkeley: University of California Press, 1989.

Hughes, Ted. *Birthday Letters*. New York: Farrar, Straus and Giroux, 1998.

Jamison, Frederic. *Postmodernism: Or The Cultural Logic of Late Capitalism*. Durham: Duke University Press, 1991.

Johnson, Barbara. *The Critical Difference: Essays in the Contemporary Rhetoric of Reading*. Baltimore: Johns Hopkins University Press, 1980.

———. *The Feminist Difference*. Cambridge: Harvard University Press, 1998.

———. "Malarme as Mother." *Denver Quarterly*, vol. 18, no. 4 (Winter 1984).

Joyce, James. *A Portrait of the Artist as a Young Man*. New York: Penguin, 1944.

Kalstone, David. *Becoming a Poet*. Ed. Robert Hemenway. New York: Farrar, Straus and Giroux, 1989.

———. *Five Temperments*. New York: Oxford University Press, 1977.

Kaplan, Justin. *Walt Whitman: A Life*. New York: Simon and Schuster, 1980.

Klein, Melanie. "Love, Guilt and Reparation." *Love, Hate and Reparation*. New York: W.W. Norton, 1964.

———. *The Selected Melanie Klein*. Ed. Juliet Mitchell. New York: The Free Press, 1986.

Kristeva, Julia. *Black Sun: Depression and Melancholia*. Trans. Leon S. Roudiez. New York: Columbia University Press, 1989.

———. *Tales of Love*. Trans. Leon S. Roudiez. New York: Columbia University Press, 1987.

Lacan, Jacques. *Ecrits: A Selection*. Trans. Alan Sheridan. New York: W.W. Norton, 1977.

Lehman, David and Charles Berger, ed. *James Merrill: Essays in Criticism*. Ithaca: Cornell University Press, 1983.

Leibowitz, Herbert A. *Hart Crane: An Introduction to the Poetry*. New York: Columbia University Press, 1968.

Lentricchia, Frank and Thomas McLaughlin, ed. *Critical Terms for Literary Study*. Chicago: University of Chicago Press, 1987.

Lewis, R. W. B. *The Poetry of Hart Crane: A Critical Study*. Princeton: Princeton University Press, 1967.

Lowell, Robert. *Life Studies and For the Union Dead*. New York: Farrar, Straus and Giroux, 1956.

———. *Notebook*. New York: Farrar, Straus and Giroux, 1971.

Malcolm, Janet. *The Silent Woman: Sylvia Plath and Ted Hughes*. New York: Alfred A. Knopf, 1994.

Mariani, Paul. *The Broken Tower: The Life of Hart Crane*. New York: W.W. Norton, 1999.

McCabe, Susan. *Elizabeth Bishop: Her Poetics of Loss*. University Park: Pennsylvania State University Press, 1994.

McClatchy, J. D. "Monsters Wrapped in Silk: James Merrill's *Country of a Thousand Years of Peace.*" *Contemporary Poetry*, 4 (1982).

McKinnon, Karen. "Catachresis and the Identity of Opposites: Alexandria as Transitional Object in Lawrence Durrell's *Justine.*" Unpublished M.A. Thesis, CUNY Graduate Center, 1992.

Melville, Herman. *Moby Dick or The Whale.* New York: Penguin Classics, 1988.

Merrill, James. *Braving the Elements.* New York: Atheneum, 1972.

———. *Changing Light at Sandover.* A Poem. New York: Alfred A. Knopf, 1993.

———. *Collected Poems.* Ed. J. D. McClatchy and Stephen Yenser. New York: Alfred A. Knopf, 2001.

———. *Country of a Thousand Years of Peace and Other Poems.* New York: Atheneum, 1983.

———. *A Different Person: A Memoir.* New York: Alfred A. Knopf, 1993.

———. "Four Letters to Stephen Yenser." *Poetry: James Merrill, A Memorial Issue.* (September 1995).

———. *Late Settings.* New York: Atheneum, 1985.

———. *Nights and Days.* London: Chatto and Windus, 1966.

———. *Recitative: Prose by James Merrill.* Ed. J. D. McClatchy. Berkeley: North Point Press, 1986.

———. *Selected Poems 1946–1985.* New York: Alfred A. Knopf, 1992.

Middlebrook, Diane. *Anne Sexton: A Biography.* Boston: Houghton Mifflin Co., 1991.

———. *Walt Whitman and Wallace Stevens.* Ithaca: Cornell University Press, 1974.

Millier, Brett. *Elizabeth Bishop: Life and the Memory of It.* Berkeley: University of California Press, 1993.

Monteiro, George, ed. *Conversations with Elizabeth Bishop.* Jackson: The University Press of Mississippi, 1996.

*Oxford English Dictionary.* Second edition. Oxford: Clarendon Press, 1989.

Parker, Robert Dale. *The Unbeliever: The Poetry of Elizabeth Bishop.* Urbana: University of Illinois Press, 1988.

Perloff, Marjorie. *The Poetic Art of Robert Lowell.* Ithaca: Cornell University Press, 1973.

Phillips, John and Lyndsey Stonebridge, ed. *Reading Melanie Klein.* New York: Routledge, 1998.

Plath, Sylvia. *Ariel.* New York: HarperPerennial, 1965.

Plato. *Phaedrus and Letters VII and VIII.* Trans. Walter Hamilton. New York: Penguin Classics, 1973.

Polito, Robert. *A Reader's Guide to James Merrill's The Changing Light at Sandover.* Ann Arbor: University of Michigan Press, 1994.

Rich, Adrienne. *Adrienne Rich's Poetry and Prose.* Ed. Barbara Gelpi and Albert Gelpi. New York: W.W. Norton and Co., 1975.

Rilke, Rainer Maria. *The Selected Poetry of Rainer Maria Rilke.* Trans. Stephen Mitchell. New York: Vintage International, 1989.

Rotella, Guy, ed. *Critical Essays on James Merrill.* New York: G.K. Hall and Co., 1996.

Sedgwick, Eve Kosofsky. *Between Men: English Literature and Male Homosocial Desire.* New York: Columbia University Press, 1985.

———. *Epistemology of the Closet.* Berkeley: University of California Press, 1990.

Selinger, Eric Murphy. *What Is It Then Between Us? Traditions of Love in American Poetry.* Ithaca: Cornell University Press, 1998.

Sexton, Anne. *Complete Poems.* Boston: Houghton Mifflin Co., 1981.

———. *Love Poems.* Boston: Houghton Mifflin, 1969.

Smith, Murray. *Engaging Characters: Fiction, Emotion, and the Cinema.* Oxford: Clarendon Press, 1995.

Stevens, Wallace. *The Collected Poems.* New York: Vintage Books, 1982.

Stevenson, Anne. *Elizabeth Bishop.* New York: Twayne, 1966.

———. "The Iceberg and the Ship." *Michigan Quarterly Review.*

Symons, Arthur. *The Symbolist Movement in Literature.* New York: E.P. Dutton and Co., 1958.

Trachtenberg, Alan. *Brooklyn Bridge: Fact and Symbol.* Chicago: University of Chicago Press, 1979.

Unterecker, John. *Voyager: A Life of Hart Crane.* New York: Farrar, Straus and Giroux, 1969.

Vendler, Helen. "Domestication, Domesticity, and the Otherwordly." *Elizabeth Bishop and Her Art.* Ed. Lloyd Schwartz and Sybil Estess. Ann Arbor: University of Michigan Press, 1983.

———. *The Music of What Happens.* Cambridge: Harvard University Press, 1988.

Wehr, Wesley. "Elizabeth Bishop: Conversation and Class Notes." *Antioch Review*, 39 (Summer, 1981).

Whitman, Walt. *Leaves of Grass.* Ed. Sculley Bradley and Harold Blodgett. New York: W.W. Norton & Company, 1973.

Yeats, William Butler. *The Collected Works of W.B. Yeats.* vol. 1. Ed. Richard Finneran. New York: Macmillan Publishing Company, 1983.

Yenser, Stephen. *The Consuming Myth: The Work of James Merrill.* Cambridge: Harvard University Press, 1987.

Yingling, Thomas. *Hart Crane and the Homosexual Text.* Chicago: University of Chicago Press, 1990.

# INDEX

affect, 78, 117, 121, 128, 135,
  142–3
  production of, 104–5
aggression, 43–4, 78, 130, 131,
  133, 156n51
Althusser, Louis, 156n46
ambiguity, images of, 74, 102, 103,
  106–7, 110, 113, 118, 129,
  131, 146
ambivalence, 49, 54–5, 108, 135,
  142, 146, 147
  affect and, 121, 129–30
Auden, W.H., 145
autobiographical impulse, 1–3,
  54, 67

Bersani, Leo, 157n9, 165n24
Bidart, Frank, 146–7
Bishop, Elizabeth, 4, 65–6, 70, 76,
  121–2
  collections: *Geography III*, 66,
    78,129, 133; *North & South*,
    53–4, 67–8, 70, 75, 76, 121,
    122, 135;*Poems: North &
    South – A Cold Spring*, 76,
    122, 125, 135
  confessional poetry and, 66
  friendship with Marianne Moore,
    94–7
  shore ode, 36, 40
  style, 35
  poetry: "At the Fishhouses," 39,
    76–8, 128, 148, 149,
    155n38; "A Miracle for
    Breakfast," 70–3, 75;
    "Crusoe in England," 35,
    129–33, 137; "Insomnia,"
122–4, 127, 129, 137; "It is
  marvelous to wake up
  together," 124–5; "In the
  Waiting Room," 32–6, 50,
  156n44; "Love Lies
  Sleeping," 121, 123, 137;
  "One Art," 133–5;
  "Sestina," 73–6; "Sleeping
  on the Ceiling," 70, 75;
  "Sleeping Standing Up,"
  123; "The Bight," 150; "The
  End of March," 36–41, 130,
  132, 155n38; "The Map,"
  68–9; "The Moose," 78–9;
  "The Roosters," 94–5; "The
  Shampoo," 125–9, 133
  prose: "*Efforts of Affection*," 96,
    162n13; "*In the Village*," 67,
    73, 165n30
Bishop, Gertrude Bulmer (mother),
  4, 76, 121
Bishop, William Thomas (father), 4
Bloom, Harold, 28, 129
Bromwich, David, 72–3
Butler, Judith, 18–9, 153n17

Castle, Terry, 126
catachresis, 104–5, 118, 120–1,
  129, 146
  trope of the closet and, 146
Cavafy, C.P., 86
closet, trope of, 8, 14–15, 20, 58–9,
  145–6
  closeting structure, 60
Coleridge, Samuel Taylor,
  39, 114
Cole, Henri, 146, 147–9

confessional poetry, 1–3, 66,
122, 135
defined, 2
as literary convention, 135
Crane, Grace Hart (mother), 3,
64–5, 107, 118, 159n26
Crane, Hart, 3, 19, 64–5, 79–80
collections: *The Bridge*, 63,
79–81, 110, 117, 118; *White
Buildings*, 54, 59, 61, 62,
63, 80–1, 105, 117, 155n33
name change, 64
poetry: "The Broken Tower,"
19–26; "To Brooklyn
Bridge," 80–1, 110, 118;
"Cape Hatteras," 80; "Cutty
Sark," 119; "Episode of
Hands," 113, 124; "For the
Marriage of Faustus and
Helen," 96, 105–7, 118,
120; "My Grandmother's
Love Letters," 116;
"Legend," 59–61, 121; "At
Melville's Tomb," 23, 53,
58, 108, 115, 117, 119;
"Repose of Rivers," 26–31,
62; "Sunday Morning
Apples," 61–3; "The
Tunnel," 119–21; "The
Visible The Untrue," 124,
147; "Voyages," 107–18,
138: six part sequence: part
one, 107–9; part two,
109–12; part three, 112–13,
115; part four, 113–14; part
five, 115–16; part six,
116–18
prose: "*General Aims and
Theories*," 112; "*A Letter to
Harriet Monroe*," 58;
"*Modern Poetry*," 57

Dickinson, Emily, 40–1
disruptions, 20–1, 132, 141, 143
internal questions, 47–8, 68,
98, 141

Doolittle, Hilda (H.D.), 65
Doty, Mark, 146, 149–50
doubling (words and images), 27,
37, 39, 60, 103, 106, 123,
132, 133–4, 137, 141, 143
language and, 110, 111, 113, 120
Douglass, Ann, 60, 64, 152n6

Edelman, Lee, 104, 120–1, 154n30,
155n32
Eliot, T.S., 5, 57, 92
"Tradition and the Individual
Talent," 92
*Elizabeth Bishop: Life and the
Memory of It*, see Millier
Emerson, Ralph Waldo, 1, 101

Foucault, Michel, 66–7
Frank, Waldo, 107
Freud, Sigmund, 3, 42, 54–7, 73,
88, 99, 102–3
drives theory, 23
work: *The Ego and the Id*, 8, 55;
"Three Essays on the Theory
of Sexuality," 12; "Female
Sexuality," 12, 152n2;
"Femininity," 157n7; *Group
Psychology and the Analysis of
the Ego*, 18; *On Dreams*, 57;
"On Narcissism," 111; "The
Uncanny," 93–4, 129;
Fuss, Diana, 13, 151n1, 160n42,
155n40

gender
identification, 18–19, 38, 41
imagery, 21, 25–6, 32–3, 47, 50,
62, 133–4
voice, 30
Gilbert, Sandra, 15
Goldensohn, Lorrie, 121, 124,
160n38
Gray, Thomas, 108

Hammer, Langdon, 118, 154n25,
154n26, 155n34

hand, trope of, 86, 87, 113, 115–16, 120, 138
Hardy, Thomas, 65
Harrison, Victoria, 67, 69
Herbert, George, 72, 167n48
Hollander, John, 108–9, 145
homosexual desire, 28–9, 60–1, 105, 106, 108, 115, 121, 124–6, 137
Hughes, Judith, 127, 159n37
Hughes, Ted, 1

Jarrell, Randell, 53
Johnson, Barbara, 67, 93, 123
Joyce, James, 34

Kalstone, David, 34–5, 159n27
Klein, Melanie, 3, 8, 13, 38, 55–7, 62–3, 65, 67, 72, 73, 76, 93, 102–3, 127, 159n37
"Love, Guilt and Reparation," 8, 55–7, 67
Kristeva, Julia, 12, 22, 103, 111, 142, 153n14, 154n29, 166n44
Black Sun, 103
Tales of Love, 111

Lacan, Jacques, 35, 60
Lewis, R.W.B., 106
liminality, 31, 39, 60, 76–7, 124, 129
loss, 16–18, 24, 37, 56, 77, 117, 130, 133, 135
homosexuality and, 58
love and, 86
love, 101, 117–19, 121, 133, 135, 136 138, 139, 140, 143, 146, 165n28
doubling and, 103, 106
Lowell, Robert, 2, 5, 65–6, 83, 98, 121–2, 165n30

McClatchy, J.D., 50, 90–1, 99
Melville, Herman, 111

Merrill, Charles, 4, 83
Merrill, Hellen Ingram (mother), 82–3, 97
Merrill, James, 4–5, 83
collection: Braving the Elements, 86, 90, 97; Changing Light at Sandover, 81, 91 142; Late Settings, 140; Nights and Days, 84, 135–6, 138
poetry: "Annie Hill's Grave," 135; "Between Us," 136; "Book of Ephraim," 81; "Clearing the Title," 140–2; "Days of 1935," 86–90; "Days of 1964," 138–40; "Days of 1971," 86, 90; "A Dedication," 99; "Her Craft," 143; "Nightgown," 136; "A Renewal," 99, 101–2; "Scenes of Childhood," 41–6, 50; "The Country of a Thousand Years of Peace," 84–6; "The Mad Scene," 138; "An Urban Convalescence," 46–50, 100, 138, 149; "The Victor Dog," 97, 135, 147
prose: A Different Person, 82–3, 84, 85, 98, 145
Middlebrook, Diane, 92–3
Millier, Brett, 73, 166n33, 167n47, 160n39
Milton, John, 132
"Mirror Stage, The," 35, 60
Mitchell, Juliet, 73
Monroe, Harriet, 53, 58, 61
Moore, Marianne, 94–7, 125, 162n13
"Marriage," 95–7

Narcissus, 111, 113, 143
Nerval, Gerald de, 22, 103

Object Relations, 3, 13, 38, 127; see also Klein and Mitchell

Page, Barbara, 135
Plath, Sylvia, 1–2
Plato, 102
   Platonic love, 107
Psychoanalysis, 22, 54, 55, 102–3,
   104–5, 111, 151n4, 152n4,
   154n21
   narcissism and, 106, 111, 123

repetition, *see* doubling
Rilke, Ranier Maria, 57, 99–100,
   163n4
Rosenthal, M.L., 2

Sedgwick, Eve Kosofsky,
   158n17–18
Selinger, Eric Murphy, 138
shore ode, 15, 36, 40, 107–18
Sommer, William, 61–2
Stevens, Wallace, 5, 36, 41, 101,
   114, 139, 142, 168n8

subterfuge, 101–2, 118
   'infinite mischief' and,
   66–67, 102

Tate, Allen, 80

Unterecker, John, 107

Vendler, Helen, 160n45
*Voyager: A Life of Hart Crane*, *see*
   Unterecker

*Waste Land, The*, 57
Whitman, Walt, 11, 15–18, 36, 46,
   80, 92–3, 107, 108–9, 111
Winters, Yvor, 63
Wordsworth, William, 68, 130

Yeats, William Butler (W.B.), 5, 19,
   57, 85, 120, 140
Yingling, Thomas, 21, 28, 151n6

CPSIA information can be obtained at www.ICGtesting.com
Printed in the USA
LVOW040048041212

309980LV00003B/20/P